Publi

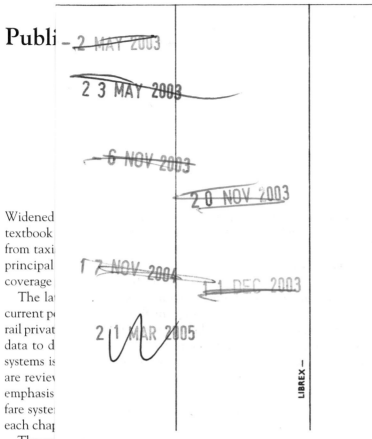

- 2 MAY 2003

2 3 MAY 2003

- 6 NOV 2003

2 0 NOV 2003

1 7 NOV 2004   1 DEC 2003

2 1 MAR 2005

LIBREX —

Widened   l
textbook   :
from taxi
principal
coverage
  The la   l
current p   l
rail privat   r
data to d   l
systems is
are revie   r
emphasis
fare syste
each cha

The concluding chapter examines long-run policy issues and developments likely to influence the role of public transport in the near future, including the British government's Ten Year Plan for 2000–2010, global warming and the role of the European Union in transport.

This book serves as a textbook for both specialist students in transport and those in related fields – such as planning, geography, civil engineering and business studies – taking optional courses in transport. Any reader concerned with transport as a policy issue will find the book useful as a contemporary account of a crucial dimension of any advanced economy.

Peter White is Professor of Public Transport Systems at the University of Westmi

Avril Robarts LRC

Liverpool John Moores University

D0308346

The Natural and Built Environment Series
Series Editors: Professor John Glasson and Professor Mick Bruton

Public Transport

Its planning, management and operation

Fourth Edition

Peter White

LIVERPOOL JOHN MOORES UNIVERSITY
Aldham Roberts L.R.C.
TEL. 0151 231 3701/3634

London and New York

Third edition, first published in 1995 by UCL Press
Reprinted 1998
Second edition 1986
First edition 1976

Fourth edition, first published 2002
by Spon Press
11 New Fetter Lane, London EC4P 4EE

Simultaneously published in the USA and Canada
by Spon Press
29 West 35th Street, New York, NY 10001

Spon Press is an imprint of the Taylor & Francis Group

© 2002 Peter White

The right of Peter White to be identified as the Author of this Work has been
asserted by him in accordance with the Copyright, Designs and Patents Act 1988

Typeset in Goudy by Keystroke, Jacaranda Lodge, Wolverhampton
Printed and bound in Great Britain by Biddles Ltd, Guildford and King's Lynn

All rights reserved. No part of this book may be reprinted or reproduced
or utilised in any form or by any electronic, mechanical, or other means,
now known or hereafter invented, including photocopying and recording,
or in any information storage or retrieval system, without permission in
writing from the publishers.

British Library Cataloguing in Publication Data
A catalogue record for this book is available from the British Library

Library of Congress Cataloging in Publication Data
White, Peter, 1948–
    Public transport : its planning, management, and operation / Peter White.—4th ed.
      p. cm. — (The natural and built environment series)
    Includes bibliographical references and index.
    1. Transportation—Great Britain. 2. Transportation and state—Great Britain.
I. Title. II. Series.

HE243.A2 W48 2002
388'.068'4—dc21
                                                                2001049081

ISBN 0–415–25771–9 (hbk)
ISBN 0–415–25772–7 (pbk)

Contents

LIVERPOOL JOHN MOORES UNIVERSITY
Aldham Roberts L.R.C.
TEL. 0151 231 3701/3634

Preface

This book aims to provide a comprehensive introduction to the public transport sector, covering the public institutions, operating industries and market served. A fairly wide definition of 'public transport' is adopted, ranging from taxis and private hire vehicles, to intercity rail and domestic air services, and including most aspects of the bus, coach and rail sectors. The institutional framework described is that within the British Isles, but a broader range of countries is considered in examining developments in technology and future policy options.

Since the first edition of this book appeared in 1976 many changes have taken place in the public transport sector in Britain. So far as rail-based systems are concerned, the picture is much more encouraging than at that time. In place of an apparent trend of decline, the national rail network has grown slightly in extent, and strikingly in patronage. The light rail concept has been reintroduced to Britain, with five systems now in operation and more under construction or in planning. The London Underground carries its highest-ever annual ridership.

In the bus and coach industry a more mixed picture can be seen. The rapid growth in express coach ridership after deregulation in 1980 was not sustained, but none the less a higher passenger volume than that seen in the late 1970s has been retained. Local bus deregulation in 1986 did not produce an overall growth in use, and a general decline in ridership has occurred, except in London and some other centres. However, increased emphasis is being placed on service quality and marketing to attract new users.

The awareness of the link between public transport and land use planning evident when the first edition was produced, having almost disappeared in the 1980s and early 1990s, has re-emerged in government policy.

The basic framework of this book has been retained from earlier editions, beginning with an examination of the structure of the industry, followed by the market served. This is followed by chapters dealing specifically with bus and rail technology, and with network structures. Costing and pricing issues are examined. Specific attention is devoted to rural and intercity issues in separate chapters. Concluding chapters examine short-run and long-run policy issues.

The whole text has been revised to incorporate the latest statistical data, changes in the law, and organization of the industry. Certain chapters have been rewritten more extensively, notably those on network structures and policy. However, it has not been my aim to give detailed guidance on current government policy implementation or financing mechanisms, since these are prone to change at short notice (an issue illustrated by restructuring of the main government department dealing with transport as this text was being finalized). Chapter 10 identifies the main current policy issues in Britain over the timescale of the ten-year plan, while Chapter 11 examines broader long-run issues relevant in Britain and other countries.

While a considerable range of descriptive statistics has been included in the text, complex modelling concepts and analysis have been avoided. As far as possible jargon has been minimized, the aim being to provide a book accessible to a fairly wide audience, as well as serving as a reference volume for those engaged in transport studies at professional, undergraduate or postgraduate levels. However, some familiarity with economic concepts, especially that of demand elasticity, will be found useful.

Throughout the period in which all four editions have been produced I have been based at the University of Westminster (until 1992 known as the 'Polytechnic of Central London'), in its Transport Studies Group. The first edition and successive updatings have been closely related to teaching and research work, especially the MSc Transport Planning and Management course. Thanks are due to colleagues at Westminster, especially to Dr Nigel Dennis for assistance in updating the material related to air transport.

Reference is also made to outputs of research work in other organizations, including other universities, and the Transport Research Laboratory. Extensive use has been made of the National Travel Survey (NTS) and other data collected by central government. The NTS in particular enables a very comprehensive picture to be drawn, setting out the role played by public transport within the wider transport market. Inevitably, specialists in any particular field may find the coverage of their subject somewhat brief, given the wide range covered in this book, but I hope they will consider that the main aspects have been highlighted.

All responsibility for conclusions drawn and analysis presented is that of the author alone.

Peter White

Acknowledgements

Thanks are due to many friends and colleagues for assistance. John Glover provided helpful comments on the draft of Chapter 1. Graphic designer Jonathan Sargent undertook the preparation of new diagrams for this volume. Data for the train pathing diagram (Figure 9.3) was provided by Railtrack plc. Tony Cross of Lincolnshire County Council helpfully clarified recent developments, as illustrated in Figure 8.1.

1 Organization and control of transport in the British Isles

Within this chapter the organizations and legislation relevant to public transport in the British Isles are outlined. The situation described is that applying from spring 2001. The overall framework is that provided under the European Union – influencing, for example, the structures for railway finances, and safety regulation – as discussed further in Chapter 11. Detailed coverage is given of the structure in the United Kingdom of Great Britain and Northern Ireland, and within the Irish Republic.

Great Britain and Northern Ireland

Central government

Following devolution of powers to the Welsh and Greater London Assemblies, and the Scottish Parliament, together with the separate arrangements in Northern Ireland, considerable variation exists between different regions of the United Kingdom. Below, the situation applicable in the UK and England as a whole is described first, followed by national and regional variations.

Until June 2001 overall responsibility for transport policy was placed under the Department of the Environment, Transport and the Regions (DETR), whose statistical publications are quoted extensively in this book. Following the General Election, its transport and local government functions were placed under a new Department of Transport, Local Government and the Regions (DTLR) whose scope covers all modes, including shipping and aviation, together with most issues affecting planning and local government expenditure, including approval of land-use plans. Regional government offices (jointly representing the DTLR, and the Department of Trade and Industry, DTI) appraise local authority transport plans.

The 'environment' aspects of DETR were transferred to a new Department for Environment, Food and Rural Affairs (DEFRA). Hence, the link between transport and environment is now less close, although rural aspects of transport may receive more attention than before.

Both Departments are headed by a Secretary of State, with cabinet rank, assisted by several Ministers of State. Their power is exercised directly in England, and within Wales through the Welsh Assembly, although generally under identical legislation. Regional aspects of policy are handled through DTLR, the Cabinet Office and the Department of Trade and Industry (DTI). Within Scotland, the Scottish Executive's Development Department, under a Minister of the Scottish Parliament, covers much of the DTLR role, with separately determined legislation on certain aspects, such as the Integrated Transport (Scotland) Act 2000. Within Northern Ireland, a variable structure applies, depending on the political situation. Either the local Legislative Assembly ('Stormont') exercises powers through its own Ministers, or the Northern Ireland Office administers the province on behalf of central government; here also different legislation may apply. The Department for Regional Development is responsible for transport planning. The self-governing Channel Islands and Isle of Man determine their own local policies, but are strongly influenced by central government in aviation and shipping policy.

The DTLR determines overall policy, but management of assets still in the public sector is mainly exercised through agencies, such as the Highways Agency (HA), responsible for the construction and maintenance of the trunk road and motorway network, whose role has been broadened to cover management of the system use – for example, through introduction of bus and coach priority lanes. Others include the Vehicle Inspectorate (VI), responsible for annual inspection and other safety controls over road vehicles, and the Health and Safety Executive (HSE), responsible for railway safety through its subsidiary, Her Majesty's Railway Inspectorate (HMRI).

Within the DTLR, several Ministers and Under Secretaries assist the Secretary of State. These responsibilities are not rigidly determined by law, and may vary as individual appointments change, but typically comprise posts covering public transport, transport in London, national policy on roads and traffic, and a fourth for aviation and shipping. The civil service staff of the Department is headed by a Permanent Secretary, to whom are responsible various Deputy Secretaries, each in turn responsible for a specialist sector (whose definitions and responsibilities change from time to time).

A quasi-independent role is played by the Commission for Integrated Transport (CfIT) which provides inputs to government policy, and responses to its implementation. Its role in the 1998 Transport White Paper is defined as 'to provide independent advice to Government on the implementation of integrated transport policy, to monitor developments across transport, environment, health and other sectors and review progress toward meeting our objectives'.

Two other government departments also have substantial influence on transport policy. The Department of Trade and Industry (DTI) is involved in certain aspects of industrial strategy, and the operation of competition policy, exercised through the Competition Commission, and the Office of Fair Trading (OFT). This aspect has gained increasing importance in the transport sector since deregulation of local bus services.

The Treasury is responsible for overall allocation of expenditures between departments, fiscal policy such as fuel duty, and taxation of 'company car' benefits. The role of financial control has become particularly strong in the transport sector in recent years, and tends to determine other aspects of policy.

Local government

Two types of structure exist:

1 Single-tier, or 'unitary', authorities. These cover all of Wales and Scotland, and some parts of England. They have responsibility for all functions below regional level. Examples include Cardiff, Edinburgh, Plymouth and East Yorkshire.
2 Traditional two-tier authorities. Most parts of England are placed under county councils (sometimes known as the 'shires'): examples include Surrey and Norfolk.

Both unitaries and counties are highway and transportation authorities, being directly responsible for local road maintenance and construction (apart from motorways and trunk roads, which are placed under the Highways Agency). They provide support for non-commercial bus services through seeking tenders for such operations. They have a role in the promotion of public transport which may involve provision of comprehensive timetable information. As education authorities, they may spend large sums on school transport (often exceeding direct support to public transport), in order to fulfil their statutory duties stemming originally from the Education Act of 1944 (discussed further in Chapter 10). A positive role in stimulating rail use is often adopted, albeit rarely with major responsibility for meeting operating losses, but including, for example, re-opening of rural stations.

Within the two-tier system, the districts are typically of 50,000 to 200,000 population and each is based on a small to medium-sized town, but also including some larger centres. Districts are usually responsible for concessionary fares for the elderly and disabled, although children are normally a county responsibility. In some counties a common county-wide scheme has been established for the pensioners and disabled. Parking is generally managed at district level. Districts are also the licensing bodies for taxis and private hire cars.

The remaining bus operations in public ownership are provided through unitary or district councils. Counties do not operate services directly (except, in a few cases, some school buses, for example, in Norfolk).

Under the Road Traffic Act 1991, districts or unitaries may also create Special Parking Areas (SPAs), in which they take over responsibility for on-street parking control from wardens controlled by the police. From July 1994, this power has been used by all London boroughs (LBs), and has been applied in some other cities outside London.

Within the major conurbations in England a 'single tier' system of local government exists. In the six metropolitan regions (West Midlands, Merseyside, Greater Manchester, South Yorkshire, West Yorkshire, Tyne and Wear) local government is provided through metropolitan district councils (36 in all), under-taking almost all transport and planning functions, with some *ad hoc* co-ordinating bodies covering each metropolitan area as a whole.

In London, the Greater London Authority (GLA) together with the directly elected Mayor, controls strategic transport and planning policy, with a lower tier of some 32 LBs (plus the City of London Corporation) responsible for functions such as parking and traffic management. The GLA, through Transport for London (TfL) controls most aspects of public transport, including buses, the Underground (following transfer of its control from central government when the funding arrangements are finalized), taxis and river services. Within this structure, the Public Carriage Office (PCO) acts as the licensing body for taxis and private hire cars ('minicabs'). TfL's street management division is also responsible for a strategic major road network (covering roads that would be the responsibility of the HA in other areas), including the 'Red Routes' on which stricter traffic control is applied.

Another feature of the governmental structure in England is the role of regional assemblies (such as that for the South East), but this is at present largely an advisory function. However, Regional Planning Guidance (RPG) through DTLR provides general advice on land-use and transport planning, and Regional Transport Strategies (RTSs) are now being developed.

Under the Transport Act 1968, Passenger Transport Authorities (PTAs) were set up in six conurbations (West Midlands, Merseyside, Greater Manchester, and Tyne and Wear, South Yorkshire and West Yorkshire). These took over the existing municipal bus operators, and also acquired a general responsibility for the integration and planning of public transport as a whole in their areas. Following abolition of the metropolitan counties in 1986, the PTAs became bodies composed of elected members from district councils in their areas. They are also dependent upon transfers from district budgets for their financing, together with central government grants.

Within each PTA area, day-to-day responsibility for its public transport role is placed upon the Passenger Transport Executive (PTE), a body of professional managers. The PTEs are responsible for agreements with Train Operating Companies and provision of tendered bus services and concessionary fares (under the 1985 and 2000 Transport Acts). They also play a major role in providing comprehensive passenger information systems, provision of school transport, co-ordinated ticketing arrangements (such as multi-operator travelcards), infra-structure investment (notably interchanges) and the planning, construction and financing of light rail systems such as those in Manchester and Sheffield.

A Passenger Transport Authority and Executive also functions in Strathclyde, the largest of the Scottish conurbations, covering Glasgow and the surrounding region (SPTA). It also operates a small underground railway. One other PTE, Tyne and Wear, runs a larger system, the local Metro.

Within Wales, some influence on transport policy is exercised by the Assembly (for example, it has extended free concessionary travel to all of pensionable age, in contrast to the minimum standard of a half-fare set out in the Transport Act 2000 which applies in England), but overall policy and structure are similar to that found in England.

Within Scotland, the Parliament exercises a greater role, having its own legislation (the Integrated Transport (Scotland) Act of 2000) and corresponding powers. This differs in some respects from that applicable in England and Wales – for example, within bus 'quality partnerships' (agreements between operators and local authorities to enhance services) fare levels and minimum service frequencies can be specified. A Minister for Transport and Planning occupies a role equivalent to the Secretary of State and Ministers in England and Wales. The Parliament has also set out its own strategic priorities for rail policy and will work with the Strategic Rail Authority (SRA) and SPTA in respect of the renewal of the 'ScotRail' franchise.

In Northern Ireland, there are some 26 district councils, but these have a very limited role in transport.

The Irish Republic

Within the Irish Republic, policy in respect of public transport is exercised primarily through the Department of Public Enterprise and its Minister. Traditionally, the major role has been that of Coras Iompair Eireann (CIE), a nationalized industry, transformed through an Act of 1986 into a holding company controlling the national rail system (Ianrodd Eireann, IE), plus bus networks in Dublin (Bus Atha Cliath), and of regional/long-distance services (Bus Eireann). A more flexible structure is now proposed, notably in the Dublin city region through the Dublin Transportation Office (DTO), introducing competitive franchising of bus services on a pattern broadly similar to that elsewhere in Europe (such as London and Copenhagen). Urban rail services within Dublin are provided principally through the DART operations of IE, and the LUAS light rail network now under construction.

Independent bus and coach operators play a growing role, in school, tour and express services, which is likely to increase through competitive franchising.

Public spending in Great Britain

Although the majority of expenditure on transport is that incurred by private individuals in running of cars, and fares paid to public transport operators, public finance plays a major role. The principal categories of expenditure in Great Britain in 1999–2000 are identified in Table 1.1.

It will be seen that the expenditure via local authorities is dominated by concessionary fares compensation, mainly for bus use, followed by support to rail services in PTE areas (the latter, however, implies a much higher expenditure per rail passenger trip given the volumes involved). While London forms about one-quarter of concessionary fares compensation (due to the generosity of the free off-peak pensioner travel and volumes involved), its bus operations were close to break-even in 1999–2000. The 'bus service support' figure represents the total relevant spending by local authorities (including TfL and PTEs), i.e. in addition to payments for tendered services provided by bus operators, it covers expenditure by the authorities themselves on the tendering process, passenger information, and historic debts. It also includes grants for rural services.

'School transport' is not usually classified within transport expenditure as such, but as can be seen represents a very large sum, and in many rural counties or

Table 1.1 Public transport expenditure by central government and local authorities, 1999–2000

Local Authorities – Current Spending	*£mn*
PTE grants to rail services	312
Concessionary fare compensation	496
of which　London	143
English PTEs	195
rest of England	102 [a]
Wales	10 [a]
Scotland	46
Local bus service support (total)	294
of which　London	10
English PTEs	120
Rest of England	123
Wales	14
Scotland	27
School transport	576 [b]
Central Government – Current Spending	
Bus fuel duty rebate	333
SRA rail passenger grants (net)	1031
Other government support to rail services and freight grants	98
Capital spending	
Total	130 [c]

Sources: Department of the Environment, Transport and the Regions Statistics Bulletin SB (00)26 *A Bulletin of Public Transport Statistics:* GB 2000 edition, tables 19, 20, 21, 22 (current spending).

Notes
a Buses only.
b England and Wales only. Source: CPT.
c 1998/9 figure, from Transport Statistics Great Britain 2000 edition, table 1.17 (TSO, October 2000).

unitaries is much greater than other types of public transport expenditure (for example, in Kent).

The central government element is dominated by support to the passenger rail system via the SRA (which is additional to that via the PTEs), together with the partial fuel duty rebate (FDR) to local bus services – in effect, a lower rate of tax rather than additional public expenditure as such.

The capital spending element is very small, being mainly related to light rail schemes in progress. However, it should be borne in mind that most spending is through the private sector, in the form of Railtrack, rolling stock leasing companies, and bus operators' own investment. Railtrack is becoming increasingly dependent upon large amounts of public finance, discussed separately in Chapter 10. Rail freight operators generally operate commercially, although receiving some grants for track access costs.

In practice, much of the expenditure handled through local authorities is supported through central government grants. Some of this is specific to certain purposes (such as rural bus subsidy grant, discussed further in Chapter 8). However, most current transport expenditure (such as that on most tendered bus services) comes from the local authority's budget as a whole, rather than specific grants for transport purposes. Central government funding to local authorities is determined by the Standard Spending Assessment (SSA), which takes account of factors such as total population, density of the area, etc. The proportion of revenue received directly from the tax on local households (the 'council tax') is relatively small. Rates levied on business (the National Non-Domestic Rate, NNDR) are collected by central government and reallocated to local authorities.

Each London borough, metropolitan district council, unitary authority and 'shire' county prepares a Local Transport Plan (LTP) document – known in London as an Interim Local Transport Implementation Plan (ILTP), covering in detail the forthcoming financial year, with an outline programme for capital spending over five years. This is assessed for grant purposes by the DTLR, with an approved total spending announced around the end of the calendar year, effective for the next financial year. The development of the system is discussed further in Chapter 10. Grants for major public transport capital schemes can be made under Section 56 of the 1968 Transport Act, under which (subject to an economic evaluation) central government may contribute a grant of up to 50 per cent of the capital cost.

The operating industries in the United Kingdom

The bus and coach industry

The bus and coach industry comprises five main segments:

1 The 'independent' operators

These are firms which have always been in private ownership, generally running small fleets, except for some of the larger coach operators. The typical fleet size is around one to ten vehicles. This sector is concentrated mainly in the 'other' services market, although the opportunities to enter local scheduled services were substantially enlarged by the Transport Act of 1985.

2 Regional bus companies

In most areas, regional companies can be found, providing the main interurban network and services within most towns. Traditionally state-owned, these were privatized following the Transport Act 1985, and the Transport (Scotland) Act of 1989.

Many companies were purchased by management buy-outs, sometimes with employee shareholdings. Others were purchased by new holding companies which have subsequently grown through purchase of many of the earlier management buy-outs, and were later 'floated' (public sale of shares on the stock exchange). The largest three such groups are Stagecoach, FirstGroup and Arriva, followed (at the time of writing, May 2001) by Go Ahead Group (GAG) and National Express Group (NEG). Together, they represent about 70 per cent or more of the local bus market measured in terms of turnover. All five groups also operate passenger rail franchises, which in the case of NEG comprise the greater part of its business.

The regional bus companies owned by such groups (such as First Eastern Counties) typically provide a mix of rural, interurban and urban services (with the exception of NEG, which runs express coaches and some urban networks). In some cases they have also replaced or taken over local authority bus fleets.

In Northern Ireland, Translink is a state-owned operation also responsible for rail services in the province, incorporating Ulsterbus and Citybus, the main bus operators. A few bus services are operated by independents and education bodies.

3   London

Bus services within the area of the Greater London Authority (GLA) are mainly provided under contracts with Transport for London (TfL) through its subsidiary London Bus Services Ltd. Many of these were once operated directly by London Transport, but its subsidiaries were privatized during 1994, and most subsequently sold on to the major groups mentioned above. In addition, contracted services are provided by independents, and regional companies based around Greater London. Through its role as provider of a comprehensive bus network, TfL is able to ensure greater stability and comprehensiveness of services than in deregulated areas of Britain, although possibly with a more rigid approach (see further discussion in Chapter 10).

Some other bus services within, and entering, Greater London, are provided commercially by private sector bus and coach operators, notably the 'commuter coach' services. Where agreements are made with TfL these may also carry local passengers using the travelcard and concessionary pass tickets. Cross-boundary services, such as Kingston-on-Thames to Epsom, effectively operate under both regimes, that of TfL within London, and the deregulated framework outside.

4   Local authority fleets

Following the Transport Act of 1985, fleets owned by local authorities and PTEs were restructured as 'arm's length' Passenger Transport Companies (PTCs). Privatization was not mandatory, but was strongly encouraged by central government. All seven ex-PTE companies have now been privatized, and over half of those owned by district or regional councils have ceased trading or been privatized. One of the remaining local authority-owned companies, Blackpool Transport, also runs a tramway. About fifteen fleets remain in district or unitary council ownership, the largest being Lothian Buses in Edinburgh.

5 Express coach services

Although opened to competition under the Transport Act of 1980, the express coach network is dominated by one operator, National Express Ltd, originally a part of the National Bus Company, and initially privatized through a management buy-out in 1988. Subsequently it was floated as a PLC in 1992, and has expanded into other activities, notably through the franchised rail services. The similar Scottish-based 'Citylink' network is a subsidiary of the Delgro group of Singapore. Very few vehicles are owned by National Express or Citylink as such, and almost all are hired in from other companies.

The internal structure of bus and coach companies, apart from informal structures found in the very smallest concerns, has been traditionally based on a separation of 'Traffic' and 'Engineering' functions, the former encompassing the planning and operation of services, the latter provision of vehicles to operate them. This was also associated with a centralized structure in which the two functions were brought together at the level of senior management. A much more decentralized approach is now taken, with greater power given to managers of subsidiary companies, and to area or depot managers within those companies.

The railways

Under the Railways Act of 1993, the nationalized British Rail system was disbanded and privatized.

Its passenger services were transferred to twenty-five Train Operating Companies (TOCs) – for example, South West Trains (a Stagecoach subsidiary), operating the network of services from London Waterloo.

The allocation of franchises, and the financial support most of them need from central government, was initially handled by the Office of Passenger Rail Franchising (OPRAF), under its Franchising Director. This role has been taken over by the Strategic Rail Authority (SRA) under the Transport Act 2000, under which the first set of franchises is being renegotiated, with some changes in the areas originally specified. About twenty-two franchises are likely to be in place once this process is complete. The possibility of 'micro-franchising' (of individual services, or much smaller groups of services) has also been raised.

There is also a local franchise within London, through TfL, the Docklands Light Railway (DLR).

In addition to franchised operations, Eurostar provides services via the Channel Tunnel to Paris, Brussels and beyond, and 'open access' operators provide some additional services competing with the franchised network. The only example to date is Hull Trains, a subsidiary of GB Railways who also operate the Anglia franchise.

All infrastructure, including track, signalling and stations are the responsibility of Railtrack Plc. The track maintenance and renewal work is contracted in from other private sector companies, but signalling is managed directly. Most stations are managed by TOCs but Railtrack runs several of the major stations itself.

Railtrack's costs are covered by charges made to train operators and government grants (further comment on this made in Chapter 10).

From 1994, the then passenger rolling stock fleet was transferred *en bloc* to three rolling stock leasing companies (ROSCOs), who charge the TOCs for the provision of stock, and remain responsible for overhauls. TOCs may also purchase or lease stock directly from other providers, such as manufacturers.

The rail freight operations were also privatized. Most are now run by English Welsh and Scottish Railways (EWS), including the major 'trainload' (bulk freight) operations, Royal Mail and Railfreight Distribution services. The principal exception is Freightliner, operated by a management buy-out company. Railfreight Distribution's major responsibility is developing freight services through the Channel Tunnel. There are also some private freight operations, making use of open access rights on the rail system, mainly for carrying their owning companies' traffic, notably the 'Mendip Rail' aggregates business, and DRS (British Nuclear Fuels).

Within the seven PTA areas, TOC services rely on local support paid through the PTEs. These enable the PTEs to establish common fares and service-level policies for TOC and tendered bus services, but also result in a substantial financial burden on local budgets (see above) which is not felt by local authorities elsewhere. Conversely, funding for TOCs' services in the London area comes through the SRA, although greater co-ordination with transport strategies of the GLA is now proposed. This can also be seen in initiatives dating from the Greater London Council era, the common Travelcard introduced in 1985, and planning of the 'Crossrail' scheme.

The rather limited rail network in Northern Ireland – on the common Irish gauge of 1,600 mm, slightly wider than in mainland Britain – is operated by Northern Ireland Railways (NIR), part of Translink.

Many preserved steam railways are operated by private companies and semi-voluntary organizations, generally providing seasonal tourist services. Historic steam and electric lines on the Isle of Man are owned by its government.

Sea and air transport

Following privatization policies in the early 1980s, all of these operations are in the private sector, except for many smaller airports, some major regional airports (notably Manchester) and Caledonian MacBrayne ('Calmac') ferries, operating many of the Scottish island services (due to be franchised as single network).

The largest ferry operator is Sealink P&O, whose services dominate the cross-Channel market. Most operators have shifted toward roll-on/roll-off services for cars, coaches and lorries as their major activity, but also remain important for 'foot' passengers interchanging from rail and bus services. A large share of the short sea cross-Channel market is held by Eurotunnel, using its 'Shuttle' services to carry lorries, coaches and cars. Other ferries in Britain are operated by numerous private companies, some very small.

Trunk domestic air services are provided by the two largest UK-based carriers: British Airways (BA), and BMI British Midland, competing directly on major routes from the London area to Scotland. Other major operators in this sector are the low-cost operator easyJet, and Air UK. Regional services may be operated by local 'third level' carriers such as Manx Airways, and Aurigny in the Channel Islands. BA also provide some local services through their Scottish network, and Scilly Isles helicopter service. Although the UK domestic air scene has experienced the arrival of many new small operators under increasingly liberal regulatory policy in recent years, the market has grown slowly on the minor services (see Chapter 9), resulting in a large turnover of small operators on marginal routes.

Major international airports, including Heathrow, Gatwick, Stansted, Glasgow, Edinburgh and Aberdeen, are operated by BAA plc. Many other airports are operated through local authority companies, such as Manchester, or have now been privatized through individual sales, such as that of East Midlands. Minor airports in Scotland, which have little hope of functioning commercially, are run directly by the Civil Aviation Authority (CAA), a body which also provides the national air-traffic control system.

Regulation

Regulation may be considered in three aspects: quality, quantity, and price. In many countries they are closely linked, but in Britain very little quantity and price regulation remains, apart from the effective control over some prices for rail passengers and London area services by central government and the GLA respectively. Capacity constraints at major airports and on the rail network also act as a form of quantity control.

Quality regulation

The bus and coach industry

Quality control of bus and coach operators is exercised through the area Traffic Commissioners (of which there are presently eight) under the Public Passenger Vehicles Act 1981. This established a system of 'operator licensing' (or 'O-licensing'), under which a person or company seeking to operate public service vehicles has to establish good repute, adequate financial support and satisfactory maintenance facilities. The term 'Public Service Vehicle' (PSV) largely corresponds to the everyday definition of a bus or coach (there is a minor legal distinction between them – see Chapter 3), except that certain small vehicles of sixteen seats or less, and those used other than for public service (such as school buses owned and operated by a local education authority) are excluded. A licensed taxi 'plying for hire' may have up to eight seats, but a vehicle of nine to sixteen used in public service (other than with a Minibus Permit, or as a community bus – see Chapter 8) requires a PSV licence.

The number of buses and coaches which the holder of an operator's licence is permitted to run (which may vary according to the quality of maintenance, financial resources, etc.) is specified by the Traffic Commissioner. For each vehicle permitted, a disc is issued, which it must display. The Traffic Commissioner has the power to revoke an operator's licence, or change the number of vehicles it covers.

Each PSV is subject to a strict annual inspection, following which a new licence is issued. A 'certificate of initial fitness' is issued to a new vehicle, provided that it meets the standard regulations regarding dimensions, etc. (see Chapter 3). Each driver is required to hold a Passenger Carrying Vehicle (PCV) driver's licence, issued following a specialized driving test and medical examination.

The Public Passenger Vehicles Act 1981 is a piece of consolidating legislation, incorporating the regulatory changes of the 1980 Act and those of the late 1970s (such as the Minibus Act 1977), and continues to form the basis of bus and coach 'quality' regulation.

The Transport Act of 1985 removed the need to obtain a road service licence for a bus or coach service. A distinction is now drawn between a 'local' service – one carrying some or all passengers distances of less than 15 miles (24 km) – and all others. For the local service, the proposed route must be registered with the Traffic Commissioners at least 42 days before operation is due (56 days in Scotland) – for others, not even this process is required. Provided that the person or organization registering the service is the holder of an operator licence, the process is automatic, and objections from other parties are not accepted. The only restriction on operation is through Traffic Regulation Conditions, which on grounds of road safety or congestion may, for example, prevent buses from using certain streets, or picking up at some points, but may not discriminate between operators. They are used very sparingly in practice.

Outside London and Northern Ireland, companies determine which services they will operate on a commercial basis. Other services may then be provided by the local authority under contract, following a competitive bidding procedure. Typically, these are for parts of the day and week (e.g. evening and Sunday services) rather than entire routes throughout the week, in contrast to the situation within London where contracts normally apply to the entire operation throughout the week of the services concerned.

Taxis and private hire vehicles

Taxi regulation was also changed under the 1985 Act, although not to the same extent. Quality and quantity control are handled by district or unitary councils, all of whom now exercise powers to license hackney carriages ('taxis', i.e. vehicles permitted to pick up in the street or at ranks, for separate fares). Most authorities also exercise their powers to license 'private hire vehicles' (PHVs), i.e. those hired by prior arrangement (such as a telephone request, or through an office). In London, the Public Carriage Office (PCO), under the GLA, licenses the hackney carriages (commonly known as 'black cabs'), through a strict system of quality regulation (both for vehicle and driver), but quantity limits have never applied. From 2000, private hire vehicles (locally known as 'minicabs') have also been subject to a basic quality licensing system, but prices remain totally uncontrolled.

Railways

Regulation of rail safety is exercised through the Railways Inspectorate of the Health and Safety Executive (HSE), which is empowered to approve new installations and rolling stock, and carries out a very thorough investigation of all major accidents.

Under the Railways Act 1993, the Office of the Rail Regulator (ORR) was created, responsible for regulating the privatized passenger railway, including matters such as charges made to operators by Railtrack, and open access arrangements. Parts of its functions were transferred to the SRA under the 2000 Act.

Quantity and price regulation

Road

The 1985 Transport Act discouraged the application of quantity restrictions on taxi services (i.e. limiting the total number of taxis, or 'plates' in each district's area), but some district councils do retain this power, subject to showing that 'no significant unmet need' would remain as a result. Powers to set fares for taxis remain. Shared taxi operation (splitting the costs of a hired journey between individual passengers), and 'taxibus' operation (running a vehicle of eight seats or less on a timetabled service at advertised individual fares) were also legalized, but with little impact nationally.

The local bus deregulation of the 1985 Act does not apply to the London area (i.e. that covered by the GLA, within which TfL is the licensing body), nor to Northern Ireland.

Air

Both quality and quantity control of civil air transport are exercised through the Civil Aviation Authority (CAA), a body appointed by central government. The general framework of regulation was set out in the Civil Aviation Act 1971, modified in subsequent Acts. However, much of the regulatory policy has been determined by government directives to the CAA, and the Authority's own policy statements. From September 1985, the controls over domestic air fares were largely removed. Domestic air service regulation thus became increasingly liberalized, although not to the same extent as road transport. Under EU policy international services within Europe gradually became subject to a more competitive regim.

Slots at congested airports could be seen as the principal barrier to entry into the scheduled air service market.

Other organizations

Other organizations involved in the public transport industry include trade unions, user groups and professional institutions.

LIVERPOOL JOHN MOORES UNIVERSITY
LEARNING SERVICES

Trade unions

Road

The largest trade union is the Transport and General Workers (T&GWU), covering many aspects of public transport, including bus and coach drivers, and airport and seaport staff. Some bus and coach drivers in district council companies are represented by the General and Municipal Workers (GMWU). The Rail Maritime and Transport (RMT) Union (incorporating the former National Union of Railwaymen) also represents a number of drivers in regional bus companies, a legacy of railway holdings in earlier regional groups. Engineering workers in the bus industry are represented by a wide range of craft unions, who co-operate in national bargaining procedures.

Following deregulation and substantial privatization of the bus and coach industry, and parallel changes in labour legislation, the former pattern of national negotiations over wages and conditions has been replaced by local bargaining, but generally retaining a role (albeit limited) for the trade unions.

Rail

In the railways, there has traditionally been a sharp demarcation between the manual, 'skilled', and clerical staff. The majority of staff are represented by the Rail, Maritime and Transport union (RMT), including guards, station staff and signalmen. Clerical and supervisory staff are represented by the Transport Salaried Staffs Association (TSSA). Most drivers are represented by the Associated Society of Locomotive Engineers and Firemen (ASLEF). Until 1993 negotiations over wages and conditions were carried out nationally with British Rail, but a pattern of local bargaining has emerged following the creation of franchises, and privatization (see above).

User groups

Passengers' interests are represented both by statutory and independent groups. The regional rail passengers' committees report to the national Rail Passengers' Council (RPC) which submits an annual report to the Secretary of State.

In the London region, the London Transport Users' Committee (LTUC) represents the interests of users of Transport for London (TfL), TOCs and other public transport services. Its members are appointed by the Secretary of State for Trade and Industry. It is the only statutory consumers' committee with responsibility for bus, river and taxi, as well as rail, services.

A number of local consumers' committees and user groups have been set up, such as that in Merseyside. Others arise from spontaneous action by consumers themselves, notably rail users' associations on routes to London. Ironically, these may relate to some of the more prosperous and well-served users. However, a National Federation of Bus Users (NFBU) was set up in 1985. The most poorly served, those in rural areas, find it difficult to organize, in part because facilities are so thin already. More enlightened operators have sought to consult the public on matters such as extensive service revisions, sometimes by calling public meetings.

Bus user interests are, however, considered by the Bus Appeals Body, an organization set up by the bus industry and the NFBU, which considers appeals from passengers not satisfied with the response from the operator concerned, analogous in its role to the LTUC.

External effects of transport modes have received increasing attention, together with concern about the need to encourage sustainable modes. Nationally based pressure groups may combine this interest with a support for public transport and its users – for example, in seeking to encourage use of public transport rather than cars in congested cities. They include groups such as the Friends of the Earth (FoE) and the Council for the Protection of Rural England (CPRE). The organization Transport 2000 is supported by a range of such organizations, together with the rail trade unions, in seeking to encourage a national policy more favourable to public transport.

Industry associations and professional institutions

Interests of road and rail public transport operators are represented nationally by the Confederation of Passenger Transport UK (CPT), incorporating the former Bus and Coach Council (BCC). Most members are bus and coach operators – from both the private and public sectors – covered in two sections (Section 1 for operators with fewer than fifty vehicles, Section 2 for all others). Another section comprises urban rail operators such as Sheffield Supertram. Its role within the independent bus and coach sector has become greater in recent years, although many small operators are not members. Local coach operators' associations also represent the interests of the independent sector.

Within the rail industry, the Association of Train Operating Companies (ATOC) represents the TOCs, with particular roles in allocation of revenue, and joint marketing of the network.

Local government associations concerned with transport matters include the Local Government Association (LGA), representing both levels of authority in England and Wales. In London, interests of the boroughs in transport are represented by Association of London Government (ALG). Within Scotland, the Convention of Scottish Local Authorities (COSLA) plays a similar role.

The principal professional body for the transport operating industry in Britain is the Institute of Logistics and Transport (IoLT), whose membership grade (MILT) is the main qualification. (It was formed from a merger of the Chartered Institute of Transport (CIT) and the Institute of Logistics (IoL). The former continues as an international body with sections in many countries, now known as the Chartered Institute of Logistics and Transport (CIoLT).) In the field of highways and transport planning a similar role is taken by the Institute of Highways and Transportation (IHT).

Transport co-ordinating officers in the county and unitary councils are represented by the Association of Transport Coordinating Officers (ATCO), which liaises with other local authority and operator organizations.

References and suggested reading

An annual review of the activities of the DTLR's activities is published as part of the government's overall expenditure plans. This, and other publications of the DTLR, may be accessed through its web-site http://www.dtlr.gov.uk. Similar websites cover other organizations listed in this chapter such as CfIT http://www.cfit.gov.uk and the SRA http://www.sra.gov.uk.

The overall role and current policies of the SRA are described in its *Strategic Agenda*, published in March 2001.

The law regarding bus and coach operations is extensively described in *Croner's Coach and Bus Operations* (Croner Publications Ltd, New Malden, Surrey) in loose-leaf form, updated quarterly.

Policy issues in transport are covered extensively in many journals, notably *Local Transport Today* and *Transit* (both fortnightly).

2 The role of public transport

The overall pattern

The role played by public transport in Britain has changed considerably in recent decades, from a semi-monopoly in the late 1940s – under somewhat artificial conditions – to a small share of the national market in the 1990s. In the case of bus travel, this has been associated with an absolute decline in the volume of travel; for rail an approximately stable absolute volume, growing in the late 1990s, but a fall as a percentage of a growing total market. The overall share of motorized domestic passenger-kilometres (km) taken by public transport – 13 per cent in 1999[1] – is fairly typical of Western Europe, but the absolute decline is highly untypical. In most other European countries the volume of passenger-km on local public transport, as well as rail, has often remained roughly stable, or increased, despite similar or higher levels of car ownership.

Definitions

For the purposes of this book I define 'public transport' to include all modes available to the public, irrespective of ownership. In addition to the scheduled services of bus, coach and rail operators, I include taxis, private hire buses and coaches, and the tour/excursion market served by the coach industry.

Provision of school services by hired-in buses and coaches (which may in some cases be restricted to pupils of a specific school or education authority) is also included.

Within this scope, the use of public transport may be measured in various ways:

1. The *absolute number of trips*, usually as reported by operators, derived from ticket sales. In some cases this gives passenger 'boardings' rather than trips as such, i.e. each time a passenger boards another vehicle or mode a new ticket may be issued, and hence a new 'journey' recorded. In Britain this often applies when different operators are involved: for example, a bus feeder journey to an urban railway would be recorded separately from the rail journey itself, even though both form part of the same 'linked trip' (for example, from home to work). Where greater ticketing integration exists, this problem is less likely to occur, or operators themselves draw the distinction (for example, between 'voyages' and 'deplacements' in French urban systems).

For example, in 1992–4, the ratio of 'boardings' to 'stages' (as defined in the National Travel Survey – see below) by bus was 1:17 in London, and 1:08 in the other major conurbations.[2] The higher ratio in London partly reflects the more complex network, but also the greater use of concessionary passes and travelcards which enable users to board the first bus to arrive and then interchange en route, rather than wait for a less frequent through service.

In some cases, operators may produce very little data (for example, for taxi and private hire car use), and household surveys may form the main basis. In Britain, the National Travel Survey (NTS) is the principal source of such data, together with studies in specific urban areas (notably the London Area Travel Survey, LATS). By collecting data via households, the NTS can also avoid the double-counting of trips. A 'journey' is defined as a movement between one activity and another (e.g. from home to work), a 'stage' is that part on a particular mode of transport. This may be further sub-divided (although not usually in the published data) into 'boardings' where more than one vehicle is used within the same mode (e.g. two different bus routes).

The NTS is an exceptionally comprehensive data source, since it covers all days of the week, and since 1989 has taken the form of a continuous sample survey throughout Britain. Within this chapter, urban and local movement is primarily considered – more detailed consideration of rural and long-distance travel using NTS data may be found in Chapters 8 and 9.

2. The *distance travelled*, expressed in passenger-kilometres. This may be derived by multiplying the number of 'trips' (howsoever defined) by an average length estimated from surveys, either on-vehicle or through household surveys. It is unwise, however, to derive such data from distances paid for, since these will generally exceed the distance actually travelled, especially where zonal or flat fares apply.

3. *User expenditure* on public transport may also be used as an indicator of the minimum economic benefit derived. This forms a means of distinguishing cases where much higher expenditure per kilometre is incurred for higher quality services (for example, a taxi instead of local bus, or first class instead of standard class rail travel). However, it does not indicate the total benefit derived by the user (which would include consumer surplus) and particular care must be taken in assessing changes over time where elasticities are low. For example, a 10 per cent real fare increase on an urban network with a short-term price elasticity of –0.4 would produce a drop in demand of 4 per cent and revenue growth of about 6 per cent, but the growth in revenue simply reflects a transfer of consumer surplus from the remaining users to the operator (not to mention the loss of consumer surplus of those no longer travelling).

4. These absolute measures may be converted to *trip rates per head of population*. In the case of operator-derived annual data, an annual trip rate may be estimated by dividing the total trips reported by an estimate of the catchment population served (which is not necessarily the same as the administrative district after which an operator may be named). Where data have been derived from a household survey (such as the NTS, which covers seven consecutive days of travel), the data

may be used directly in this form, or expanded to an annual figure (allowing for any seasonal factors at the time of data collection). The 'trips per head per annum' indicator, while crude in some respects, does provide a useful quick comparison between different areas and countries, in the absence of more detailed survey information (see further discussion below). Where appropriate data exist, these rates may also be estimated for different groups in the population.

Even where the only source is operator ticket-based data, it is none the less often possible to estimate separate rates for passengers on concessionary fares and/or travelcards. Where the number of such cards on issue is known, an average rate may likewise be estimated for their users.

5. *Market share* may be estimated where data on other modes are available, as in the case for the NTS. It is particularly important to ensure that comparable definitions are used, since other modes rarely involve *en route* interchange in the same fashion as public transport. The extent to which non-motorized trips are included is also critical, since when short trips are included they may represent up to about one-third of all journeys (although obviously a much smaller proportion of distance travelled).

These basic concepts are illustrated in Table 2.1 for Britain, using data from the latest National Travel Survey, and annual totals reported by operators.

It will be noted that the data derived from the NTS generally give a slightly lower estimate of use of bus and rail services than that derived from operators, especially in respect of trips per head for rail, despite lack of operator-derived data for 'other bus and coach services'. This is partly owing to differences in definition mentioned above, but also to the coverage of the NTS being more limited – its sample covers only households resident in Britain, and hence omits travel by non-residents within the country. Certain other categories, such as students in university halls of residence, are also omitted. This may explain some of the differences found (which are more noticeable in respect of rail travel than for local bus). However, the NTS is the only practicable source of data for taxi trips, in the absence of any data being reported by the operators themselves. Note that the 'journey stages' definition is used here, so that if more than one mode were used in the same one way trip, each is counted. If the NTS 'journeys' definition was used (in which only the principal mode is classified), then a greater difference exists.

The term 'National Railways' (or 'surface railways') is used to describe the services provided by the twenty-five privatized Train Operating Companies (TOCs) running the network formerly provided by British Rail. 'Other urban railways' includes the systems in Glasgow, Tyne and Wear and recently developed light rail networks such as Manchester.

Operator data unfortunately give little information on journey length or trip purpose, and hence in analysing the market in this form, NTS data will be used as the main source. However, its possible understatement of rail travel should be borne in mind.

Table 2.1 Public transport use in Britain

Data refer to 1999–2000 (financial year) for that from operators, and an average of the calendar years 1997–9 for the National Travel Survey (NTS)

Operator data (1999–2000)

	Trips (m)	Passenger-km ('000 m)
Local bus services	4,279	⎫
Other bus and coach services	n/a	⎬ 45
		⎭
National railways	947	38.3
London Underground	927	7.2
Other urban railways	109	0.7
Grand total	6,262	91
Population (1999)		57.81 million
Implied public transport trips/head		108[a]
Implied distance/head		1,580[a]

Data from NTS (1997–9)   Averages per person per year

	Journey stages	Distance (km)
Local buses	64	395
Other bus and coach[b]	8	335
Railways[c]	21	623
Taxi/private hire vehicles	12	90
Other public (including rail, ferries, air)	2	97
Total	104	1540
As a percentage of all travel		
– all trip lengths	8.9%	14.1%
– of trips over 1.6 km	11.6%	n/a

Sources: A Bulletin of Public Transport Statistics Bulletin GB: 2000 edition. Bulletin SB(00)26 DETR London, December 2000, tables 1, 3.1, 5, 10.

Notes
a Excluding domestic air (17 m trips; 7,300 m pax-km)
b Express, excursions, tours and private hire
c Surface rail, London Underground, urban metros and light rail

Comparisons of bus and rail trip rates with the NTS

The local bus journeys of 4,279 m implies 74 per head per annum on population base of 57.81 m, compared with 64 'stages' in NTS. This difference is explained by 'boardings' effect, and possible omission of some categories of user from NTS.

Rail differences are larger, the operator-reported data giving a rail combined total of about 34 per head compared with only 21 in NTS. This is partly explained by double-counting between TOCs in National Railways data, also foreign tourist use of London Underground and other systems, and rapid growth in the late 1990s.

Composition of the rail and bus markets

It can be seen from Table 2.1 that National Railways and the London Underground rail networks are of similar size in terms of passenger trips, but that the former is much greater in terms of passenger-km, owing to the higher average length of journey (about 40 km, compared with 13 km). The average trip length by local bus is much shorter at about 4 km.

Within the total 38,300 million passenger-km on National Railways in 1999/2000, about 13,200 were made on long-distance (formerly InterCity sector) services, 17,600 on London and South East (mostly commuting into London), and 7,500 on regional services.[3] In terms of passenger trips, a large proportion is made on the network focusing on London and the South East, around 650 million. Rail use is thus highly concentrated in and around the London region, and on the long-distance flows.

Within the bus and coach industry, the 'local' trips, i.e. those on public local scheduled services, are handled mostly by the larger urban and regional operators, while the independent sector (of smaller companies, always in private ownership) has predominated in the 'other' market, as discussed in Chapter 1. The latter is largely composed of school services, together with private hire and excursion and tour operations. The express service category – based on the Transport Act 1985 definition of those carrying all their passengers a distance of at least 15 miles (24 km) measured in a straight line – is a fairly small one, around 15–20 million trips. In practice, many long-distance and commuter coach services also carry intermediate traffic, and are therefore registered in the 'local service' category.

Use of the 'trips per head' measure

In most cities of the world, the annual public transport trip rate per person varies between about 100 and 400, with some cases of higher values. For example, in Britain one may derive a figure of about 275–300 in London (including all public transport modes), which is similar to that in Paris. However, in medium-sized conurbations of about 1 to 2 million people (such as West Yorkshire) the rate is often less than 150, and in smaller urban areas less than 100. A figure of about 300 per head is fairly common in large cities, both in Europe and elsewhere, often associated with extensive rail systems, and constraints on car use.

So far, I have made comments mainly on Britain, where buses form the majority of the public transport system, and hence growing car ownership may have direct impacts on ridership. However, Britain is not typical of Europe as a whole. In Western Europe, public transport use has often grown, or at least remained stable, during a phase of further car ownership growth. This is associated in particular with provision of high-quality urban rail and tramway systems, albeit at very high investment levels. There are often much higher levels of operating support in other European countries (enabling fares to be kept down).

High per capita use is particularly associated with German, Dutch and Swiss cities, notably Zurich. Conversely, some of the growth in French urban systems since the 1970s (associated with innovations such as VAL in Lille, for example) was from a low per capita ridership base, and even today is not necessarily higher than in Britain, for cities of equivalent size.

These high per capita trip rates have been retained by public transport in cities with high-quality public transport systems, despite car ownership levels of over 300–400 cars per 1,000 people, notably in Germany and Switzerland.

Among the highest per capita trip rates in the world are Hong Kong and Singapore at about 500 per annum, in this case associated with high levels of real income and employment, and good quality public transport systems, but also with deliberate restraints on car ownership (through high taxation) and use (notably through road pricing in Singapore). High urban density is also an obvious contributory factor.[4]

Until the late 1980s, conditions in Eastern Europe were particularly favourable to public transport – low car ownership, high subsidies (permitting low fares), high population density, and high economic activity rates. Per capita trip rates of 500 or more were found in some cities. One should add, however, that this was a highly artificial situation, based on an economic structure that was not sustainable, and unacceptable constraints on personal freedom.

The last few years have seen a very abrupt reversal of this situation, in effect a greatly accelerated form of the 'vicious circle' of decline as seen in the British bus industry. Unemployment has directly reduced the demand for transport, and fares have risen rapidly in real terms as subsidies have been reduced. At the same time, growing prosperity among those remaining in employment has caused a very rapid growth in car ownership, often to levels of 0.3 per head or even above within 5–10 years (for example, in Warsaw). There is a danger that a previously favourable public transport situation could change to one of exceptionally rapid decline, perhaps to below Western European ridership levels. Cities in eastern *Länder* of Germany showed sharp falls – for example, from about 400 per annum in 1990 to about 200 in 1997.

Variations in public transport use by age and sex

Use of NTS data enables us to indicate variations in public transport use by age and sex, both in terms of absolute trip rates and the percentage share it represents.

Overall, NTS respondents made 1,046 journeys per person per year in 1997–9, of which about one-third were 'short' trips (under 1.6 km) mainly on foot or cycle, the remaining two-thirds over 1.6 km, and largely motorized. Although most public transport trips are over 1.6 km, there are a small number of shorter trips, especially when feeder journeys are counted separately.

By age, trip rates and distances travelled are highest in the 'working age' groups, from 18 to 59, averaging around 1,200 trips and 15,000 km per year (by all modes combined). Bus and coach use tends to be concentrated at each end of the age spectrum, representing about 6 per cent of all trips, but up to 12 per cent in the age groups 17–20, and over 70, although at its lowest in the 'working age' groups 30–59, at only 4 per cent. This is associated with car availability, the youngest groups not yet being able to own cars, and the oldest group never having done so. Conversely, rail use shows much less variation, its highest share being in the 21–9 age group (at 3 per cent) and taxi/private hire car use is fairly well spread over the age groups (an average share of 1 per cent, highest at 3 per cent in the 17–20 age group).

By sex, females tend to make greater use of public transport than males, their average bus and coach share being 7 per cent (compared with 5 per cent for males), with a similar distribution by age category. Rail use is marginally lower among females than males, but taxi and private hire car use similar. A more noteworthy difference between males and females is the split between car driver and car passenger use. Whereas for males 47 per cent of all trips are made as car drivers and 17 per cent as car passengers, for females these proportions are 32 per cent and 28 per cent respectively. The differences are much less marked in the youngest groups.

For the public transport operator, there are some worrying implications. While rail and taxi use are fairly well spread by age and sex, bus use is clearly associated with lack of access to cars. In the case of the older groups, it is also associated with lower fares due to provision of concessionary travel. In future, older age groups are more likely to retain car use they now display in the working age range.

There may, however, be some prospect of retaining and increasing public transport use among the younger age groups, provided that an acceptable quality of service and price can be offered. School and education travel as such may be offered at concessionary fares (or free travel in some cases), but in many instances the full adult fare may be payable from the age of about 16 (dependent upon operator policy). Greater interest is now being shown in differential pricing policies aimed at this group, which ease the shift from child rates to full adult pricing. For example, Brighton & Hove (one of the most successful privatized bus operators in Britain) now sells a card to those attaining the age of 16, entitling them to continue travelling at the child rate for each trip made. The price of this card is then successively increased at six-month intervals up to the 18th birthday, after which a quarterly travelcard is sold by direct mailing at a gradually increasing price. In London, a one-third discount is now offered to 16/17-year-olds for period travelcards on TfL and Underground services. In Paris, RATP has been successful in targeting this group with its 'Imagine R' annual pass.

One unfortunate aspect of the perception of bus and coach travel by young people is that much of their experience may be gained on crowded school bus journeys, rather than the moderate load factors typical of off-peak travel.

Car occupancy levels are often much higher for non-work purposes – in 1997–99 averaging 1.9 for leisure, and 1.6 for shopping, reaching 2.4 for holidays or day trips.[5] Hence for these purposes, perceived cost per person by public transport may compare unfavourably where car running and parking costs are split. Tickets such as the 'family railcard' or 'family travelcard' (in London) can be seen as response to this.

The proportion of public transport trips – both for all purposes, and work – falls gradually with size of urban area, associated with absence of rail services, lower levels of bus service, higher car ownership and less constraint on car use.

Variations by time of day, and day of week

The internal structure of the public transport market may also be examined in terms of trip length distribution, and split by time of day and day of week. Within the Monday to Friday 'working day', work and education trips tend to be concentrated at peak periods (around 0800–0930, and 1600–1730). However, they do not usually coincide in both peaks, since the school day is generally shorter than the adult working day. Where service industry employment predominates, working hours are typically around 0900–1700, causing the morning school and work peaks to coincide, but with a spread in the late afternoon, as schools finish around 1530–1600.

In many areas, it is the school peak which causes almost the entire additional peak vehicle demand above a 'base' level from 0800 to 1800. This is evident in almost all smaller towns, and in most cities up to about 200,000 population, such as Plymouth and Southampton. Although journeys to work by public transport are substantial, they do not necessarily require more vehicular capacity (given the higher load factors accepted in the peak) than for shopping, and other trips between the peaks. Even in the largest conurbation bus networks, it is only on the radial routes to the central area that journeys to work create sharp peaks, school travel causing the peak within suburban areas.

Rail networks display a very different peaking ratio, however, being oriented almost entirely to the centres of large cities, and thus the adult work journey.

The ratio of peak to base demand may be somewhat greater in terms of passenger-km than passenger trips, since the journeys to work are often much longer than local shopping and personal business trips within the suburban areas. The 1997–9 NTS shows that for all modes, work commuting trips tend to be longer (at 13.0 km average) than those for education (4.8 km) or shopping (6.4 km), with an 'all purposes' average of 10.5 km.[6] Conversely, in smaller towns employment and shopping may show a similar degree of concentration, leading to similar trip lengths, and hence a good balance of demand during the base period. This is particularly noticeable in towns of about 50,000 to 150,000 people, such as Oxford, or Grimsby. Many work trips are by car, and much school travel within walking or cycling distance. Shopping is fairly concentrated in town centres, generating good levels of demand on radial networks.

In recent years, a similar flattening out of the public transport demand ratio between peak and inter-peak periods (the latter being the shopping hours from about 0930 to 1600) has been observed, as work trips have shifted to the private car, the inter-peak demand has often held up better, owing to the rising proportion of pensioners in the population, often without cars, whose use of public transport is further encouraged by concessionary fares at such times. The availability of cars within the car-owning household during this period is also limited by the use of cars for the work trip, creating a potential public transport market among those based at home during the day, perhaps stimulated by lower off-peak fares. The growth of high-frequency minibus services has also stimulated non-work travel to a greater extent than peak demand, aiding this process.

This flattening out, while occurring within an overall decline, has thus enabled some improvement in vehicle and crew utilization through more efficient scheduling.

A sharper decline has occurred in early morning, evening and Sunday public transport use, car availability to the household as a whole being much greater in the latter two periods, and the first affected by loss of work journeys and changes in working hours. Evening travel has also been hit by the long-term drop in cinema attendance (albeit recently reversed), and a reluctance in some areas to go out in the dark for fear of assault. However, very late evening and all-night bus travel has grown rapidly in London following the revamped network introduced during the 1980s and subsequently expanded.

Since deregulation of local bus services outside London, it has been common to find that a Monday to Saturday service is registered to run commercially from about 0800 to 1800 (even in some low-density areas), while early morning, evening and Sunday services become the responsibility of local authority tendered operations. Operators may also be unwilling to register additional peak-period journeys required largely for school travel (see further discussion in Chapters 6 and 7).

Within the week as a whole, Mondays to Fridays display similar demand patterns, although Friday is often busier for shopping, and has an earlier afternoon peak, especially where the working week has been shortened by shorter hours on this day. Saturday continues to be a busy day for shopping trips, especially where car ownership is low, but has suffered a marked decline in high car-ownership areas, owing to use of the car by the family as a whole on that day. Within larger conurbations, the shopping activity is often concentrated in the secondary centres.

The 'market gearing' concept

A further general concept which may be introduced at this stage is that of 'market gearing', i.e. the share of demand which may be attributed to a specific category of users. In addition to talking of average trip rates, even broken down by age or sex, for example, we can show that certain categories of individuals produce a substantial part of total demand. This may be derived from operator ticket data where defined individuals hold certain types of ticket or pass (such as a pensioner concession, or working age adult travelcard) and the number of trips attributable to such users can be estimated. Surveys such as the NTS also enable such estimates to be made. For example, in Greater London, there are about 1 million holders of the pensioner pass, and in the wider region about 0.9 million rail/bus travelcard holders,[7] each representing a substantial share of all public transport trips.

A notional example is shown in Table 2.2. Hence, in this case, pensioners comprise 15 per cent of the population, but 26 per cent of public transport trips. The highest ratio is found for adult travelcard users (travelling between home and work about 200–225 days per year) in which 7.5 per cent of the population produce 30 per cent of all trips. For the less frequent users, it may be difficult to identify them separately from 'non-users' (since they do not hold separately issued cards), and some boundary definition may need to be adopted (e.g. use less than once a month).

Table 2.2 A notional example of 'market gearing': city population 1 million

Types of person	Number (m)	Trips per person per year	Total trips (m)	(%)
Pensioners	0.15	200	30	(26)
Adult travelcard users	0.075	450	34	(30)
Child pass holders	0.05	400	20	(18)
Other users	0.3	100	30	(26)
Non-users	0.425	0	–	
Average trip rate			114	

(26%) etc – share of total trips represented by this category

A shift to smart card use may assist, in that they will become attractive to less frequent users who now pay in cash.

Although notional, this pattern does compare fairly well with NTS data, as shown in Table 2.3. In addition to the travel diary, a question is sometimes included in the NTS on overall frequency of use of different modes. In 1998/9 this question showed that 20 per cent of the population travelled by local bus or rail three or more times a week, and a further 12 per cent once or twice a week. However, 44 per cent reported use of local buses 'once a year or never' and 53 per cent likewise for rail.[8] The last closely matches the 'non-user' share of 42.5 per cent assumed in Table 2.2. Bear in mind that published NTS data give an average for the whole population, including small towns and rural areas, and hence the share of the population using public transport with high frequency would be less than assumed for a city as above.

Table 2.3 shows data from a special tabulation, relating frequency of local bus use to size of settlement.

Table 2.3 Frequency of local bus use by size of settlement, 1997–9: percentages of respondents

Settlement size type	Frequency of use		
	Once a week or more	Less than once a week, more than twice a year	Once or twice a year, or less
Greater London	45	26	29
Metropolitan built-up areas	38	20	41
Large urban area (over 250,000)	33	25	42
Urban area (25,000 to 250,000)	24	15	61
Small urban (3,000 to 25,000)	19	19	62
Rural	12	14	74

Source: Special tabulations from NTS 1997–9.

The journey to work

Table 2.4 shows the shares of the journey-to-work market by different modes, from the 1997–9 NTS. Note that the principal mode of transport used is shown – for example, if someone commutes to central London by surface rail, and then makes a shorter ride on the Underground to reach their final destination, only surface rail will be shown as the mode used.

Overall, buses account for about 9 per cent of all journeys to work, and rail about 5 per cent (or, as shares of the motorized market, about 11 per cent and 6 per cent respectively). As one would expect, the public transport mode share is greater for central London, with 49 per cent of journeys to work by surface rail or Underground, and 10 per cent by bus. Note that these figures are for the whole day: during the morning peak (0700–1000), the rail share is substantially greater at about 75 per cent. The proportions vary substantially between different parts of outer London (Croydon is well served, for example) and between the conurbation centres. The greatest share handled by bus and coach is for conurbation centres (16 per cent). Note that almost six times as many car commuters travelled as drivers than passengers, giving an average car occupancy for this purpose of only 1.2.

Other journey purposes

Although public transport's role tends to be associated mainly with the work journey, it is evident that this is not necessarily where bus takes the greatest share. In many cases, buses take a larger share of the shopping market, and this in turn forms a larger share of all bus trips other than work, as Table 2.5 shows. The largest share taken by local bus is often within the education trip market. In 1997–9, local bus (i.e. scheduled services open to the public) represented 24 per cent of journeys between home and school by children aged 11–16, higher than car at 21 per cent. 'Private bus' (typically, buses and coaches hired to carry children on behalf of local education authorities) accounted for another 8 per cent. This is also a sector in which the scheduled local bus share has been increasing, having risen from 20 per cent in 1985–6.[9] As many home to school trips lie above walking distance, a major demand for public transport is created, especially in rural areas.

Table 2.4 Usual means of travel to work by usual place of work 1997–9: percentage (rounded to nearest whole number)

Area	Walk	Pedal/ motor cycle	Car driver	Car pass	Bus or coach	Surface rail	London Underground	Other
Central London	7	3	26	4	10	29	20	–
Outer London	10	6	63	6	9	4	3	–
Conurbation centre	8	2	54	13	16	6	n/a	1
Other urban	11	5	61	12	10	1	n/a	–
Not urban	13	4	65	12	4	–	n/a	–
Average	10	4	60	11	9	3	2	1

Source: National Travel Survey 1997–9, as quoted in DETR Statistics Bulletin SB(00)02, table 4.4.

Table 2.5 Composition of the market for each mode, by journey purpose, 1993–5

Purpose	*Local bus (outside London)*	*Surface rail*
Work (commuting)	21	51
Business	1	6
Education	15	7
Shopping	34	9
Personal business	10	7
Visiting friends	13	11
Sport/Entertainment	4	5
Other	2	4
Total	100	100

Notes: Derived from table 2A of the National Travel Survey 1993–5 (HMSO, July 1996). Percentages sum down the columns.

Conversely, the role of rail is generally small for non-work purposes (1 per cent in the case of home to school trips by 11–16-year-olds, for example).

Trip chaining

Patterns of travel during the day may be best understood in terms of trip chains. Just as individual journeys are better analysed as linked trips from one activity to another, the day's travel can be seen as a 'chain' of such links, starting at home, then via various activities and destinations until home is reached again. The simplest consists of 'home – one activity (for example, work) – home', but more complex patterns may be found, such as returning home for lunch (mainly in smaller towns), or returning in the evening via the shops, or place of entertainment. Analysis of travel diaries from the 1985/6 NTS enables us to understand such chains more clearly.[10]

In analysing such data, short walk links must also be considered. For example, someone working in a city centre might walk to a shopping street open in the evening, then return home by public transport: although only two public transport journeys would be recorded, the trip chain is none the less a 'complex' one in terms of individual behaviour.

Complex public transport-based trip chains are found mainly in larger cities, often associated with the use of tickets such as the travelcard which permit additional linking trips at zero money cost.

Trip chain analysis also enables us to understand how trips made by the same individual are linked by time of day: for example, a substantial proportion (around 40 per cent) of one-way trips made on bus services after 1800 are in reality the return leg of trip chains which began earlier in the same day, rather than new home-based trips. Hence, cutting out a poorly loaded evening service has implications for ridership on daytime services, should the inability to make the return leg of the trip result in the user switching to another mode for the whole trip chain. This has implications for the extent to which evening services are in fact 'cross-subsidized' by profitable daytime operation.

The more complex chains may explain why cars are used sometimes for the peak work journey into large cities even when public transport may appear more convenient, as the car is available for indirect homeward journeys in the evenings, or business trips during the day. To capture a high share of the work market, public transport may need to offer good evening services, and facilities such as travelcards which permit complex trip patterns without financial penalty or the inconvenience of checking fares for occasional journeys.

Time spent in travel

Irrespective of income, status or modes used all individuals ultimately face the same constraint in terms of time – 24 hours per day. Allowing for time spent in work, sleeping and household activities, the discretionary time in which travel and other activities may be fitted is fairly limited, especially within the Monday to Friday 'working week'. Although the amount of time spent by individuals in travel obviously varies, the average time spent in travel per person per day is surprisingly constant. Increased travel may thus be seen as arising from faster modes being used within the same time budget to cover greater distances.

For example, the NTS shows that average time spent in travel per person per year has hardly changed between 1972/3 (353 hours) and 1997–9 (357 hours), albeit with some fluctuation in the intervening period. The overall average is thus very close to one hour per day. However, over the same period distance travelled rose by 52 per cent (for all modes), implying a corresponding rise in average speed.[11]

A more detailed time-activity diary enables such trends to be examined in greater depth. Work by Brög[12] in German cities indicates that for intra-urban travel the average time spent per person per day is very stable (at about 60 minutes), as is the number of activities outside the home. For example, in comparing surveys carried out in Essen and Hanover in 1976 and 1990 it was found that average travel time per person in Essen had changed from 60 minutes to 59 minutes, and in Hanover from 61 to 62. Activities per person per day likewise changed very little (stable at 2.7, and from 2.9 to 2.8 respectively). Thus one could see the urban transport market as a whole as a 'saturated' market, with little scope for dramatic expansion. More substantial changes were seen in the mix of modes used, and total travel distance (a shift from non-motorized modes to car driver and public transport). However, in Hanover in particular, public transport did not decline as a share of total trips, but rose from 16 to 22 per cent over this period.

Such time budget constraints are less likely to apply to weekend, leisure and long-distance travel.

Changes in individuals' travel over time

So far, although we have disaggregated the market into certain categories of person, we have not looked at individual behaviour.

Individuals shift from one category to another, not simply as their ages change, but also their status – from child to student, to adult, to married person possibly with children, to pensioner, etc. These stages in the 'life cycle' are associated with changes in household size and structure, car availability and trip purpose. Thus the work journey is a major factor determining household travel behaviour for certain stages, the need to get children to school at others.

Changes in travel behaviour are often associated with critical events in the life cycle, such as setting up a new home, or changing jobs. Many people may change their mode of travel for this reason, at least in the short run, rather than because of modal characteristics as such. This leads to a high turnover in the market, such that net changes between one year and the next are often small compared with the gross changes that produce them. For example, panel surveys in Tyne and Wear showed that a net reduction in the public transport share for the journey to work of 2 percentage points between 1982 and 1983 was the net result of 7 per cent of respondents ceasing to be public transport users, while 5 per cent became new users in that period. A net change of 2 per cent thus involved about 12 per cent of the sample in changing modes.[13]

These changes are likely to be particularly noticeable if an individual service is examined, since people may change routes used when changing homes and/or jobs, while remaining in the public transport market. Even in a zone of apparently stable land use and total population, such as a well-established residential area, constant change is occurring. On a typical urban bus or rail route, as many as 20 per cent of users may have begun to use that specific service within the last twelve months. Hence, if examining the impact of a recent change (such as introduction of a 'Quality Partnership' upgraded bus service) it is important to distinguish users who have switched to a route for such personal reasons, as distinct from those attracted by service characteristics as such.

Patterns of individual behaviour may influence trip frequencies over a very long period. For example, based on work in South Yorkshire and elsewhere, Goodwin and others have suggested that trip rates developed in early adult life may strongly influence subsequent modal use.

The implications of this for transport operators and planners is that responses to changes in fares and service quality should be assessed not only in the short run, but over long periods, since much short-run change is caused primarily by non-transport factors, but in the long run transport characteristics will affect other choices. For example, individuals may be firmly committed to a specific mode of travel for their existing home to work trip, which may not be affected even by large changes in price or service quality, but when relocating, will have to reconsider the routing, and perhaps mode, of that trip. If a good public transport service is offered, then relocation may take account of access by that mode; if not, then car might be the inevitable choice.

Taxis and private hire cars

The total number of taxis and private hire cars has grown rapidly in recent years, associated with legislative changes, which have liberalized previous restrictions, and (until the mid-1990s) increasing unemployment stimulating more entry into the trade. Licensed taxis as such in Great Britain grew from about 39,100 in 1985 to 69,000 in 1999, or by 76 per cent.[14] Use of taxis and private hire vehicles (miles per person per year) grew by about 107 per cent between 1985/6 and 1997–9.[15] While representing only about 13 per cent of all public transport journeys in 1997–9 (and hence just over 1 per cent of all motorized trips), they account for about 25 per cent of all personal expenditure on public transport, due to the very much higher cost per trip.

In some respects, the roles of taxis/private hire vehicles and other public transport could be seen as complementary: they are used particularly for late-night travel. Some of the growth since 1985–6 may have been associated with reduced quality of bus services since deregulation. However, London displays both a high level of conventional (bus and rail) public transport use, and the highest taxi/minicab mileage per person per year within Britain.

Public transport and car use

As car ownership has grown, it has had a direct effect on public transport use. First, the individual having first choice in use of the car (usually corresponding to the 'main driver' in the NTS, and typically the working head of household) will tend to use it, unless other specific factors apply (such as commuting into a large city centre, for which public transport may be more convenient). His or her trips will then be lost to public transport, except for occasional journeys. In addition, however, other members of the household may also transfer some of their trips to the car, as passengers – a child being given a lift to school, or the family travelling together at weekends. The loss of trips to public transport will thus be greater than those of one person alone, although this could depend upon price and quality of the service offered: if it is good, then other members of the household may be less inclined to arrange their trips so as to travel as passengers in the household car. Teenagers, for example, may prefer the greater independence of travel by public transport to being given lifts by their parents (and the latter appreciate the reduction in chauffeuring).

Overall, each new car may reduce local bus trips by about 200–250 per annum. For example, Table 2.6 shows that persons in no-car households made 156 local bus trips per person in 1995–7, falling to 43 in one-car households. At an average household size of approximately 2.3, the drop in bus trips per annum would thus be about 250. The effect is greater for the first car than the second, since the latter will be used in part to take trips that were being made as car passengers in the first (the children acquiring their first cars, for example). The effect on public transport use is that the members of a one-car household still make substantial numbers of public transport trips, although these are concentrated into categories such as school and Monday to Friday shopping trips, with much less evening and weekend public transport use. A two-car household may make very little use of public transport, except where larger than average, or employing public transport for the work journey.

Rail trip rates are also affected by car ownership, but to a lesser degree, and rail distance in fact rises with car ownership.

Table 2.6 Relationships between car ownership and public transport use: per person per year, averages for 1995–7

Cars per household	Local bus trips	Bus km	Rail trips	Rail km
None	156	544	22	335
One	43	193	17	336
Two or more	22	124	13	366
Average	62	252	17	345

Source: National Travel Survey 1995–7 as quoted in *Focus on Personal Travel* 1998 edition (TSO, November 1998), table 6.5.

The majority of rail users come from car-owning households, and in many areas this is also true for bus use.

In 1999, 22.8 million private cars were licensed in Britain, corresponding to about 0.39 per head, or 1.02 per household. The most common category was the one-car household, some 44 per cent of the total. Another 27 per cent of households had two or more cars, thus leaving 28 per cent without a car. The proportion of households with one or more cars has grown less rapidly than car ownership in total, as average household size has fallen. Its rate of growth has also declined. For example, between 1963 and 1973 this proportion rose from 36 per cent to 54 per cent, but by 1984 by only another 7 points to 61 per cent, and a further 8 points to 69 per cent in 1993, and 72 per cent in 1999.[16] It should be noted that the average household size in non-car owning households is lower than in those with cars, being typified by pensioner households with only one or two persons per household. Hence, only about 20 per cent of the population are resident in non-car-owning households.

Marked variations occur by area. In 1997–9, about 38 per cent of households in London and the metropolitan areas did not have a car, but this fell to 29 per cent in urban areas of 25,000 to 250,000, and to 16 per cent in rural areas.[17]

The London case

London is of importance in its own right as a part of the public transport market – the majority of rail travel and about 30 per cent of all bus journeys in Britain – and also displays markedly different trends to public transport use elsewhere in Britain. Following a period of gradual decline from a peak of use around 1950, the Underground network saw very rapid growth in use during the 1980s, from 498 million trips in 1982 to 815 million in 1988/9 (by 64 per cent) exceeding the previous peak around 1950 when car ownership was a fraction of the present level. Following recovery from a recession in the early 1990s, it reached a further peak of 927 million journeys in 1999–2000. Bus use, while not experiencing such dramatic growth, remained fairly stable at about 1,100 million trips per year in the 1980s, and has now risen to about 1,300 million, in contrast to sharp drops elsewhere. Surface rail peak period commuting into central London also rose during the late 1980s, falling with the recession and rising again in recent years.

The growth in central area peak demand (concentrated wholly on rail) is explained by growth in central area employment, notably in the financial services sector. Off-peak Underground ridership growth and the high level of bus use may be explained largely by the stimulus resulting from the travelcard (see also Chapter 7), and, in the latter part of this period, improved bus service frequency and reliability.

Aggregate forecasting of public transport demand

As described earlier, public transport demand may be measured in several ways at the aggregate level. For forecasting purposes, either trips or passenger-km may form the basis. Revenue then becomes an output, through multiplying the forecast physical volume by unit revenue. Price level will itself be a significant factor in demand.

A trip rate per capita may be derived for selected urban areas from operator data and/or sources such as the NTS. The simplest 'default' forecast would be to assume that the same trip rate will apply, and hence total volume changes only in response to population. In Britain and Western Europe this factor alone is generally marginal, although it does explain some differences between urban areas in the recent past (for example, the modest population growth in London since the 1980s partly explains some bus and underground growth – around 4 per cent between 1991 and 1998[18] – prior to considering factors affecting trip rate. Conversely, areas such as Liverpool have suffered population decline.)

However, in the developing world, with urban population growth of 3–5 per cent p.a. compound, this may well be the strongest factor, the crucial issue being whether transport supply can expand to meet demand growth.

As the next step, the population growth forecast may be broken down by age groups, to which specific trip rates may be applied. An obvious division in Britain and Western Europe is to treat separately the oldest groups, aged 60–65 upward, possibly sub-dividing between an 'active' younger group, and an older group more likely to suffer infirmity (usually 75 upward). The 60–65 upward age group also coincides with availability of concessionary fares.

Current forecasts indicate very rapid growth in the older categories, especially the very oldest. This is even more marked in some other European countries such as Italy and Germany (subject to fluctuations in future birth rates and immigration). Currently, on a 1998 base, British forecasts envisage total population rising from 58.7 m to 60 m in 2020, within which the over-65s will rise from 12 m to 16 m, implying a net reduction in other age groups.[19] Unless a marked change occurs in life expectancy (or its assumed current trend) a high degree of confidence may be expressed in the forecast of absolute numbers of older people.

Similarly, the school age group could be predicted (with less certainty, due to variations in birth rate), and matched with a ticket category.

By applying existing public transport trip rates to these age group categories, a crude aggregate forecast can be produced, assuming no other factors are applicable. The growth in pensioners would imply, *ceteris paribus*, a corresponding growth in public transport use, given that their trip rate is higher than for 'working age' adult categories.

The impact of car ownership

Bus use is in general affected much more by growth in car ownership, than rail, since for most journeys (even under congested conditions) it will offer a faster and more convenient alternative, except into congested city centres where parking is limited by volume or price. Hence, a forecast which simply assumed a constant trip rate per head by bus for each population category over time would overstate bus use if car ownership were rising.

Data such as the NTS can be used to determine average trip rates by car ownership category for a base year (see Table 2.6). The loss of bus trips per additional car has tended to decline over time, due to a lower trip rate in the 'captive' non-car owning groups (from which any decline due to a shift to car use would occur), and also the fact that a growing proportion of the net additions to the car fleet takes the form of second or third cars in households already with one car. While having some further impact on public transport use (through household members previously using public transport due to non-availability of a car for certain journeys they wish to make), the second or third car also affects use of the first, through journeys previously being made as 'second drivers' or passengers being transferred to the additional car.

At recent rates of car ownership growth, a reduction of about 1 per cent to 1.5 per cent per annum in urban bus use might be expected from this factor alone. However, there will also be 'second order' effects where the bus operator has to react to the resultant loss of revenue through cutting costs and/or increasing real fares paid by the remaining users, in the absence of efficiency gains which might absorb the loss.

For example, suppose an operator carries 100 units of passengers per annum, at an average revenue of £1. All costs, including a 'normal' return on capital, are covered from revenue. If demand falls in one year, due to rising car ownership, by 1.5 per cent, then if revenue falls by the same proportion, the operator must take action to compensate for this gap. If no additional public funding is available, nor efficiency gains to compensate, nor marketing/quality initiatives to increase demand, there are two main methods: 1. By increasing real fare per trip for the remaining passengers; 2. By cutting services to reduce costs (assumed *pro rata*).

However, both these factors are subject to their own elasticities, implying a further drop in ridership (and hence revenue) as a result. The extensive work collated by the Transport and Road Research Laboratory in 1980 suggests short-run elasticities of about the same magnitude, i.e. +0.4 for real fares, −0.4 for service level (the latter expressed as vehicle-km). Hence, within a year, say, an operator would have to allow for these effects as well as initial savings/revenue gains produced.

For example, if the operator tried to offset the trips/revenue loss of 1.5 per cent due to rising car ownership with a fare increase of about 1.5 per cent this would not fill the gap, since a further loss of patronage would occur, i.e. −0.4 × +1.5 per cent = 0.6 per cent.

'Second order' effects of responding to car ownership impacts

Initial revenue/volume	100 units
Revenue/volume after car ownership effect	98.5
Volume after further fares increase of 1.5%	97.9
(−0.6% reduction on 98.5)	
Resultant total revenue (97.9 × 1.015)	£99.4
Further fares increase of 1.1%	
(giving −0.44% drop in demand), total volume	97.5
Total revenue (97.5 × 1.026)	£100.0

As can be seen from the above, a further fares increase would be needed to fill the gap, of approximately 1.1 per cent (i.e. producing a further −0.44 per cent reduction in demand, from 97.9 to 97.5; each remaining passenger would pay a real fare about 2.6 per cent higher than before, restoring total revenue to 100 units). The overall ridership drop of 2 to 3 per cent per annum from a combination of the initial car ownership effect and the secondary effects of fares/service level changes is consistent with the broad long-term trend of bus use in Britain outside London both before and after deregulation.

Given the similar magnitude of the fares and service level elasticities, there is no obviously 'better' approach in terms of further raising fares or reducing service levels as means to regaining a break-even position (it may well be the case, however, that users would be prepared to pay more for a 'package' of higher service quality including reliability, comfort, accessibility, etc. – changes in vehicle-km alone are a crude proxy for this).

In practice, bus operators in Britain followed a mix of both measures up to deregulation. A 'cause and effect' relationship is easier to demonstrate for fares, since network-wide increases were generally introduced simultaneously, and clear 'before and after' periods could be observed. In the case of service level reductions the effects were less clear-cut, since these generally occurred on a piecemeal basis, often in response to earlier losses of ridership (e.g. where loadings on Sunday or evening services had become very low). However, time series modelling over a number of years enabled average elasticity values to be derived.

The extensive introduction of high-frequency minibus services in the mid to late 1980s, and the introduction of bus deregulation outside London enabled these factors to be examined over a much larger short-term range of values than previously.

A range of such minibus conversions was examined, and showed short-term elasticities of around +0.4 in a number of cases, typically where daytime frequencies were doubled (for example, from three to six journeys per hour) and provision under a single operator ensured a reasonably regular spacing of journeys (i.e. in this case from every 20 to every 10 minutes). Hence, convenience to the user was maximized. However, in one case where bunching tended to occur (due to traffic congestion) the gain in ridership was much less.[20]

However, in other cases where deregulation resulted in extensive competition on already well-served routes, the gain in ridership seemed to be much less: for example, in Preston a 4 per cent ridership growth on a 118 per cent vehicle-km increase in a period in which no substantial fare changes occurred.[21]

A simplistic view would be that improved service frequency would lead to a passenger gain through reducing waiting time at the roadside. While this is true at high frequencies, it is less applicable to wider intervals. For example, if buses already run every 10 minutes at regular intervals and passengers arrive randomly at stops, average waiting time will be 5 minutes. An increase in frequency to give a 6 minute headway would reduce average waiting time to 3 minutes, a 2 minute saving (possibly valued at 4 minutes in-vehicle time on the usual assumptions). However, a time saving of less than 5 minutes may be given little value by users – the recent study by Accent and Hague Consulting suggests for non-work-related journeys 'a time saving of five minutes has negligible value'.[22]

Conversely, in a situation where frequency is raised from two to four buses per hour (headway reduced from 30 to 15 minutes), passengers may still tend to plan their journeys around the printed timetable (if sufficiently reliable), allowing about 5 minutes' wait at the roadside. Hence, apparent time savings may be negligible. However, the probability of the timetable matching the passengers' desire to travel from one activity to another may be greatly increased, leading to less 'wasted time' at home (prior to departure), or at a shopping centre, etc.

This aspect was illustrated in a study of route 282 in London, converted to higher-frequency minibus operation in 1990, the typical inter-peak service level rising from every 20 minutes to every 10. Peak and evening/Sunday levels changed less, giving an aggregate growth in vehicle-km of about 50 per cent. Observations at a roadside stop indicated that waiting time was about 5 minutes both before and after the service level change. However, demand rose by about 20 per cent (corresponding to the short-run elasticity value of +0.4). Hence, users must clearly have been obtaining some benefit. Interviews with them indicated that before the service changes most were 'planning' their journeys to match a particular departure; afterwards almost all went randomly to the bus stop, i.e. in the 'before' case the 5-minute wait represented a margin to ensure catching a particular bus; in the 'after' situation half the headway. By using the 'demand curve shift' concept, a monetary estimate of user benefits may then be derived.[23]

The extent to which higher vehicle-km provide benefits for users will also depend on distribution by time of day. For example, if daytime frequencies are raised while at the same time evening and Sunday levels are reduced, potential for making trip chains extending through the day and week is reduced, so that even if growth occurs within the period in which frequency is increased, it could be offset by losses elsewhere.

If the short-term elasticities are applied to changes since bus deregulation, then it would appear that ridership has fallen by more than would be 'expected', given an underlying trend decline owing to rising car ownership, and the traditionally applied short-run elasticities of about –0.4 for fares and +0.4 for vehicle-km. This was observed by White[24] for the period up to 1990, with similar conclusions reached by Mackie for a longer period.[25] Likely factors explaining the 'gap' include:

- a growing dispersal of land use patterns, which disadvantage public transport over and above car ownership growth;
- negative effects of deregulation, including instability in networks, poor passenger information, etc.;
- the distribution of additional vehicle-km: if this is largely in competing routes on well-served corridors it may be more marginal;
- reductions in concessionary fares in some major cities outside London.

Conversely, the London bus trends perform 'better' than expected on the same assumptions.

Longer-term elasticities

It is likely that elasticities are higher in the longer term, i.e. the same change, if maintained over several years, will have a greater impact. For example, a real fares increase of 10 per cent in one single year might thereafter be maintained by indexing with inflation. Whereas in the short run, passengers will have little option but to pay higher fares or tolerate lower service levels especially for purposes such as the journey to work, in the longer run there are possibilities such as:

- relocate home;
- relocate place of work (or other activity);
- shift mode, e.g. accelerate car purchase.

In addition, the 'turnover' effect tends to result in new individuals replacing those formerly using the services (due to changes in household structure, etc. rather than transport effects *per se*) who may be much more sensitive to fares and service levels than habitual users.

Recent work has indicated that such elasticities are typically about twice the magnitude of short-term values, while the short-term values from these new studies are themselves consistent with earlier work, e.g. the service level elasticities being around +0.4 in the short term, +0.8 to +0.9 in the longer term (about 5–7 years).[26] Hence, fares increases would have a greater long-term impact on demand than in the short term, and a greater share of losses in bus ridership since deregulation might be attributed to fares increases (this also implies possibly a greater positive contribution from increased vehicle-km than short-run values suggest). There could, however, be some contradiction with the clearly observed differences in households of differing car ownership levels from sources such as the NTS if a very high proportion of bus decline were attributed to real fare rises.

Policy implications

In policy terms, both short- and long-run elasticities imply that changes in one factor may be offset by another, and/or are reversible: for example, that service levels could be increased to compensate for increased real fares (although this would imply a marked reduction in average loads). A previous fares increase could be reversed. Where greater public financial support is available, this could be used to lower fares and/or increase service levels, producing ridership growth to offset the decline due to car ownership (this may explain much of the differences in trends between Britain and mainland Europe, for example).

Other aspects of 'perceived' quality of service may also be critical to the user, such as helpfulness of staff, ease of boarding and alighting, or convenience of ticket purchase. As in other models, the elasticity-based technique should not be seen as giving a totally deterministic prediction, but a general guide

Notes

1 *Transport Statistics Great Britain*, 2000 edition, TSO, London, October 2000, table 1.1.
2 Unpublished data from 1992–4 NTS, as quoted in White, P.R. 'What conclusions can be drawn about bus deregulation in Britain?' *Transport Reviews*, vol. 17, no. 1, January–March 1997, pp. 1–16.
3 Strategic Rail Authority. *National Rail Trends 2000–01*, Bulletin no. 3, March 2001, table 1.1b.
4 From UITP Millennium Cities database 2001.
5 From DETR Statistics Bulletin SB(00)02, table 5.3.
6 From DETR Statistics Bulletin SB(00)02, table 4.1.
7 Briefing note 'Railway Fares and Ticketing in London', issued by ATOC/LT/ Railtrack, May 2000.
8 From DETR Statistics Bulletin SB(00)33, table 5.4.
9 Data derived from table 4.6 in DETR Statistics Bulletin SB(00)02.
10 Dennis, N.P., Turner, R.P. and White, P.R. (1991) 'Understanding the behaviour of public transport users through trip chain concept', PTRC Summer Annual Meeting, September 1991, seminar H, pp. 15–30.
11 Derived from DETR Statistics Bulletin SB(00)22, table 2.1.
12 Brög, W. (Socialdata, Munich) (1993) 'Behaviour begins in the mind – possibilities and limits of marketing activities in urban public transport', paper at ECMT (European Conference of Ministers of Transport) Round Table No. 92, Marketing and Service Quality in Public Transport, Paris, December 1991 (published 1993).
13 Smart, H.E. (1984) 'The dynamics of change – application of the panel survey technique to transportation surveys in Tyne and Wear', *Traffic Engineering and Control*, December pp. 595–8.
14 From DETR Statistics Bulletin SB(00)26, table 4.1.
15 From DETR Statistics Bulletin SB(00)26, table 3.1.
16 Car ownership data derived from *Transport Statistics Great Britain*, 2000 edition, tables 3.4 and 3.14; DETR Statistics Bulletin SB(00)22, table 1.2.
17 *Transport Statistics Great Britain*, 2000 edition, table 3.14c.
18 *Transport Statistics for London 1999*, table 1a.
19 Glenn Lyons et al. (2000) (Transportation Research Group, University of Southampton) 'Society and lifestyles', first report from *Transport Visions Network*, Landor Publishing, September 2000. (See section 2.)
20 Watts, P.F. et al. (1990) *Urban Minibuses in Britain: Development, User Response,*

Operations and Finances, Transport Research Laboratory report RR269, Crowthorne, Berks.

21 Mackie, P.J. and Preston J.M. (1988) 'Competition in the urban bus market: a case study', PTRC Summer Annual Meeting, 1988, Seminar C.

22 *The Value of Travel Time on UK Roads – 1994*, Accent Marketing & Research/Hague Consulting Group report for DETR, 1999, p. 9.

23 White, P.R., Turner, R.P. and Mbara, T.C. (1992) 'Cost benefit analysis of urban minibus operations', *Transportation*, vol. 19, pp. 59–74.

24 White, P.R. (1990) 'Bus deregulation: a welfare balance sheet', *Journal of Transport Economics and Policy*, September, pp. 311–32.

25 Mackie, P. (2001) 'Principles of public policy for bus services', Chapter 2 (pp. 19–39), in Grayling, T. (ed.) *Any More Fares? Delivering Better Bus Services*, IPPR, London.

26 Dargay, J. and Hanly, M. (1999) *Bus Fare Elasticities: A Report to the Department of Environment, Transport and the Regions*, ESRC Transport Studies Unit, University College London, December 1999.

References and suggested reading

Extensive use has been made of three national reports, which are updated annually:

'*NTS*': *National Travel Survey* (latest issue 1997–9). An annual update is provided as a DETR Statistics Bulletin.

Transport Statistics Great Britain, TSO, London (principal statistics for all modes).

A Bulletin of Public Transport Statistics (DETR). More detailed information on bus and rail modes.

The *Demand for Public Transport* handbook produced by TRRL in 1980 is currently being updated by a consortium including the present author, to be published in 2002/03.

3 The technology of bus and coach systems

Design of the vehicle

General issues

In this chapter, general principles will be described, together with conditions specific to the UK market. Most references are to local bus requirements, with coach design issues identified where applicable.

The designer has to produce a compromise between many conflicting requirements: to minimize fuel consumption, maintenance and purchase costs; to maximize passenger capacity within certain comfort limits; to permit ease of boarding and alighting; to provide a smooth ride through use of appropriate transmission and suspension systems. Some of these may be quantified more easily than others. In particular, fuel, maintenance and capital costs can be combined in a single measure, whole life cost. Forecast fuel consumption and maintenance costs – for a given service pattern – may be discounted over the proposed life of the vehicle and added to capital cost to identify the vehicle which is cheapest overall. This enables trade-offs to be identified, such as the purchase of a heavy-duty vehicle – with its higher initial cost – to give subsequent maintenance cost savings, and hence a lower overall whole life cost.

Such trade-offs will depend partly on the local circumstances. For example, in Western Europe and North America, labour-intensive maintenance costs have risen rapidly in recent years, making these a major factor in vehicle choice, whereas fuel costs represents only about 8 per cent of total costs. In many developing countries, where labour costs are low, fuel costs may form up to 20 per cent of total costs, and thus become a critical factor.

The designer is also constrained by the legal limits on length, width, height, gross vehicle weight, and maximum weight on any one axle. In Britain, for two-axle vehicles these are:

Length	12.0 metres
Width	2.55 metres
Height	4.57 metres
Gross vehicle weight	18.0 tonnes
Maximum axleload	11.5 tonnes

The 18-tonne gross weight was introduced in 1999, bringing Britain into line with other EU countries – and most vehicles in operation were designed to the previous limit of 17.0 tonnes (maximum axleload 10.5 t). A rigid three-axle variant is also permitted (used mostly for long-distance coach work) with a gross weight of up to 26 tonnes within the same length.

Recently, the EU has agreed to permit rigid vehicles of up to 15 metres length, as already found in some countries outside Britain. These are most likely to be used on longer-distance coach work rather than local services within built-up areas. However, a three-year derogation has been granted within Britain.

Unlike most other countries, Britain has traditionally not imposed a maximum height limit as such, but a 'tilt test' is applied, in which a single decker must be tilted to 35 degrees from the horizontal before toppling over (for a double-decker 28 degrees applies). Under harmonization of standards within the EU, a height limit of 4.57 metres applies to all newly constructed vehicles, some versions being slightly lower than this where bridge clearances are limited. In many other countries more severe constraints may apply, making double-deckers largely impracticable (for example, in The Netherlands).

The 'unladen weight' is defined as the weight of vehicle structure. The term 'kerbside weight' is also employed to describe the vehicle as ready for service (including fuel, driver, etc.). The effective payload is thus the gross weight minus kerbside weight. An average weight per passenger of 65 kg was generally assumed until recently (hence, for example, a vehicle of 17.0 tonnes gross with a kerbside weight of 10.5 tonnes could carry 100 passengers). In practice, for a two-axle double-decker, the typical maximum capacity is about 85–90 (75 seated plus 10–15 standing). The gross weight constraint is more likely to cause difficulties in coach operation, when passengers are carrying heavy luggage or duty-free goods.

Legal constraints have changed over time. For example, not until 1981 did the articulated single-decker become legal for regular service with a maximum length of 18 metres, and gross weight of 27 tonnes. Today, maximum dimensions are about as large as the designer would wish, and smaller limits may often be imposed by road network conditions.

Types of buses and coaches

Major types of bus and coach found today include:

Minibuses

The term 'minibus' has a specific legal meaning in Britain, being a vehicle of 9 to 16 seats or less, constructed and used for work other than public local bus services (for example, vehicles operated under 'minibus permits' by voluntary groups). These are typically mass-produced vehicles based on integral van designs, modified to incorporate passenger seating. More specialized designs, often fitted with wheelchair lifts, are used for 'dial-a-ride' operations in many urban areas. It should also be noted that the term 'taxi' applies to a vehicle of up to 8 seats (i.e. a small minibus), used for public service.

However, the term 'minibus' is also widely used to cover the smaller passenger-carrying vehicles (PCVs) used in public service, especially following their rapid expansion in Britain from 1984. These are typically vehicles of 16 to about 30 seats, usually based on mass-produced van chassis with a purpose-built body (such as the Mercedes Vario series), or vehicles of a similar layout, with front engine, built as integral minibuses (notably the Optare Metrorider). The earlier, smaller, models such as the Ford Transit are now being replaced by larger models offering slightly greater seating capacity, wider passenger doorways and more luggage space. Improved suspension and transmission systems are now incorporated to improve comfort and reduce maintenance costs. However, the benefits of low-priced spares through commonality with light goods vehicle models remain.

Midibuses

This term has no specific legal meaning, but typically applies either to the large front-engined minibuses (such as the Mercedes 811 series), purpose-built vehicles replacing earlier minibuses (such as the Optare Solo) or in effect a shorter version of a conventional single-deck chassis, such as the Dennis Dart or Volvo B6 – a rear-engined vehicle typically seating around 30 to 35 – which may be employed in a similar role to the smaller minibuses (i.e. replacing larger vehicles to offer a higher frequency, as in many parts of London), or to substitute on a '1 for 1' basis for larger vehicles where average loads have fallen.

Standard single-deckers

These are typically 10 to 12 metres in length: (a) Front engine, forward of the front axle and alongside the driver. A simple, robust layout, but with a high floor and interior noise levels. Popular in many developing countries, where mechanical reliability is the major factor, but no longer purchased in Britain; (b) Underfloor engine, mounted centrally or at the rear. This permits a wide front entrance adjacent to the driver. The underfloor version (for example, the Volvo B10M) is common both as a coach (in which case high-floor bodies are often specified to increase luggage space and improve the passenger view), or as a local bus. However, to minimize floor height the rear-engined layout is more common for local bus work (such as the Volvo B10LB, or Optare Delta), albeit requiring a sloped floor, or step towards the rear of the vehicle, in order to accommodate engine and transmission. To improve access further, notably for wheelchair users, very low floor models (or 'super low floor', SLF) have been developed, such as the Neoplan N4014, or Dennis Dart SLF, or Volvo B7L.

Initially, these were purchased largely in mainland Europe, where a substantial price premium of about 25–30 per cent over standard models was found. Reduced manufacturing costs within Britain brought the premium down to about 10 per cent, and even before the application of the Disability Discrimination Act (see below) such models accounted for the great majority of new bus purchases in Britain.

The seating capacity of single-deckers varies with length and pitch. For local service work, 45 to 54 seats is typical, with some layouts using 'five across' seating (two persons one side of the gangway, three on the other) to give over 60, usually for school work. For intensive urban services, layouts with a high proportion of standing passengers may be used, such as 44 seats plus 20 standing. By further increasing the ratio of standing space, over 70 may be carried. For coaches, up to about 50 may be carried in the 12-metre length, with space for toilet, and a reasonable seat pitch.

Double-deckers

These are usually on two axles, typically about 10 metres long, seating about 75, of two configurations: (a) Rear-mounted transverse engine. This permits low entrance and floor level. Current types include the Volvo B7L and Dennis Trident, of SLF layout, although for double-deckers this can lead to an awkward layout on the lower deck, limiting seating capacity; (b) Underfloor horizontally mounted engine (Volvo D10M Citybus). This has a slightly higher floor, but better weight distribution.

Articulated single-decker

This usually comprises a four-axle front section with steered two-axle rear section linked by flexible connection permitting through passenger movement, based either on underfloor-engined chassis (such as Volvo BIOM), or rear-mounted 'pusher' design. Very popular elsewhere in Europe, with a high proportion of standing passengers to give a capacity of over 100, but rare in Britain, as a high ratio of seated capacity is usually preferred, and on this basis the traditional two-axle double-decker gives a similar capacity at lower cost. However, Stagecoach group use this layout for interurban coach work, and FirstGroup use SLF variants for busier urban routes. A high proportion of off-bus ticketing is necessary, if excessive boarding times are to be avoided.

It should be borne in mind that the above examples do not include some minor design variants, or types now becoming obsolete in Britain (such as the 'Route-master' in London – a front-engined, rear open-platform double-decker, with a roving conductor).

Some current issues in bus and coach design

Vehicle life and replacement policy

Assumptions regarding optimal vehicle life remain somewhat crude, being based on accounting conventions and engineers' 'judgement' as much as precise calculation. In Britain, a figure of 15 years was typical on both criteria for full-sized vehicles. This has tended to be revised upwards, especially for some of the types such as the Leyland National, following the abolition of the new bus grant – which until the early 1980s covered up to 50 per cent of the cost of new vehicles – and the inability since deregulation of many operators to generate sufficient cash to meet full replacement costs. Up to 20 to 25 years may now be observed, where vehicles are extensively refurbished and re-engined.

Vehicles are required to pass a strict annual test, and the operator thus faces a trade-off between increasingly costly work to bring a vehicle up to the required standard as it ages, and complete replacement. The average life now found in Britain is exceptionally high, and while refurbishment may enable some improvements to be incorporated, it does not, for example, provide the accessibility benefits now offered by very low-floor designs. Some operators that had been pursuing a policy of refurbishment have reverted to complete replacement.

The increased complexity of modern vehicles has in many cases led to a rise in maintenance costs, both in real terms and as a proportion of total costs. Following local bus deregulation in Britain, sharp cuts in engineering staff reversed this trend, but this factor itself is now being offset by rising average vehicle life (see above). After driver costs, vehicle maintenance forms the second largest element within total costs. If real labour costs begin to rise, then a shift back toward a shorter vehicle-life may be justified, especially if newer designs offer significant improvements in reliability and ease of maintenance. As a reasonable target, one might expect fleet availability of 85 per cent to 90 per cent (i.e. the proportion of vehicles in a fleet available for peak-period service), but this may fall as average age rises.

Following the 'bus summit' with government in 1999, the industry agreed to work to an aim of reducing average fleet age to 8 years (i.e. close to 7.5 implied by a maximum life of 15 years for full-sized vehicles, although minibus/midibus types would normally have somewhat shorter lives). Following improved levels of new deliveries in recent years, it fell from 9.9 years in 1994 to 8.6 in June 2000. None the less, at the end of 1999 21 per cent of the bus and coach fleet was over 15 years old.[1] The latest data on new deliveries indicate a drop as large groups complete their updating programmes. The problem lies with smaller operators still incurring poorer profit margins.

Following extensive experience in Britain, a somewhat longer life than initially anticipated may be acceptable for minibuses, in the order of 5 to 7 years for van-derived models, or up to about 10 years for 'midibus' vehicles such as the Metrorider or Dart. None the less, the anticipated life is shorter than that for full-sized 'heavyweight' vehicles, and hence for intensive public service, low initial capital cost may thus be offset by a high annual depreciation charge. As a rule of thumb, the initial capital cost per seated passenger is about £2,000 for a wide range of vehicles, from minibuses to double-deckers (slightly higher for some midibuses and articulated buses).

The role of mass-production

Bus and coach manufacture remains in many respects a craft industry, with small-scale production characteristic of both developed and developing countries.

Although this has some advantages, in permitting numerous variations to meet users' requirements and local bodywork manufacture in countries not large enough to make chassis or engines, it results in high unit costs. Only one model in Britain has been made on a production-line basis, the Leyland National single-decker, manufactured on a large scale during the 1970s, but ceasing production in 1985.

Energy consumption

Typical consumption of derv for a large single-decker, or double-decker, is about 35–40 litres per 100 kilometres, or somewhat better for longer-distance services with fewer intermediate stops. As Figure 3.1 shows, this is strongly influenced by stop spacing. For minibuses around 25 litres per 100 km may be consumed in urban service. At loads of about 15 passengers over the whole day (full-sized vehicles) or 10 (minibuses), this is about half the energy consumed per passenger-km for private cars. In practice, the current averages in Britain are somewhat below this – overall fuel consumption for local bus services (including rural and urban routes, and averaged over all sizes of vehicle) is about 3.0 kilometres per litre (33 litres/100 km), and with an average load of about 9, thus providing about 27 person-km per litre used, around 50 per cent higher than the average figure for cars.[2] In London the ratio is somewhat better, and of course in peak urban conditions consumption per occupant will be very much lower than for car travel.

Some opportunities for improvements exist, although less marked than in the case of urban rail (Chapter 4), as unladen weight per seated passenger space is already low (about 125 kg, compared with 250 kg for 'heavy' urban rail systems). Regeneration – converting energy otherwise wastefully converted during the braking phase – may be incorporated, through flywheel storage, giving energy savings of up to 25 per cent. However, at present fuel prices the necessary investment and added mechanical complexity are unlikely to be justifiable in financial terms. The main current problem in Britain is the low average load at which buses are operating since deregulation, reducing the relative energy advantage over private car previously displayed.

Electric vehicles

As in the case of long-distance rail (see Chapter 9), electric traction gives significant advantages over diesel in maintenance costs, availability, local pollution impacts and increased acceleration. Regenerative braking may also be incorporated more easily. Although often thought outdated, the trolleybus – using a pair of overhead wires mounted above the vehicle – offers all of these features. Redesign of the overhead equipment has reduced its capital cost and environmental intrusion. The last of many trolleybus systems in Britain closed in 1972, but following the oil cost increases from the following year, many elsewhere were renewed and extended, such as Seattle, Wellington and Lyon. Reintroduction has been proposed within Britain, but is currently deferred due to complexities arising from local bus deregulation, and the high unit capital costs of a small installation.

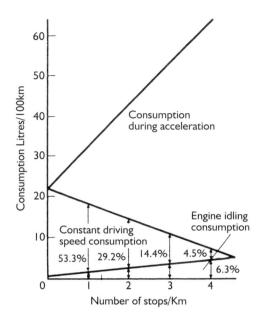

Figure 3.1 Energy consumption of an urban bus, related to stop spacing. Consumption
during acceleration and engine idling increases with the number of stops per
kilometre. (From *Motor Transport*, 27 October 1982.)

A much smaller range of benefits is offered by battery buses, whose theoretical
attractiveness is offset by limited range, high unladen weight and high cost
of battery replacement: an experiment using a battery-powered version of the
Metrorider minibus began in Oxford in November 1993 but has now ceased due
to cost and reliability problems.

Noise levels and local pollution

Although buses generally emit less pollution per passenger-kilometre than private
cars (notably in carbon monoxide, CO, and lead, Pb), localized concentrations in
busy central area streets may result in pressures to remove buses, unless pollution
and noise levels can be reduced. Acceptability within residential areas may also
be critical.

Within the EU, tighter requirements now exist for both passenger and goods
diesel vehicles, notably in emission of particulates (smoke). Under 'Euro 1'
regulations, applying to new vehicles from October 1993, the maximum allowance
for particulates was 0.36 g/kWh. Under 'Euro 2' from October 1996 this maximum
fell to 0.15 g/kWh. Lower limits are also set for Nitrous Oxides (NOx), CO, and
hydrocarbons. While new vehicles, and those fitted with replacement engines, will
meet these criteria, current fleet replacement rates mean that up to twenty years
may pass before all buses meet such standards.

An exterior noise level is now specified according to power (in Kw) for new vehicles with over 9 passenger seats – 81 dB4 if under 75 kW; 83 dBA for vehicles of 75–150 kW; and 84 dbA for vehicles over 150 kW.

In December 1998 the EU adopted the following further tightening of pollution standards (in g/kWh):

	CO	HC	NOx	Particulates
Euro 3 (from Oct 2000)	2.1	0.66	5.0	0.1
Euro 4 (from Oct 2005)	1.5	0.46	3.5*	0.02

* May be reduced to 2.0 from October 2008

In the shorter term, very substantial benefits may be obtained by adopting ultra-low sulphur fuel (ULSD) which also assists in reducing particulates. Existing vehicles may operate now on this fuel without modification, and many operators have switched over. A tax differential of 3p per litre is now offered in Britain, which offsets additional oil company production costs.

Tests by London Transport in 1997 indicated that a combination of ULSD with particulate traps or an oxidizing catalyst could produce results with Euro 2 engines that give similar results to use of alternative fuels such as compressed natural gas (CNG) – indeed a combination of ULSD and continuously regenerating trap (CRT) gave lower particulate emissions than a CNG engine, and slightly lower CO_2 emissions.[3]

Under EU Directive 98/79 standard diesel is in any case subject to a lower sulphur content – from 500 mg/kg to 350 since January 2000, and 60 by 2005.

Trials with alternative fuels and means of reducing pollution from existing diesels continue in a number of countries. These include liquefied natural gas (LNG), compressed natural gas (CNG), and methanol.

Where CNG is used as a fuel, a major factor is not only the storage on the vehicle itself, but also the refuelling arrangements. At normal pressures, this is very slow (typically overnight), and for efficient operation high-pressure refuelling is desirable. This incurs substantial capital costs (in the order of £0.5 m upward per depot), favouring concentration of such vehicles at a limited number of points. However, in some cases energy suppliers such as British Gas are willing to meet this capital cost in return for long-term contracts.

Although considerable interest continues to be shown in alternative-energy buses, some manufacturers such as Volvo remain sceptical. Further developments are, however, occurring in battery/diesel vehicles, enabling extensive operation in environmentally-sensitive areas on the battery alone.

A further review of the environmental factors affecting buses and comparisons with other modes is provided by Ferguson.[4]

Safety of passengers

Most casualties in local service operation are associated not with vehicular accidents, but in boarding, alighting and movement within the vehicle by the

LIVERPOOL JOHN MOORES UNIVERSITY
LEARNING SERVICES

passengers themselves, especially the elderly.[5] Appropriate positioning and shape of grab rails, use of low step heights, and careful design of entry and exit, may all assist. New and refurbished vehicles now follow the guideline specifications produced by DPTAC (Disabled Persons Transport Advisory Committee). One commonly used technique until the advent of super low floor buses was to create a 'split step' in the front platform, so that three small steps replace two bigger ones.

Another feature is to ensure that stairs in double-deckers rise toward the front of the vehicle so that passengers are not thrown downwards should sharp braking occur. A particularly dangerous feature is the retention of open rear-platform vehicles in London (the 'Routemaster' type). Alighting casualties have also been associated with the use of driver-controlled centre exit doors, to which stricter design criteria (to detect obstructions in closing) now apply. Many operators have reverted to a single entry layout, the time savings offered by simultaneous exit being marginal in most cases.

Overall casualty rates (expressed as killed and seriously injured (KSI) per 1,000 million passenger-km) fell from about 25 in the early 1970s to 15–20 per year from the late 1970s, associated especially with reduction in open rear-platform operation. The most recent years give a slightly lower figure of about 14.[6] The rate of reduction lessened partly owing to the elimination of the open-rear-platform type in many areas, and also reflects the fact that absolute safety is in any case an impractical expectation. In absolute terms the number of fatalities is very small, around 10–20 per year. The total number of KSI fell by 35 per cent between the 1981–5 average and 1999, thus attaining the government's target of a one-third reduction (albeit due in part to a reduction in the absolute volume of bus and coach travel).

In London, KSI casualties as a percentage of all bus and coach occupant casualties tend to be somewhat higher than in Britain as a whole (about 11 per cent compared with 6 per cent). However, boarding casualties fell markedly as a proportion of all bus passenger casualties in London between the early 1980s and the 1990s, probably due to a lower level of 'Routemaster' operation.[7]

Provision for the disabled

Making boarding and alighting easier assists not only the elderly and the partially ambulant disabled, but also other types of passenger, such as those with heavy shopping. Those suffering more severe disabilities, and the rapidly growing numbers aged over 75, may not be able to use conventional systems. Provision of wheelchair lifts on full-size buses is one solution, and some urban systems run such buses on specially selected routes and timings, able to carry both the disabled and non-disabled passengers. However, a more commonplace solution is the provision of special 'dial-a-ride' services using minibuses, such as 'Readibus' in Reading, and those in many parts of London. Another type of specialized service, often more cost-effective than dial-a-ride, is the 'Taxicard' scheme in London, using standard taxis (now constructed to incorporate wheelchair access).

However, a better solution may be to adopt very low floor buses, operated in place of standard vehicles on all-day services, thus offering a wider choice of travel opportunities to elderly and disabled users, and incorporating access for all types of passengers. The first such services in Britain commenced in Liverpool in 1993, followed by London in 1994.

Under the Disability Discrimination Act 1995 (DDA), all new buses and coaches over 22 seats on scheduled public services will have to be wheelchair-accessible – in practice of super low floor layout – (and non-compliant vehicles withdrawn) by the following dates:

	New vehicles	*Old ones withdrawn*
Double-deck buses	31.12.00	01.01.17
Single-deck buses	31.12.00	01.01.16
Single-deck coaches	31.12.00*	01.01.20
Double-deck coaches	01.01.05	01.01.20

* Postponed

In many cases, operators have already shifted to SLF models for commercial reasons, due to the growth in ridership resulting from improved accessibility (not usually in wheelchair use as such, but mainly pushchairs and shopping trolleys). A growth of about 5 per cent upward is sufficient to meet the higher capital and maintenance costs which result, and higher figures have been reported in some cases.

Difficulty in boarding buses and coaches is also not restricted to wheelchair users as such, but generally increases with age and infirmity. About 36 per cent of the elderly in households without cars experience some difficulty in using buses, notably in boarding or alighting, or within the bus itself.[8]

The problems applying to coaches arise from the fact that a high-floor layout is generally desired, to provide luggage space and a view for tour passengers – hence a wheelchair lift is needed, with consequent displacement of seating capacity. However, adoption of a slightly longer vehicle might permit this without displacing existing capacity. It is likely that fuel duty rebate will be extended to express services in return for such access and provision of concessionary fares at the same level as local bus services.

Ticketing systems

One-person-operation of buses is now almost universal in North America and Western Europe, apart from some busier routes in London. Two approaches to revenue collection and ticket issue may be taken:

1   All passengers are required to pass the driver, to pay a cash fare, produce a return ticket, or display a pass/travelcard.

This system is general in Britain, with a tradition of most fares being collected in cash (see Chapter 7), and ensures that almost all passengers are entitled to travel, but imposes the penalty of extra boarding time, ranging from about 2.5 seconds for passholders or those with the exact change, to about 6 seconds where many passengers pay in cash and require change. As a result average journey speeds are reduced, and greater variation occurs between successive runs on the same route, as boardings vary. Statistical data may be collected through the machine issuing a ticket for each cash fare, and the driver may record each pass holder as they board. Developments in magnetic card and smart card technology now make it practicable to validate passes automatically (without physical contact being required), enabling a higher degree of inspection, and a more comprehensive statistical record, to be obtained.

2   Most passengers have purchased tickets off-vehicle, either as passes, travelcards or self-cancelling multiride tickets.

Drivers only deal with a very small proportion still paying in cash, and other passengers may board by any entrance. This gives much more rapid boarding, especially useful on articulated buses or tramcars, but a significant risk of revenue loss, despite checks by groups of inspectors who have power to levy fines or 'penalty fares'. On the Dutch system, for example, virtually no cash fare collection on vehicles now takes place.

Most single cash fares are now handled by driver-operated electronic ticket machines (ETMs), such as the 'Wayfarer' which can print extensive information on the ticket (such as time of issue) and store comprehensive data for management analysis (although its use in practice is very limited). They may be linked with payment of the exact cash fare into a farebox to speed boarding. However, these systems do not reduce boarding times if cash fares are still applicable.

The adoption of magnetic re-encodable, and smart card, technology offers a partial solution. Where a fixed decrement is made for each trip, then manual self-cancellation may be replaced by a card offering a fixed total value for travel, re-encoded by a contactless reader each time a trip is made (for example, in Greater Manchester, the concessionary flat fare is now handled in this manner). ETMs such as in newer models of 'Wayfarer' may incorporate card validators/encoders for this purpose. The 'Prestige' smart card system should become network-wide in London (on bus and Underground) toward the end of 2002. However, retention of the graduated (distance-based) fare scale in most parts of Britain makes such automation of cash-paid adult trips of little value in reducing boarding times on buses unless automatic re-encoding on alighting becomes effective. The technology of fare collection cannot be divorced from the need for simplicity in fare structures (see Chapter 7).

On urban rail networks, however, with a 'closed system' in which all stations are fitted with entry and exit barriers, re-encoding of tickets for variable sums per journey (by time of day, distance covered, etc.) is far more practicable, for example as already seen on the Hong Kong Mass Transit Railway, or the Washington Metro.

Control and supervision of bus services

Unlike railways, buses do not necessarily require any special control systems beyond those for road traffic in general. However, it is desirable that drivers can communicate with supervisors in emergencies, such as breakdown or assault. On denser urban routes measures are needed to cope effectively with frequent crew changeover and the irregularities caused by traffic congestion. Traditionally, inspectors at depots, stations and on-street stands have monitored buses and crews, using telephones and hand-held radios. However, this method is very labour-intensive and may give poor results if inspectors themselves do not work on a co-ordinated basis. A central control point is better able to detect overall patterns and take the most appropriate action to maintain regularity, while using fewer staff.

Cab radios

The simplest approach is to fit all vehicles with cab radios, for direct-voice contact. Most urban fleets are now fitted, and many coach operators also use such systems (or employ standard cellular mobile phones). Their value in emergencies is clear, but on large networks they are often limited through the small number of wavelengths allocated to operators. Around 100 drivers or more may be served by a single channel, making frequent reporting of position impracticable in the airtime available.

Cab radio may be supplemented by closed-circuit TV cameras placed at strategic junctions and boarding points in the central area. In a medium-sized town, most congestion can thus be monitored through one control room which is also linked to each driver. Examples include Leicester and Nottingham.

In some cases, a common emergency contact point may be provided, independent of each operator's own management system such as the Emergency Communications Centre of London Bus Services.

Automatic Vehicle Location (AVL)

For more complex networks, and those affected by more severe traffic congestion, automatic monitoring of vehicle location is desirable. A number of systems are in use, of which the major example in Britain is that established by Transport for London (TfL) over much of the London bus network, commencing with service 18 in 1992.

The following main options now apply:

1 Use of a bus-mounted sensor which picks up signals from loops or roadside devices placed at frequent intervals, and converts the signal into coded form for transmission to a control centre. Similar coded messages may be sent and received by the driver (for example, an instruction to turn short), as in the London example mentioned above. This is the system used to support the 'Countdown' real-time passenger information system for which about 3,000 buses (half the fleet) were fitted by 2000.

2   Use of a standard commercial system, as Securicor 'Datatrak', for which the operator pays a fee to receive frequently updated signals indicating the vehicle's position, identified through a system of triangulation (as used by Hertz Heathrow shuttle buses). Communication with their drivers or a real-time information system is then handled through the operator's own system. Another commercially available system is the GEC 'Bus Tracker' (as used by Armchair Transport for tendered services in west London).

3   Use of Global Satellite Positioning (GPS) systems, using satellite signals – for example, by First PMT, the main operator in Stoke on Trent. While some problems have been perceived in the past due, for example, to the 'shadowing' effects of large buildings, these are now often seen as less significant, and accuracy has improved. Hence, this system is increasingly popular in new applications, through avoiding the need for fixed installations. It has been used in Nottinghamshire to give an accuracy within 100 metres, and is also used by other public transport modes, such as taxis.

All such systems are only of value if supported by a control strategy, such as drafting in extra vehicles and crews (if available) to fill gaps in service, re-allocating vehicles and crews between routes at termini, or turning trips short in one direction to cover a gap in the other (unpopular with passengers for obvious reasons). In many cases, scheduled running times do not reflect realistically traffic conditions often experienced. AVL systems or on-bus data recorders may be used to obtain a large sample of running times from existing operations, and hence set more reliable schedules (see also Chapter 5), reducing the need to introduce unplanned variations.

Passenger information systems

Quality of information provided on bus services remains poor. Even simple bus-stop displays of route number, destination and departure times are often lacking. Fares information is very rarely provided. Simple displays, showing departure times from each stop for each destination may be more effective than use of full timetable sheets. The introduction of comprehensive national monitoring of bus service quality in Britain has highlighted information at stops as a major cause of passenger dissatisfaction, and the aspect of service given the lowest satisfaction rating.[9] Ready availability of maps, timetable leaflets and leaflets on fares provides the user with much of the information required.

The most effective back-up would appear to be a telephone enquiry service with a well-publicised number. This has been expanded from a variety of local systems into the national PTI2000 (Public Transport Information) system, becoming operational throughout Britain in 2001, with a common national enquiry number (0870 608 2608) and links to a series of regional information centres covering all bus and rail services. However, the quality of information in the early phases has been questioned by some.

AVL systems can also be linked to passenger information displays to indicate in how many minutes the next bus for a given destination is arriving. Following introduction of the 'Countdown' system on route 18, Transport for London has now extended this concept to many other heavily used corridors, and plans wider use over the whole network. Technology giving very similar information has been adopted in other cities, such as Southampton ('Stopwatch'), Dundee and Birmingham. Actual waiting times are not reduced, but the reassurance provided to the user and information on exceptional conditions enable more effective planning of journeys. A useful review is provided by Lobo.[10]

In several Canadian cities, the 'Teleride', a computer-based telephone answering system, enables the potential user to call from home before setting out for the bus stop: this approach may be particularly appropriate in low-density suburbs. It may simply consist of a synthesized voice working from the fixed schedule, or, in more sophisticated versions be linked with an AVL to give real-time information.

A further development is to link real-time information with web page access, pioneered on 'Superroute 66' in Ipswich, enabling the user to check operations prior to leaving home or the office. The 'GOTIC' information system in Goteborg, Sweden, offers further examples of such developments. The latest scope is through direct access via users' mobile phones, notably using 'WAP' technology to give real-time information prior to departure and at interchange points *en route*.

Buses on road networks

In very broad terms, measures that benefit all road users also benefit buses. Traffic lights reduce accidents and delay at busy intersections, new roads improve traffic flow (except where additional volumes offset the initial savings in time), and traffic-management measures enable existing networks to handle heavier flows and/or higher speeds. However, the opposite may also be true. One-way schemes increase route length, and may take buses away from passenger objectives. At traffic lights, a relatively long cycle time maximizes total flow but as shown below leads to significant and variable delays for buses. A case for bus priority can therefore be made, first, on grounds that buses should not suffer adverse effects from management schemes. As a wider policy, buses can be made more attractive, for example by permitting them to use a direct route via a contra-flow lane when other traffic is re-routed around a one-way system. They can thus retain more passengers. In conditions of scarce road space, giving priority to the most efficient users of that space (buses) may reduce total travel time within the network.

Up to a third of bus journey time (especially in peak and/or congested conditions) may be spent stationary – roughly half at passenger stops, and half at traffic-light controlled intersections (together with other junctions, pedestrian crossings, etc.). These are also the periods with the heaviest passenger flows. Reduction of time at stops may be attained through appropriate ticketing/boarding systems. How can similar reductions be obtained at intersections?

For the majority of road users, average time taken to pass through an intersection is the only relevant criterion. The traffic engineer is also concerned with maximizing the flow of PCUs (passenger car units), in which a bus carrying 50 passengers traditionally receives little more weight than a single car. However, buses form a time-linked system, so that delays to one affect others.

Consider Figure 3.2. Buses are scheduled to depart from A at 3-minute intervals. Passengers accumulate at each stop at the rate of two per minute. Each takes 5 seconds to board, and hence average scheduled time at each stop is 30 seconds. Scheduled running times between stops and across intersections (20 seconds) are shown. Assume that the first bus just misses a green phase at the first traffic lights (or joins a queue of vehicles which does not discharge entirely during the first available green phase). It is delayed for 80, instead of the scheduled 20 seconds. When it reaches the next stop, more passengers have accumulated, and hence stop time is extended. This process is repeated at each stop, the bus running further and further behind schedule. The following bus has fewer passengers to pick up, and hence gains on schedule. If the first bus suffers a similar delay at the second traffic light, and the second bus only the scheduled delay at each junction, the two buses will be only 45 seconds instead of 3 minutes apart at B. Delay to passengers at stops is likely to be found particularly inconvenient and irritating, and is customarily given a value up to twice that of 'in vehicle' time.

This example also illustrates the effect of boarding times in aggravating irregularity, and the difficulty of running a regular, very high frequency service: thus, the theoretical benefits of substituting small minibuses for full-size vehicles may to some extent be offset where small headways are already offered.

A simple solution would be to reduce traffic light cycle time and hence intervals between each green phase. However, this would reduce total junction capacity by increasing the proportion of 'inter-green' time (i.e. that in which a green aspect is not displayed for any flow) and if the junction were already working near saturation, this could merely worsen congestion, in which buses would also be delayed. But if, as part of a comprehensive traffic-restraint scheme, traffic volumes over a wide area were reduced, this solution could apply. Alternatively, selective vehicle detection (SVD) could be used, linked to priority in phasing of lights for the bus.

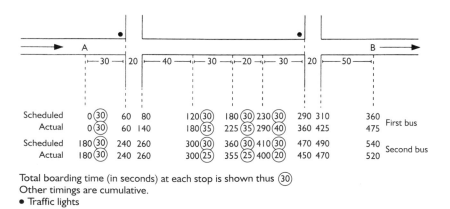

Total boarding time (in seconds) at each stop is shown thus ③⓪
Other timings are cumulative.
● Traffic lights

Figure 3.2 Effect of junction delays on bus service regularity

At the least, one can ensure that each bus reaches the junction so that the next available green phase is used. By making the nearside lane 'bus only', buses can overtake queues of other traffic. Many of these 'with flow' priority lanes were introduced during the 1970s, and they remain the most common form of bus priority measure. This success depends upon adequate enforcement (often lacking), and queues into which other traffic is placed not being so long as to obstruct other junctions which are also used by buses. Extra traffic wardens may be needed to deter kerbside parking in the bus lane. Variations in hours of operation of lanes (many are peak-only), and lack of physical separation of with-flow lanes from other parts of the road surface add to these problems. Colouring of the tarmac in the lane aids enforcement: the 'Greenways' in Edinburgh are a notable recent example.

If the with-flow lane is taken right up to the stop line at the junction, this may reduce total junction capacity (in terms of PCU) and tempt motorists turning left to use the bus lane. It is standard policy to terminate the bus lane short of the stop line: buses can still get close enough to be able to use the first available green phase, but other traffic can also make use of the junction capacity.

In order to avoid extra running time and diversion from passenger objectives when one-way schemes are introduced, buses may be allowed to continue to use a road in both directions, those against the (new) one-way flow in a 'contra-flow' lane. Although a few may be separated from other traffic merely by a solid white line (as for with-flow lanes) most are physically separated by a series of traffic islands or raised curbs. Major examples may be found in London, such as Tottenham High Road or Piccadilly. In some cases the concept may be taken further by having a segregated section of road surface for two-way bus traffic, as near Gare du Nord in Paris.

A merit of contra-flow schemes is that they are largely self-enforcing, and substantial increases in bus speeds may be obtained. However, since the tarmac surface is used only by buses, 'rutting' may develop, requiring more frequent resurfacing. One part of the Runcorn busway has been relaid in concrete slab form for this reason. There is also a problem of pedestrian safety, and it may be necessary to confine their movement to light-controlled crossings by use of barriers. In order to make them more conspicuous, buses now show their headlights throughout the day when in contra-flow lanes.

Another common means of giving buses priority is to exempt them from right turn bans, causing little delay to other traffic but giving significant time savings. Many examples can be found in London. Buses can also be given the benefits of selective detection approaching traffic lights, enabling either an extension of an existing green phase, or bringing forward the start of the next green phase. Losses to other traffic may be compensated by extending green time on the next phase. Variation in delay to buses may be markedly reduced, especially when they are turning right. Selective vehicle detection (SVD) is thus required: transponders fitted to buses enable those vehicles entitled to such priority to be detected clearly.

Such priority may be given either at junctions which are individually controlled (usually through MOVA software) or those within linked networks. Urban traffic control (UTC) schemes have been introduced in many cities, in which optimal use is made of an entire network – in terms of capacity, and/or minimizing delay – through central computer control. A common feature is the provision of a 'green wave' in which a platoon of vehicles is able to experience a green phase on most signalled junctions it crosses, by the green phases at each junction being offset to allow for the average speed of vehicles in the platoon. However, running times of buses between junctions may be longer than for cars owing to the presence of intermediate stops and lower acceleration. Buses may thus fail to benefit, or even hit more red phases than before. Traditional fixed-time linking systems such as 'Transyt' may be modified to incorporate bus characteristics. More recent systems such as 'SCOOT' (Split cycle offset optimization technique) have also been adapted to allow for buses in addition to giving overall capacity gains for traffic as a whole of about 10 per cent. However, the bus priority tends to be most beneficial at intermediate traffic volumes rather than saturation level.

It will be evident from the above that much of the benefit of bus priorities comes through reduced variability in journey time rather than any dramatic increase in average speeds. Their evaluation thus depends upon assessment of changes in passenger waiting time as much as that in-vehicle, as highlighted in the Buchanan consultancy study of London bus priorities in 1986.

The concept of allocating part of existing road space to buses and coaches has now been applied to motorway lanes, following a broader approach to its role adopted by the Highways Agency (HA). A bus and coach priority lane on the Heathrow airport spur of the M4 was opened in 1997, followed by an offside with-flow lane on the M4 itself between Junctions 3 and 2, appproaching London from the west, in 1999, both of which have provided net benefits at peak times.

Stations and interchanges

The great majority of bus passengers continue to board and alight at kerbside stops. For local services, this is in any case desirable in order to give good access to passengers' destinations, and permit cross-centre linking of services. The value of on-street stops can be enhanced by introduction and enforcement of parking restrictions, and provision of better shelters with timetable information. Their costs may be offset by advertising.

Bus stations are required for rural and long-distance services, and interchange – especially with rail in large cities. In some cases, however, they may have been built to 'tidy up' town centres rather than aid bus passengers. Under pressure of competitive services following deregulation, some operations have shifted back to on-street stops in some towns where stations are poorly sited, and to reduce charges paid.

Figure 3.3 shows some common station layouts. For high-frequency services, a through-platform design is often best, buses moving parallel to it. Space between platforms should be sufficient for buses to overtake one another. A good example is the main interchange at Sheffield. However, a large area may be needed, and many points of conflict between bus and pedestrian movement occur. The end-on and 'sawtooth' (or 'echelon') layouts remedy this by providing only one platform

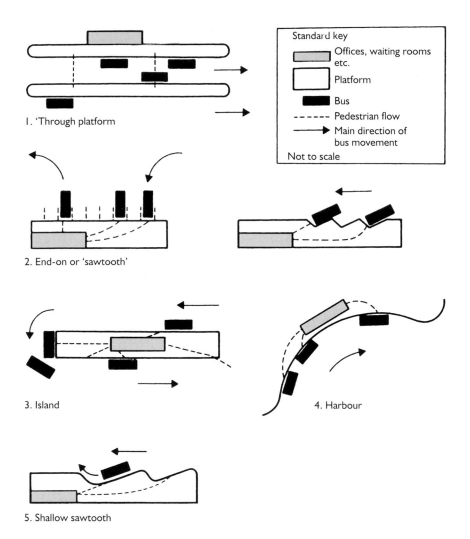

Figure 3.3 Bus station layouts

area, on which all facilities such as waiting rooms and enquiry offices are concentrated, with the front doors of buses adjoining the platform. This layout is favoured for many rural/interurban or small town stations, but is limited by the need for buses to reverse on departing, with associated accident risk: a modification introduced by Greater Manchester, the 'shallow sawtooth', overcomes this. Other layouts offering minimal pedestrian/bus conflict, and concentration of activities, are the 'island' and 'harbour' types, as found at Newark and King's Lynn, respectively. The 'island' type can be expanded by end-on loading of buses along each side, as at Preston. The main platform may also be entirely enclosed, and access to buses given through sliding doors. Many stations in medium-sized towns combine both through-platform and end-on layouts for different types of service.

All of the above layouts may be used also for bus/rail interchanges, with a further aim of minimizing pedestrian conflict in access to the rail platforms. The 'harbour' layout may be particularly suitable, or 'island' where the railway is underground, access to rail platforms being given by stairs or escalator in the centre (as at Wandsbek-Markt, Hamburg).

Busways and bus links

The concept of providing bus priorities on existing roads may be extended to that of allocating the whole road space to buses, and/or building separate busways, usually conventional road structures of about 7.0 metres width, with one lane in each direction. They may provide new direct links, access to areas not open to general traffic, or routes parallel to existing congested roads.

The simplest form is where an entire street is restricted to bus and delivery vehicle use only, typically a town centre shopping street from which other traffic has been taken by an inner relief road. Buses thus continue to serve the heart of the town, and cross-linking of services is made easy. Major examples include Queen Street in Oxford, and High Street in Exeter (the latter for smaller buses only). The traditional road surface may be retained, with separate pavements, or the whole area resurfaced to permit mixed bus/pedestrian movement, as in Oxford. Average speeds may not rise substantially, but delays owing to congestion are largely avoided and excellent access provided.

Within residential areas, bus links may be provided, in which direct routeing is provided for buses, but other traffic is banned. Buses thus benefit from efficient network structures, but intrusion from other through-traffic is prevented. Examples may be found in new towns such as Bracknell and Washington, and also in some older towns where previously indirect routeings have been replaced in this manner. Even for flows of only two or three buses per hour, operating cost savings can justify such investment, not to mention passenger time savings. However, buses in residential areas and others in which 'traffic calming' is applied, have in some cases suffered from inappropriately designed speed humps. Recent work has established more suitable designs which may negotiated safely by buses while meeting the objective of reducing car speeds.

By these means, an incremental approach to investment can be adopted, in which many of the benefits associated with rail systems can be provided through gradual improvement of existing bus networks, also retaining the better accessibility of the bus. Unfortunately, until recently funding policies in Britain made even these modest schemes difficult to plan and finance (although, paradoxically, large-scale rail projects are more readily financed). The framework under five-year Local Transport Plans should provide greater security of funding for such projects.

In terms of extensive new busway construction, the major example in Britain is in Runcorn New Town where most of the network is provided by busways, enabling services to operate at an average of over 32 km/h, compared with about 19 km/h for buses entirely on conventional streets.

The busway concept has been developed into the 'guided busway' – a narrower surface (although taking a standard-width bus of 2.55 metres), on which the bus is guided laterally by use of small, horizontally mounted wheels set adjacent to the main running wheels, running against steel guide rails. The total width required for the busway is thus reduced by about 25 per cent, and the driver's task made easier. As with other busways, incremental development is possible, as buses fitted with the guidewheels can run quite normally on the rest of the road network.

The most extensive development of this idea has been the 'O-Bahn', pioneered by Mercedes-Benz in Germany. Worldwide, the major example is the North East corridor in Adelaide, in which a guided busway serves a large residential area, both by 'park & ride' facilities, and a network of through bus services into low-density housing areas. Rapid growth contrasts with decline in bus use elsewhere in that city: the scheme has been notably successful in attracting car users, and working-age male commuters.

In Britain, the first applications have been in Ipswich (a short section east of the town centre providing a link within a housing area as part of the 'Superroute 66' corridor improvement), and on two corridors in Leeds, the first of which (Scott Hall Road) came into operation in phases between 1995 and 1998. Bus patronage has grown by about 50 to 70 per cent, albeit from a situation in which a low frequency was previously offered. A second scheme is now under construction in Leeds, on the York Road corridor, notable for the fact that financial contributions are being made by the two main operators, who will benefit from reduced operating costs and greater ridership, despite the fact that within the deregulated framework the busway cannot be made exclusive to them.

Further proposals in Britain include a scheme in Chester, serving a 'park & ride' site north-east of the city, to provide a fast direct link to the centre; and the most ambitious to date, the 'CERT' scheme linking Edinburgh airport with the city centre. However, the latter has been delayed owing to the the initially selected consortium withdrawing from the scheme.

The cost per kilometre of guided busway construction is not necessarily much less than that for light rail systems, as Crampton and Hass-Klau have shown.[11] However, whereas a new light rail system involves a minimum length of at least 8–10 km (to serve a single corridor) the busway concept may be applied selectively to the most congested parts of an urban bus corridor, coupled with conventional bus priority measures and other traffic management techniques elsewhere. Hence, the overall capital cost may be much lower, and an incremental approach to investment is made possible, in which new sections may come into use as soon as they are completed.

The most dramatic application of the busway concept is as an alternative to rail construction for heavy flows into the centres of large cities. Experience of such busways in several South American cities, and of reserved lanes in the Lincoln Tunnel in New York, indicates that passenger flows of up to 20,000 to 25,000 per hour per lane in one direction may be attainable, i.e. as great as any rail route in Britain. The critical factor is the capacity of intermediate stops, and hence passenger boarding rates.[12]

Within more affluent countries, such flows are generally already served by rail, but considerable scope exists for the busway concept in lower-density cities, and major suburban corridors. Australia has followed the pioneering Adelaide case with a second route, and a major busway in Brisbane. Studies of suburban corridors in London, such as that along the Uxbridge Road, have evaluated busways and light rail as alternatives.

In many respects, the choice between bus and rail technology (except where substantial underground operation is unavoidable) lies in passenger service quality, rather than peak capacity *per se*.

Development of the 'Quality Partnership' concept

The introduction of bus priority and supporting traffic management measures may be associated with a 'package' approach in which operators and local authorities form a 'partnership' to improve services, the local authority contributing priority measures, and perhaps also improved bus stops and passenger information, while the operator invests in new vehicles (typically low floor, low pollution) and driver training. A greater impact on ridership may thus be obtained than through such measures applied individually.

Major examples include the 'Superroute 66' corridor in Ipswich already mentioned, the 'Showcase' routes in the West Midlands (such as service 33 in Birmingham), and the 'Cotgrave connection' in Nottinghamshire. Substantial ridership growth has been reported, of up to about 30 per cent in some cases, although care must be taken to ensure that diversion from parallel bus services is excluded. The growth may also emerge largely from existing bus users, rather than car drivers.

Under the Transport Act 2000, powers are introduced to formalize such partnerships, enabling operators not within the partnership to be excluded (see further discussion in Chapter 10).

Conclusion

We can see that the most immediate technical issues in bus and coach operation are with the choice of vehicle itself. Also, however, there is great benefit to be derived from looking at urban bus operation in particular as a 'system' in which fixed investment in control and information systems and reserved track may produce many of the benefits normally associated with much more costly urban rail projects.

Notes

1   DETR Statistics Bulletin SB(00)24, Bus Quality Indicators England: Q1 2000/01, chart 6a and table 6.

2 Data derived from fuel duty rebate payments (enabling calculation of litres used), local bus km run, bus and car occupancy rates derived from NTS, and average car fuel consumption from *Transport Statistics Great Britain* 1998 edition, table 2.6.

3 Barton Mark, (1997) 'Pollution – the acid test', *Coach and Bus Week*, 11 December 1997, p. 23.

4 Ferguson Malcolm, (2001) 'Bus services and the environment', Chapter 12, in Tony Grayling (ed.), *Any more fares? Delivering better bus services*, Institute of Public Policy Research, London, February 2001.

5 White, P.R., Dennis, N.P. and Tyler, N. (1995) 'Analysis of recent trends in bus and coach safety in Britain', *Safety Science*, vol. 19, pp. 99–107.

6 Derived from annual casualty figures (published in *Road Accidents Great Britain*), divided by estimated total passenger-km for all bus and coach services.

7 See London Research Centre, London Accident Analysis Unit Factsheet 95, March 2000.

8 DETR Statistics Bulletin SB(00)26, table 3.7.

9 Bus Quality Monitor, First Quarter 2000/01. DETR Statistics Bulletin SB(00)24, table 1.

10 Lobo, A.X. (1998) 'A review of automatic vehicle location technology and its real-time applications', *Transport Reviews*, vol. 18 (1998) no. 2 (April–June), pp. 165–92.

11 Crampton, G.R and Hass-Klau, C. (2001) 'Bus or light rail – which is best?', Chapter 6 in Tony Grayling (ed.), *Any more fares? Delivering better bus services*, Institute of Public Policy Research, London, February 2001.

12 Gardner, G., Cornwell, P.R. and Cracknell, J.A. (1992) *The Performance of Busway Transit in Developing Countries*, Transport Research Laboratory Research Report 329, 1992.

References and suggested reading

'Keeping buses moving: a guide to traffic management to assist buses in urban areas', Department of the Environment, Transport and the Regions Local Transport Note 1/97, TSO 1997 (Guide to current official practice).

Institution of Highways and Transportation (IHT), *Planning for Public Transport in Developments*, April 1999.

Control, March 1996, pp. 186–92.

Quality Bus Infrastructure: A manual and Guide. TAS Partnership, June 2000. A review of current design practice (including official standards, with working diagrams), development of quality partnerships, etc.

Astrop, A.J. and Balcombe, R.J. (1995) 'Performance of bus priority measures in Shepherd's Bush', TRL Report 140.

Austin, J. (2001) 'Busways have a future in UK but should learn lessons from Australia and elsewhere overseas', *Transit* 19 January 2001, pp. 8/9.

Enoch, M. 'Can guided bus schemes lead the way in the drive towards quality public transport?' *Local Transport Today*, 12 March 1998, pp. 10–13.

Slinn, M., Guest, P. and Matthews, P. (1998) *Traffic Engineering Design: Principles and Practice*, Arnold, Chapter 12.

Smith, N. and Hensher, D. (1998) 'The future of exclusive busways: the Brazilian experience' *Transport Reviews*, vol 18, no. 2, April–June 1998, pp. 131–64.

York, I. and Balcombe, R.J. (1998) *Evaluation of Low-floor Bus Trials in London and North Tyneside*, Transport Research Laboratory Report 271.

4 Urban railways and rapid transit systems

Early developments

During the nineteenth century, railways served almost all demands for mechanized transport, including those within urban areas. Specialized urban railways developed in the largest centres, notably the London Underground system from the opening of the Metropolitan Line in 1863. A number of main line railway companies also developed a strong interest in suburban traffic, especially where long-distance demand was limited. Thus, the railways to the south of London displayed markedly greater interest than those to the north and west. In smaller British cities, frequent steam-hauled services played an important role towards the end of that century, as in Stoke on Trent, Edinburgh and Birmingham.

The growth of electric tramways at the turn of the twentieth century caused a rapid transfer of short-distance trips to this new mode, which offered much better accessibility and frequency than railways, whose routes had been located primarily from the viewpoint of long-distance traffic. It was the tramcar, not the railway, which gave the first opportunity to the majority of the population to make frequent use of mechanized transport. The railways responded by closing some minor routes – leading eventually to the complete closure of local systems in cities such as Stoke or Edinburgh during the 'Beeching' era of the 1960s – and concentrating on longer distance suburban flows, and movement within congested centres of very large cities, such as London.

Suburban lines were electrified to improve speeds from the first decade of the twentieth century (for example, Liverpool to Southport, Ormskirk and Birkenhead; Manchester to Bury; and on Tyneside). In the London region this process greatly accelerated during the 1920s and 1930s to produce much of the present network south of the Thames. After World War Two this was followed by further extensions south of London, east London, and Glasgow. A renewed spate of investment led to further schemes north of London in the 1970s, notably extensions of the Glasgow and Merseyside networks. Main line electrification had also permitted local schemes as a by-product, notably in Manchester.

A more dramatic development was the growth of self-contained urban railway schemes, typically located underground in city centres. These are often known as 'metros' after the Paris system, inaugurated in 1900. Other early examples included

Hamburg, New York, Chicago and Madrid. By 1940, seventeen such systems were in operation, including Moscow, Osaka and Tokyo. A boom in metro construction then followed from the 1950s. A further forty-nine systems were opened by 1984, and more than another twenty have opened since. Within Europe, successively smaller cities, such as Oslo and Marseille, have opened metros, but some of the most heavily used systems are now found in the very large cities of Asia and South America, such as Hong Kong and Mexico City. Further growth in these regions is likely to produce much of the overall increase in metros.

In Britain, investment levels have been lower, but substantial improvements have been made to the London, Merseyside and Glasgow systems, and the Tyne and Wear 'Metro' has been created largely from former surface routes. Light rail has been introduced in the form of Docklands Light Rail (DLR) and Croydon Tramlink in London, Manchester Metrolink, Midland Metro, and Sheffield Supertram.

In Britain the street tramcar largely disappeared during the 1950s, and only the Blackpool system remains. However, many medium-sized cities elsewhere in Europe retained their systems, which have been developed into 'light rapid transit' networks, acting either as the major framework in the public transport systems (as in Göteborg or Hanover), or feeders to underground railways (as in Stockholm). New suburbs have been built around reserved track extensions, and older sections of the network placed on reserved track (sometimes in tunnel), so that most of the network is thus aligned.

Types of urban rail systems

Four types may be distinguished, the first two using German terminology.

U-Bahn

This is an 'underground' railway, usually running within the built-up limits of a city, giving good penetration of the city centre by tunnels (however, well over half the network may, in practice, be sited on the surface, or elevated track, outside the centre). Ownership is usually vested in the city transport authority, and the network largely self-contained. Close station spacing (about 1,000 metres on average) permits a very high proportion of passengers to reach stations on foot, and all-stations operation of trains is normal. Simple fare systems, often flat rate or zonal, apply. Examples include the London Underground, Hamburg, Stockholm, Munich and New York. Although often adopted as a generic title for such systems, the 'Metro' in Paris is in some respects untypical, with very close station spacing and short routes (apart from the RER regional system).

S-Bahn

This term denotes those routes of main-line surface railways on which a frequent service geared to local traffic is offered. Station spacing within the inner city may approximate to that of the U-Bahn, but intervals of 2 to 3 km are more common.

White, Lee (2002) recognises that

Average speeds are higher, despite lower acceleration rates. Peak service levels have often been limited by lack of track capacity, although there has been a general trend to segregate such services from long-distance operations through provision of separate tracks and stations. This may be taken further, to construction of new extensions purely for such systems, including city-centre routes in tunnel: this may offer a much cheaper alternative to building a new 'Metro', while giving many of the same benefits. Examples include Hamburg, Frankfurt, Merseyside, Cairo and Glasgow. The 'Thameslink' service, reusing an old tunnel between Farringdon and Blackfriars to create strategic cross-London links (such as Bedford–King's Cross–Gatwick) may also be placed in this category, albeit serving somewhat longer-distance traffic.

Light rapid transit (LRT) (also known as light rail)

This term is applied to electrically powered systems with characteristics similar to U-Bahn, but generally without block signalling (see below), full-height station platforms or ticket issue at all stations. Trains of up to three or four single cars, or one or two articulated cars, are usually operated. Many of the advantages of the 'heavy' U- or S-Bahn systems are given, together with better accessibility, for a much lower investment, albeit also less capacity. Except in the largest cities, such systems are generally adequate for peak flows. Most have been developed from upgraded street tramways, but entirely new systems have been opened since the 1970s, including Calgary and Edmonton (both in Canada), San Diego and St Louis (USA), Manila (Philippines) and Utrecht (The Netherlands). The Tyne and Wear system uses some of the same techniques, but is closer to 'heavy' transit. The Greater Manchester 'Metrolink', opened in 1992, represents the first British example of this new generation, using street-based technology to provide a cross-city link, while incorporating through running over former suburban lines. France offers many examples, notably the Nantes system, whose first line opened in 1985 reintroduced the modern 'street tramway' concept, followed by others such as Grenoble, Rouen and Montpellier.

   In some cases, tramways have been upgraded to form an intermediate stage to 'heavy' urban railways or metros. For example, the 'premetro' in Brussels comprises city centre tunnels and stations served initially by trams, and later by conventional metro trains. In other cases, a tramway may be upgraded by extensive construction of city-centre tunnels, and some stations at which all tickets are sold prior to boarding the vehicle ('semi-metro'), for example in Stuttgart. An advantage of such systems is that trams can be diverted into relatively short sections of tunnel as they are built, rather than waiting for a major portion of the system to be completed before operations can commence.

Automated systems

For some years, control technology has made fully automated operation (with no drivers or station staff) quite feasible. A number of airport systems have been built, mainly in the USA, of which the Gatwick peoplemover offers a British example; but the first such systems for general public use opened in Japan (Kobe and Osaka) in 1981. They have since been joined by several other Japanese systems, and the 'VAL' in Lille (France), opened in 1983. The latter was the first to penetrate a traditional city centre, providing the same function as a traditional 'metro', and has operated very successfully. Further systems include the Vancouver's 'Skytrain', now being extended. In most cases, flows handled are of similar size to those suited to LRT, hence the term 'ALRT' (automated light rapid transit) being used sometimes. The DLR, the first part of which opened in 1987, also falls into this category, albeit retaining on-train 'captains' for customer contact.

The most important example is Line 14 ('Méteor') of the Paris Metro opened in 1998, the first 'heavy' urban line to be fully automated, with headways potentially down to 85 seconds.[1]

Basic system characteristics

White (2002) identifies that

Capacity

This is a function of three variables:

1 *Passenger capacity of each car.* Typically about 100 to 150, dependent upon the proportion of standing-to-seated passengers, level of comfort accepted, and size of car (LRT cars generally being smaller, and some 'heavy' systems, such as Hong Kong, being built to a larger track and/or loading gauge than normal). A distinction may be drawn between 'tolerable' loads, including some standing, and 'maximum crush' (with greater standing densities) at the peak: in the case of London Underground 'tube' stock, about 800 and 1,200 per train respectively. The proportion of seated passengers may be greatly increased by use of double-deck stock. This is found extensively on the Paris system for longer-distance commuting, and several other major cities, but is currently impractical in Britain due to the restricted loading gauge.

2 *Average length of train.* Up to ten or twelve cars may be possible in the case of S-Bahn, but U-Bahn lines are generally limited by platform length to seven or eight (although newer systems may take more), as in the case of London. For LRT, up to three or four single cars, or two articulated cars, is typical.

3 *Headway between trains.* Block signalling applies to all U-Bahn and S-Bahn lines, and some newer LRT routes, implying a minimum headway of about 90 seconds. To allow some margin for minor operating delays, 120 seconds may be taken as a practical minimum (i.e. 30 trains per hour). LRT cars may operate at intervals of down to about 45 seconds with control by drivers on sight distances.

Putting these factors together, the maximum passenger flow in one direction per hour (for a double-track route) can be estimated. For example, if each car takes 150 passengers, there are 8 cars to a train and 30 trains per hour, the flow will be

$150 \times 8 \times 30$, or 36,000. In Europe, rarely is more than 25,000 required, although heavier flows may be encountered for 15–30 minute periods at the height of the peak (for example, on the Victoria Line). S-Bahn routes may have lower capacity owing to sharing of track with other services and LRT routes a maximum of about 5,000 to 15,000 per hour. In large cities of the developing world, higher capacities may be required: the Hong Kong Mass Transit Railway, for example, attains up to 80,000 per hour. RER line A in Paris attains about 65,000 passengers per hour on a 2 minute headway.

The DLR offers an interesting example, having been built to a modest capacity, partly as a means of stimulating land use development in London Docklands, rather than catering for existing passenger flows. However, development occurred more rapidly than initially envisaged, thus requiring the system to be rebuilt soon after coming into operation. Initially, single articulated cars with a capacity of 220 each offered 8 trips per hour on the section between the City and Canary Wharf (1,760 passengers per hour). This was increased first by expanding frequency to 16 trains per hour and doubling train length (giving 7,040 per hour). By bringing the headway down to 2 minutes (i.e. 30 trains per hour) this could be further increased to 13,200 passengers per hour.

It is clear from the above that the time taken to clear a block section is a critical factor. This is determined first by the length of the section (in resignalling schemes, introduction of shorter sections thus becomes one means of raising capacity), and second by the average speed through the section. This will be affected by presence of station stops, whose duration ('dwelltime') may be minimized by setting platform and train floor heights equal, and providing a large number of doors per car, of sliding or plug form. Lower platforms on some S-Bahn, and many LRT lines, may cause delay. Trams for operation on both street and in tunnel often have steps adjustable for loading at various heights. On some automated systems, a platform edge screen with sliding doors to match those on the train (as for a lift) are fitted, preventing passengers from falling on the track, and also minimizing delays: newer conventional metro lines, such as the Jubilee Line Extension (JLE) in London, 'Météor' in Paris, and Singapore Mass Rapid Transit also have this feature.

Delays in block sections owing to stops may also be reduced by adopting higher acceleration and retardation rates to/from running speed. New stock typically attains an acceleration of around 1.2 metres/second/second, although older stock may be much slower. Higher energy consumption may be required as a result.

It will be evident from the above that one means of avoiding the need to build new tracks to raise peak capacity is to improve train performance. This may increase energy consumption and the capital cost of new rolling stock, but will generally be much cheaper than new construction.

The above statements assume implicitly that trains possess identical performance. Where speeds and acceleration rates vary, peak flows may be much lower, especially where trains with urban performance characteristics and those for long-distance work are mixed on approach tracks to main-line stations.

Power supply and control

Direct current (d.c.) supply is typical, usually at 600–750 volts, via a third rail. This form of current and voltage is suitable for use on trains without rectifiers or transformers but requires the provision of substations at very frequent intervals, about every 3–5 km. For dense urban traffic the cost of such substations is less than the extra on-train equipment, but for S-Bahn lines, especially those sharing intercity tracks, the 25 kV (25,000 V) a.c. system, favoured for long-distance movement may be adopted as standard. Britain has standardized on this system for suburban routes in north and east London, Greater Manchester and Glasgow, whereas the London and Glasgow Undergrounds, Merseyrail and the network south of the Thames are based on third-rail d.c. A third option is 1,500 d.c. by overhead supply, requiring about half as many substations as third-rail voltages, but using 750 V motors in parallel: this has been adopted for the Tyne and Wear metro (reducing substations from 13 to 7) and also on the Hong Kong Mass Transit Railway.

On trains, motors are usually mounted on the bogies, fed by current controlled through 'series resistor'; 'chopper' (d.c.) or 'thyristor' (a.c.) switchgear. The traditional series-resistor system consists of banks of resistances connected in series, through which current is passed to the motors. These are successively switched out as acceleration occurs. About fifteen such 'steps' occur in reaching full speed. A further sequence may be inserted by connecting the motors in series during the first stage of acceleration, and then in parallel.

The series-resistor system is very well-established and reliable, but involves a waste of energy as the resistances are heated (warming the passenger saloon is one use for this by-product in cool climates). The alternative chopper/thyristor system, and more recent developments such as three-phase motors with inverters, are now in general use on new stock. These are solid-state switching devices, originally applied to a.c. equipment, in which a 'gating' pulse of a few milliseconds breaks the main current flow at intervals which are varied to change its voltage. In the acceleration phase, waste of energy is avoided, and smoother performance given, of particular value where high acceleration rates are required. Provided that problems caused by high-frequency interference from the gating pulses to telecommunications equipment can be overcome, this system offers clear advantages. It also makes the use of regenerative braking (see below) much easier.

The combined impacts are considerable: for example, in the case of Hong Kong it was found worth retrofitting choppers in place of the series-resistor control initially fitted, resulting in energy consumption (watt-hours per tonne-km) falling by 50 per cent, with a payback period of under seven years.[2]

In Britain, a more conservative approach has been adopted by manufacturers and operators, and only with the introduction of the 'Networker' class 465 in 1992, and the Central Line stock for London Underground in 1993 has it become standard for new stock. Even so, the d.c. 'Networker' stock is not at present operating in this mode, due to inability of the supply system to accept regenerated current (the 'averaging out' of electricity charges to operators through Railtrack also reduces incentives to regenerate current, although the revised track access charging structure from 2001 has improved matters). London Underground is now investigating alternative forms of energy storage.

Electric urban trains are almost entirely of the multiple-unit form, in which the switchgear is carried on each power car, which picks up current direct from the third-rail or overhead, being operated by controls from the driving car. A high proportion of axles in the train can be motored where high acceleration is required, without reducing passenger capacity, as all motors and control gear are mounted under the floor. Some 'push-pull' working using separate locomotives linked to a control cab in the car at the opposite end of the train is also found, notably on SNCF lines in Paris and – using diesel locomotives – the 'GO Transit' suburban lines in Toronto.

Energy consumption

This is determined by two main factors:

1   *Acceleration.* Energy used is proportional to the mass of the train (including payload) multiplied by the square of the maximum speed attained.
2   *Overcoming rolling resistance.* Energy is used while accelerating and maintaining a steady speed, and is proportional to mass.

Aerodynamic resistance is of little importance at the fairly low speeds attained by urban railways, although critical for intercity modes. However, it is a factor in tunnels, where little clearance is provided between train and tunnel, creating a 'piston' effect. The need for frequent bursts of high acceleration, owing to close station spacing, creates a much higher energy consumption per gross tonne-km for urban stock than intercity: high acceleration may itself impose a weight penalty, owing to the higher proportion of motored axles (up to 100 per cent for rates of 1.0 metres/second/second and above) thus required.

The energy required for the acceleration phase is often the greater part of total consumption, especially where stations are less than 1,000 metres apart. Since it is proportional to mass, and urban rail stock is heavy relative to road vehicles, much of the expected energy advantage that one would expect *vis-à-vis* buses owing to lower rolling resistance disappears. Except where very high load factors are attained, energy consumption per passenger-km may be higher for urban rail than bus, as appears to be the case in Britain. A typical unladen weight per passenger space for a bus is about 125 kg; that for 'heavy' urban rail stock about 250 kg.

Many techniques for reducing rail energy consumption are available.

A *downward gradient*

On leaving a station at about 1 in 20 (5 per cent) this aids acceleration, and retardation is likewise aided by an upward gradient on entering. This is used on some London 'tube' lines, but for subway or surface routes such frequent variation in vertical alignment is less easy to incorporate.

Reduced unladen weight of train

Older motor cars may weigh as much as 45 tonnes, but new stock is much lighter. Use of stainless steel instead of conventional construction can reduce the weight of a trailer car to about 25 tonnes. Further reductions may be obtained through aluminium or light alloy construction. British EMU (electric multiple unit) stock built in the 1970s featured aluminium cladding on steel framework, but then reverted to all-steel construction, using the mark 3 intercity coach shell (classes 317–322, and 455). None the less, substantial weight savings were obtained, a four-car 455 set weighing 129 tonnes. More dramatic savings were obtained in London Underground's D78 District Line stock, in which use of longer cars, and a lower weight per car, enabled a saving of 40 per cent, through a six-car train of 146 tonnes replacing a seven-car train of 242 tonnes. Using longer cars (within limits imposed by the loading gauge) enables the number of bogies to be reduced, in addition to savings from lower body weight. Where longer cars are not feasible, articulation of adjoining cars over common bogies achieves a similar gain, as in the Tyne and Wear metro stock (an articulated set weighing 38 tonnes), or three-car sets as on the Hamburg U-Bahn.

The stock placed in service on London Underground's Central Line from 1993 uses large welded aluminium extrusions to give a weight of only 24 tonnes per car, all of which are motored.

However, when the high energy requirements for aluminium production are borne in mind, it is only for vehicles operating high distances each year that net overall energy saving is obtained.

Reduced length of train

Some systems run shorter trains at off-peak periods. However, since the cost of electricity is determined largely by the peak (see below), this is probably more useful in reducing maintenance costs.

Coasting

By cutting off power after the initial acceleration phase, energy consumption can be reduced substantially as rolling resistance has to be overcome only during the acceleration phase, i.e. that shown as phase t_1 in Figure 4.1. Where constant speed is maintained during phase t_2 a trapezoidal speed-time curve results, but an irregular curve is produced when coasting is used, as shown in Figure 4.1(b). The area under the curve represents distance (i.e. speed × time). By using a higher initial acceleration rate the station-to-station trip may be completed in the same time, even with coasting.

Owing to the low rolling resistance on steel rail, loss of speed through coasting is marginal. For example, if two stations are 750 metres apart, and a train accelerates at 0.49 metres/second/second (m/s/s) and decelerates (phase t_3) at –0.75 m/s/s then at a steady speed of 9.89 m/s during phase t_1 the trip takes 92.5 seconds. If the train

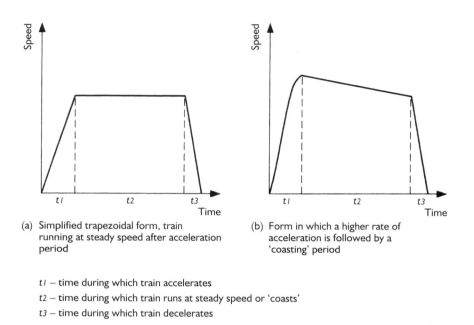

(a) Simplified trapezoidal form, train
    running at steady speed after acceleration
    period

(b) Form in which a higher rate of
    acceleration is followed by a
    'coasting' period

t1 – time during which train accelerates

t2 – time during which train runs at steady speed or 'coasts'

t3 – time during which train decelerates

Figure 4.1 Energy consumption curves for urban rail services

is allowed to 'coast' during phase t_2, losing speed at –0.025 m/s/s, the same distance is covered in 98 seconds, an increase of only 5.5 seconds, or about 6 per cent – yet an energy saving of about 25 per cent would be obtained. The additional journey time between stations might be offset by reducing station dwell time.

Use of regenerative braking

With friction braking, kinetic energy is converted wastefully into heat and noise. The electric motor of the train may be used as a form of retarder, generating current in this process. The simpler form is known as 'rheostatic braking', in which the current is fed into resistors to produce heat. This reduces wear and tear on the friction braking system, and the heat may be used inside the car where climate requires. Better use of the current may be made by feeding it back into the power supply for use by other trains, known as 'regenerative braking'. In theory, savings of up to 30 per cent or more in net energy requirements may be obtained, although in practice this may be limited by factors such as the acceptability of regenerated current at substations, and number of other trains on the system at any one time which can use the regenerated supply. This has limited the net gain in most cases to around 15 per cent to 20 per cent; but with more comprehensive system design to make better use of regenerative motor characteristics from the outset, gains closer to the theoretical maximum may be expected. Regeneration has been made much easier through the use of chopper/thyristor technology, and is now general on new systems. Substations on the Sheffield Supertram are designed to accept regenerated current.

Other forms of energy storage

As in the case of buses, energy may also be stored on the vehicle itself through high-speed flywheels or batteries, thus overcoming the problem of finding other trains to use regenerated current. Rail vehicles can incorporate the weight and bulk of such equipment more readily than buses, but conventional regeneration is probably more practical. Flywheels have also been used to store regenerated current at a substation on the Tokyo network, thus overcoming the problem of feeding it back into the main supply system.

Putting all these factors together, one can see scope for reducing energy consumption on some older systems by about 50 per cent, mainly through a combination of reduced stock weight and use of regenerative braking. The main constraint in many cases is the rate of renewal of rolling stock. Longevity of rail stock makes it possible to aim for lives as high as 35–40 years (with mid-life refurbishment), but in consequence the rate at which energy-saving technology can be introduced is very slow. If energy costs rise, a more rapid rate of renewal may be justified.

Internal layout of rolling stock

For many years, a pattern of three or four sliding doors on each side of the car, with a high proportion of standing space, has characterized U-Bahn stock. Seating is often arranged longitudinally to assist this. In some recent London Underground stock a single-section sliding door has replaced the traditional double-leaf door (for example, D78 stock on the District Line), giving reduced maintenance costs without significant extra dwell time. High rates of acceleration necessitate a large number of grab rails.

For S-Bahn services, a higher proportion of seats, and fewer doors, are usually provided. This difference can be observed in London by comparing the C69 Circle Line stock (with four sets of double doors per car to permit rapid loading), with the A60 stock on the Metropolitan Line to the north-west of London (with three sets of doors and 'five across' seating). On British Rail, the antiquated layout of slam doors was retained in new stock until the late 1970s, but here also sliding doors are now general, with the remaining slam-door stock to be phased out in the next few years.

The sliding-door layout permits driver control, and with certain other modifications (notably mirror or closed-circuit TV display at platform ends) enables driver-only operation (DOO) to be introduced. In Britain, it has applied from the start on the rebuilt Glasgow Underground, Tyne and Wear Metro, and Manchester Metrolink. It applies to a number of TOC suburban and all London Underground lines, and is being extended. On heavy rail systems, the driver remains responsible only for driving as such, and on new light rail systems all fare collection is likewise removed from the driver's responsibility.

The closing of sliding doors is controlled automatically by the guard or driver, but their opening may be actuated selectively by passengers, as on London's D78 stock. This avoids the needless entry of rain and cold air, especially on surface stations.

Where double-deck stock is used, as in Paris, this takes the form of an entry vestibule over each bogie, with steps into upper and lower saloons, the latter within a well section of the chassis.

Signalling and control

A system simpler than that found on main-line railways can be used, owing to regular timetable patterns, and lesser variation in speeds, braking distances, etc. The network of most U-Bahn systems is fairly simple, with few junctions and crossing points only at terminals or certain intermediate stations. S-Bahn may be somewhat more complex, owing to mixing with other rail traffic, but even in this case, tracks are often largely segregated from parallel main lines (between Euston and Watford, for example).

A semi-automatic sequence of trains can be programmed, with manual control as an override to handle exceptions and emergencies. An entire network can thus be controlled from a single centre, such as that on the Tyne and Wear Metro.

As on main-line railways, the basic signalling system is that of block working. A train may not enter a block section until the previous train has cleared it. Figure 4.2 shows this in simplified form. The train in section A cannot enter section B until the train in that section has entered section C. The minimum length of block section is normally at least equal to the minimum safe braking distance from the maximum speed permitted, where signals are of the simple 'two aspect' (red/green) type.

On surface railways, the presence of the train in section was observed from signal-boxes manually, as shown in Figure 4.2. On the tube lines in London such a method was clearly impracticable and at an early stage a system of semi-automatic block working was devised. Quite apart from the traction current (from third rail, or

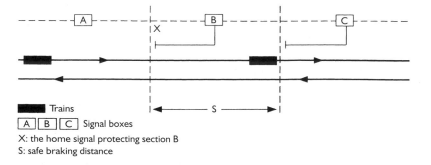

■■■ Trains

A B C Signal boxes

X: the home signal protecting section B
S: safe braking distance

Figure 4.2 Block section signalling

overhead), a low-voltage 'track circuit' current may be fed through the running rails (a.c. where traction is d.c., and vice versa). When a train enters a section it shorts the circuit set up by this current, thus indicating on a control panel that the section is occupied. The circuit can also be interlocked with signals to ensure that the section is protected. Together with a trip-arm which ensures that a train passing the red signal will brake automatically, the system makes collisions between following trains on the same track almost impossible.

Complete automation of 'heavy' urban railways is possible. To date, this has mainly taken the form of automatic control of the train running between station, with the driver remaining responsible for starting the trains, as on the Victoria Line in London, and the Paris Metro. High-frequency pulses through the traction supply determine rates of acceleration, maximum speed and retardation. A more efficient cycle can thus be followed – for example, to make the best use of opportunities for coasting described above.

French systems have pioneered full automation of heavy metros, beginning with the 'MAGGALY' system on Lyon's Line D in 1992 (albeit with some reliability problems). This also incorporates 'moving block' signalling (as distinct from the 'fixed block' described above), enabling spacing of trains related to braking distance for the speed currently performed. Opened in October 1998, the 'Meteor' line in Paris offers capacities in the order of 30,000 passengers per hour per direction (pphd) with fully automated working. Eventual headways as low as 85 seconds with 8-car trains should be feasible, giving a maximum capacity of 40,000 pph.[3]

Information from track circuits and control centres can also be used to activate platform indicators. In the traditional form in London, these simply display the sequence in which trains are due to arrive. These are being replaced by dot-matrix indicators, which display a real-time estimate of the number of minutes in which the train is due. This information has been found to be acceptably accurate, and of considerable help to passengers.

Stations and interchanges

Much of the high labour productivity resulting from one person driving a train with over 1,000 passengers on a heavy transit system may be offset by the need to staff stations throughout the day. Ticket issue may be automated to a large extent by use of machines designed to cover all destinations and ticket types. Cash sales may be further reduced by pre-sale of travelcards and stored value tickets, which are decremented on use. On some older systems, station staff are retained to handle some types of ticket issue, as in London, but complete destaffing is technically feasible, as the Tyne and Wear Metro has demonstrated since opening in 1980. Ticket inspection may be automated by use of barriers which read magnetically encoded or contactless smart card tickets, checking their validity, and if necessary re-encoding. Such 'stored value' tickets are used on the Hong Kong and Washington systems, for example. If a completed 'closed entry' system is used, they may be re-encoded at the end of each journey to allow for distance covered and rate applied (peak or off-peak).

On some systems, a simpler approach is adopted, as on the DLR, where the passenger is required to hold a valid ticket on entering the platform, but not to pass through a barrier as such. Strict enforcement through random inspections is a necessary feature on such systems, backed up by penalty fares and fines. Reliable ticket-issuing machines, to ensure that all passengers have had the opportunity of buying a ticket before commencing their journey, are also essential.

In designing stations it is desirable to minimize the number of changes of level, and make such changes as are necessary easier by use of escalators and lifts. The latter may also improve access for the disabled. Conflicting pedestrian flows should be prevented by use of separate passageways where possible. Well-lit passages and platforms, with no 'blind spots', are desirable.

Escalator width required for one person is about 60 cm, 80 cm with luggage, or about 1 metre to allow overtaking. In order to reduce energy consumption created by continuous operation, escalators may be activated by passengers breaking a photo-electric beam. Increased emphasis is now being placed on accessibility for elderly and disabled users, which may justify use of lifts in addition to escalators.

Passages and other entrances to the platform should be located at different points on successive stations so as to distribute passenger loadings throughout the train. If only one entry can be provided, the mid-point is best; if two (or separate entry and exit), then at quarter length from each end. The situation to be avoided if possible is the repetition of the same entry/exit positions at successive stations, which result in some parts of the train being overcrowded, others almost empty. The terminal layout is particularly unsuited to suburban operation, as boarding passengers may concentrate at only one end of the train, while seats at the other remain empty. Further arguments for through-running in place of terminal working may be found in Chapter 5. In some cases, platform width may be a constraint, notably on the deep-level tube lines in London, in that passengers from one train may not be able to clear the platform before the next has entered at peak times (for example, at Victoria on the Victoria Line).

Where different routes can be arranged to run parallel at an interchange, cross-platform passenger movement may be possible, as at Oxford Circus (Victoria/Bakerloo Lines) or Hammersmith (District/Piccadilly Lines) in London.

Track and structures

The cross-sectional area of rolling stock is determined primarily by the height of standing passengers, use of standard track gauge, and the clearance required for motors and equipment below the train floor. A square cross-section of about 3 metres is typical. Where power is supplied from overhead wires, a vertical clearance of about 4.5 metres may be required. More limited clearances may apply to light-rail systems, and on automated systems such as VAL (Lille) a narrower vehicle width can be adopted to reduce tunnelling costs: the high frequency possible with unmanned trains provides capacity to compensate for the reduced size of each car. On curves, swept area is a function of radius, body width and length.

Shorter vehicles, or tapered ends, may be adopted (as on street tramways) to reduce lateral clearances.

Surface tracks may be relatively simple, although use of continuously welded rail is now common as a means of ensuring a smoother ride. Conventional rail track, with sleepers and ballast is generally used, although grooved rail is still used on street tramway sections of light railways; and concrete slab-base track is now used on new tunnel sections, to reduce subsequent maintenance costs and access delays. Tramways continue to operate through pedestrianized areas, and new light-rail alignments of this sort are now accepted, as in Manchester. Bremen, in north Germany, was the first major city to pedestrianize its centre in the early 1960s, and the trams remain the only vehicles in major shopping streets. The swept area of cars is indicated by distinctively coloured paving.

Where land is not available, the cheapest alternative alignment is an elevated structure. This may also be a means of avoiding conflict on the same level with other modes. This solution was common on early systems – the DLR partly follows such an alignment first built in 1840 – and substantial sections remain in New York and Paris. However, the environmental effects of such structures are often criticized. Newer elevated structures, using concrete, are much less intrusive, and noise levels may be reduced by adoption of rubber-tyred stock, as on the Marseille and Lille systems.

An underground alignment became necessary in the largest cities because of the high land costs and environmental effects of elevated structures. Most systems are subways, i.e. usually aligned not more than 10 metres below the surface and built on the 'cut and cover' principle, often along existing major roads. The first London lines, such as the Metropolitan, were of this pattern, but at an early stage opportunities at this level were restricted by existing railways, sewers and the Thames. The deep-level tubes such as the Bakerloo were therefore built by shield tunnelling, of about 3.5 metres diameter. Reduced cross-sectional area limits train capacity and room for motors, etc.

The depth required for access by escalator or lift, instead of a short flight of stairs, increases passenger access time, which will itself deter use especially for short trips. Hence, this alignment should only be adopted if unavoidable. A subway alignment, even if incurring more disruption during the construction phase, is generally preferable. Whereas the sub-surface metro in Paris is appropriate for short trips, the deep-level tubes in London require bus duplication for such travel. Londoners' habit of referring to all underground railways as 'tubes' is inaccurate in their own city, and even more so in respect of others, Moscow being the only other major example. Construction costs vary greatly according to local circumstances, including geology: as a very rough guide, they are in the order of £100 million upward per double-track route-km for subway or tube routes, with an additional cost per deep-level station.

Elevated track may be much less than half this figure, with surface (especially if following existing alignments) cheaper still. The last point is well illustrated by the Manchester Metrolink, which uses light rail technology to provide the cross-city centre surface link, at very much lower cost than the previously proposed conventional rail with cross-centre tunnels.

Current rail developments in Britain

Prospects for 'heavy rail' systems

The urban rail 'revival' of the 1960s and 1970s is largely over so far as new 'heavy' rail systems in North America and Western Europe are concerned. Static or falling population densities make substantial new construction difficult to justify. However, those systems which have been built are generally well used, and have retained their traffic with much greater success than buses mixed with other traffic. Further expansion is likely to take the form of modest extensions to existing networks, rather than entirely new ones or additional routes involving substantial extra tunnelling. However, major renewal investment will be needed, creating the opportunity for energy saving, improved labour productivity and better conditions for passengers.

In Britain, urban rail use is dominated by London. Following the rapid growth in ridership during the 1980s (see Chapter 2), extensive proposals for improvement were put forward. These included the Jubilee Line Extension (JLE) to serve growing development in Docklands, for which the DLR was not seen as sufficient; the Crossrail scheme, linking Liverpool Street and Paddington suburban services in similar fashion to the RER of Paris; and expansion of the Thameslink service to provide a high-density north–south link across the central area.

The Central London Rail Study of 1989 evaluated a number of options in central London (but not the JLE, subject of a separate study), indicating a positive cost-benefit analysis for Crossrail, and, more markedly, for expansion of Thameslink to increase capacity. Government approval for construction of JLE was finally given in October 1993, following confirmation of previously negotiated private sector contributions. Re-evaluation of the Crossrail proposal now suggests a higher benefit:cost ratio than initially calculated, but funding remains highly uncertain. The Thameslink scheme has been delayed by the associated problems of finalizing the Channel Tunnel Rail Link (CTRL) terminal at St Pancras/King's Cross. The JLE opened at the end of 1999. Subject to planning consent, substantial expansion of Thameslink is likely to occur, and proposals for Crossrail and a south-west–north-east tube line are being actively investigated.

Improved access to airports plays a major role. Following the Piccadilly Line extension to Heathrow in 1976 (and the loop to serve Terminal 4 in 1984), the Heathrow Express (largely funded through private sources) opened in June 1998, provided by a spur from the surface rail Paddington route. The Tyne and Wear Metro was extended to serve Newcastle airport in 1991. A new spur to Manchester airport was opened in 1993, served by local and regional services. Proposals for rail access to Glasgow and Edinburgh airports are being evaluated.

As in the case of bus operation, increased interest is being shown in improving access for elderly and disabled users on urban rail systems. London Underground lifted its previous ban on wheelchair users from October 1993, and the JLE is fully accessible, together with a limited number of central area stations on other lines. The Manchester Metrolink offers improved access through raised platform sections within central Manchester (elsewhere, former suburban stations provide high-level platforms in any case), to permit access for wheelchairs. In parallel with bus design, very low-floor light rail vehicles have been developed, as in those operated on the Sheffield and Croydon systems.

Taking a broader view of 'developed' countries, a higher level of rail investment may be seen. The construction of fully automated systems is evidence of this: the initial VAL line in Lille has been followed by further routes in that city, and other systems, such as Toulouse. Some standardization of future automated systems is being attained in Japan. Capital costs are very high, but there is greater scope for covering operating costs than on traditional labour-intensive systems. A much higher quality of service, especially in terms of frequency, can be offered.

A common feature of automated systems is the nationalistic basis on which they have been developed to date, with each country designing its own system. Not only does this lead to high initial costs, but also the risk that a successful system will not be adopted for use elsewhere, nor economies of scale from mass production attained.

The major issue in terms of 'heavy rail' development in Britain at present is the need to finance extensive renewal of the existing network in London. Following further economic growth, stimulating employment in the central area, traffic grew to an all-time high of 927 m trips in 1999–2000. Current forecasts envisage a growth of around 1 per cent to 1.5 per cent per annum, largely driven by further employment growth, assuming no significant economic recession. London is virtually unique in covering all of its direct operating costs from revenues – at any rate within Western Europe and North America – and providing a contribution to depreciation and renewal from an operating surplus. However, this is insufficient to provide an adequate cash flow for all necessary renewal work.

Central government has proposed a 'Public Private Partnership' (PPP) in which the infrastructure of the underground would be transferred to three 'infracos', who would handle the major renewal work under 30-year contracts. While not providing for any radical extension of the network or capacity growth, this should enable some modest capacity increases within the existing infrastructure (for example, through higher train performance, resignalling, some station improvement works) which would probably keep pace with a demand growth of 1 to 1.5 per cent per annum. However, major doubts have been raised about the cost-effectiveness of such a programme, since the private sector builders would have to borrow money at a substantially higher rate than the state or large public bodies. Hence, a large saving in the direct costs of carrying out the infrastructure renewal work would be needed in order to offset the likely additional cost of capital.[4, 5] Alternatives have been proposed, including use of a public bond issue raised by the Greater London Authority, although in practice much of the infrastructure renewal work itself might still be carried out by private sector contractors.

Recent developments in light rail systems

Given the flows encountered in Britain's cities outside London, there is little justification for new 'heavy' rail construction apart from some minor extensions of existing routes. The flows are well within light rail capacity, which also offers the opportunity for improved accessibility through on-street running.

As mentioned earlier, the Tyne and Wear Metro incorporated elements of light rail technology, but was developed as a fully segregated system with substantial tunnelling. The Docklands Light Railway (DLR), opened in 1987 and subsequently extended, is closer to European light rail systems in vehicle design but none the less, being based on third rail current collection and automated driving, requires full segregation of tracks.

The first example of street-running light rail in Britain was the Manchester Metrolink, whose trunk Bury–Manchester–Altrincham line opened in 1992. An extension to Salford Quays and Eccles opened in 1999–2000. Ridership has been around or above forecasts, at about 13–14 million passengers per year.[6] Major extensions have been approved, and are likely to be constructed as a single package contract.

This was followed by Sheffield Supertram, opened in 1994–95, with a much larger proportion of street running. Average speeds are lower and the relative attractiveness *vis-à-vis* competing bus services somewhat less. Initial ridership was well below forecasts, at about 8 million per year, but has since grown to about 11 million per year following marketing and pricing initiatives. The third system, Midland Metro, is a single route between Birmingham Snow Hill and Wolverhampton, opened in 1999, with probable extensions into Birmingham city centre and to Merry Hill/Dudley. Further options are also being studied. Ridership is below forecast at about 6 million per year.

Potentially the most important system is Croydon Tramlink, opened in 2000, incorporating some existing rail alignments, also with street running and new reserved sections, forecast to carry 20 million per year. In contrast to the systems in deregulated areas much fuller pricing and route integration with buses is evident. A fifth system is now being built in Nottingham. Government approval has been given to proposals for new systems in Leeds, Bristol and South Hampshire (Portsmouth–Gosport).

Development has been encouraged by broader economic and social appraisal under the 'New Approach to Appraisal', in place of the restrictive 'section 56' procedure previously applying, which resulted in the charging of premium fares, thus hindering full integration potential within the public transport network, and inter-modal transfer from car. However, light rail remains a high-cost option in comparison with busways (primarily due to the need to build a minimum length of system in order to commence operation, rather than infrastructure costs per route-km as such).

Notes

1   Griffe, Pierre, 'Year one of Météor operations: an assessment', *Public Transport International*, 1/2000, pp. 15–17.
2   Ford, R. (1988) 'State of the Art: Traction refurbishment and re-engineering', *Modern Railways*, September, pp. 588–90.

3 Griffe, op. cit., pp 15–17.
4 The Industrial Society, London, (2000) 'The London Underground Public Private Partnership: an independent review', September 2000 (text may be downloaded from http://www.Indsoc\tube).
5 National Audit Office (2000) 'The financial analysis for the London Underground Public Private Partnerships', HC 54 Session 2000–01: 15 December 2000 (may be downloaded from http://www.nao.gov.uk)
6 Knowles, R. 'Transport impacts of Greater Manchester's Metrolink light rail system', *Journal of Transport Geography*, vol. 4 (1996) no. 1, pp. 1–14.

References and suggested reading

Frequent coverage of urban rail developments is given in *Modern Railways*, and *Railway Gazette International*, with further coverage of light rail system developments in *Tramways and Urban Transit* – all monthly.
Hass-Klau, C., Crampton, G. *et al.* (2000) *Bus or Light Rail: Making the Choice*, ETP, Brighton and University of Wuppertal.

5　Network planning

Typical structures

The task of a traffic manager or transport planner is to effect the optimal balance between the desired door-to-door trips of individual users and characteristics – especially speed, capacity and cost – of the mode(s) available.

A consequence is that different modes of transport serve different traffic densities, which in turn affect network structure. The minimum average load for a 'conventional' bus service to be viable – averaged over the whole day in both directions – is about ten to twelve passengers (if all costs, including replacement depreciation, are to be covered). Lower traffic densities may be handled either by a smaller vehicle, such as minibus or shared taxi, and/or by a service financially supported by a local authority. For 'heavy' rail very much higher densities are required: for a new route several thousand passengers per hour would normally be needed, although many routes at very much lower densities continue to be justified by the fact that investment in infrastructure has already taken place (or existing alignments may be reused at low cost).

A distinction may be drawn between public, scheduled services operating for most of the day, to which the above comments would apply, and those timed for specific traffic flows, such as from a housing estate to a school, on which only a few journeys may be operated. However, although total daily flows on such routes may be low, the break-even load per trip may be considerably higher when peak-only operation is involved, as discussed in Chapter 6.

Within this chapter, networks in urban areas and the adjoining rural zones are examined. Aspects of rural networks as such are considered in Chapter 8, and long-distance networks in Chapter 9.

Given the typical loadings mentioned above, many public transport services are confined to radial routes into town centres. In towns of up to 100,000 little else may be provided, save for school specials. As town size increases, inter-suburban traffic may justify regular all-day services. Such services become more firmly established in larger cities, linking inner suburbs at high frequency as in London and Birmingham. Larger cities are also parts of conurbations, such as Greater London, or the West Midlands, which have been formed from a group of formerly separate towns. Local bus networks focus upon each of these, overlaid by other bus and rail links to the main conurbation centre. Thus, local networks may be found in Stockport, Bury, Oldham, etc. together with rail services and trunk bus routes from each to the centre of Manchester. Such a situation lends itself to the creation of integrated bus/rail networks, especially where the local centre has a convenient interchange, as at Bury and Altrincham.

Within large city centres, additional distributor services may be needed where walking distances from terminals become excessive. Within London, the 'Red Arrow' buses from Waterloo are one example, although the radial bus and Underground lines provide most of this function.

Rail rapid transit's high capital cost confines it to major radial corridors and central area distribution, although the North London Link does provide a somewhat exceptional service linking inner suburbs, and further scope exists for an orbital service incorporating parts of the West, East and South London lines.

Urban form and land use

The starting point of any public transport network must be the pattern of land use, which strongly influences the potential traffic. The public transport network itself may also influence the land-use pattern: although the car is now the main influence, the past structure of rail, tram and bus routes had a major effect on urban form, and improved rail services for long-distance commuting continue to affect the housing market around London.

Density of population has a major effect on public transport demand: where it is higher, a greater level of service may be justified, and/or lower fares be viable. A longer operating day and week, perhaps including all-night services, may be sustained. Housing density is perhaps the most important factor, followed by the degree of concentration of workplaces and shops. The two are in any case correlated to a large extent, often also with the age of the city.

Two measures of residential density must be distinguished: 'gross' is that estimated from the population divided by total land area, including roads, schools, open space, etc. 'Net' density is that of the area actually occupied by houses, private gardens, access roads, etc. and thus higher than the 'gross' density for the same area. Table 5.1 relates housing type with net residential density.

In Table 5.1, a household size of about 2.4 persons is assumed, based on the national 1991 Census average. The average has declined, as more old people live

Table 5.1 Typical net residential densities

Housing type	Density (persons per hectare)
High density terrace, multi-occupation	200–350
Inner-city redevelopment, flats	150–250
Local authority estates	70–150
Private, medium density	40–80

in households of one or two persons, and size of completed family falls. Typical densities are also falling as more space per house is required – for example, to provide garage space – although it may be the case that fewer rooms per house may be needed as the number of occupants declines.

As a comparison with 'gross' densities, the Greater London average is slightly over 40, and itself somewhat higher than other British conurbations.

Although there is a general personal wish to enjoy more space per household, evident in some very low densities – or scattered rural development – of recent new construction, public costs are also incurred which may not be reflected in those perceived by the householder. There may be a case for higher densities, and a greater variety, than currently found. Much new housing is at low densities, thus incurring the following resource costs:

1   Basic utilities such as gas, telephone, electricity and water require a greater length of pipe or cable to serve each residence, increasing capital and maintenance costs.
2   Other services such as postal deliveries and public transport provision require regular servicing of the household. A lower density increases the cost of maintaining a given level of service, which rises further with growing real labour costs.
3   As urban areas expand, a loss of open space and natural habitats occurs.

Little incentive to higher densities is given by the present council tax system, and costs such as those of postal delivery are (unavoidably) averaged out, resulting in a cross-subsidy to low-density areas. From the public transport viewpoint, the situation is worsened by the stimulus given to car use and ownership in low density areas, as it becomes necessary to make trips that previously were within walking distance (for example, to the local shop) by this mode. Further arguments in favour of higher densities and illustrations of attractive designs that can be provided (retaining ground floor access for all dwellings) are given by Sherlock.[1]

The densities of shops and workplaces have also tended to fall over time, although less so for some types of office work. From the public transport operator's viewpoint, it is not so much the density as location of such development which is important. New 'out of town' superstores are obviously far more attractive to car users, although some bus services are generally provided. If new office development outside traditional city centres can be encouraged to locate at public transport interchanges rather than 'greenfield' sites, then there is a higher chance of retaining traffic. This pattern can be seen in the London area, where much new development has been outside the traditional conurbation centre, but near suburban rail stations such as Croydon, Wimbledon, Hammersmith, etc.

The emphasis on 'brownfield' development in recent planning guidance has helped offset some earlier trends, by encouraging development of pockets of land within existing urban areas (such as former factories) which are more likely to be accessible to the existing public transport network, and thereby help to sustain it through generating additional ridership.

Design of public transport networks

Stop and route spacing

The total time for a one-way door-to-door trip comprises:

Walk to public transport stop or station
Wait for vehicle
Board vehicle
Vehicle accelerates to steady speed
Vehicle runs at steady speed   Cycle repeated
Vehicle decelerates to stop   for each stop
Intermediate stop
Alight from vehicle
Walk to destination, or to an interchange point for further public transport ride as part of a trip.

For urban bus services, a simple average speed may be taken (typically around 18 km/h) for the in-vehicle ride, varied according to traffic congestion and boarding time (see Chapter 3). For rail systems, where acceleration/deceleration rates and maximum running speed can be specified more precisely, they may be considered explicitly.

As shown in the Appendix to this chapter, an expression can be derived for the components of total time listed above, incorporating speed and average length of line-haul trip, and vehicular characteristics. The 'line-haul' part of the trip is that which takes place on the major public transport mode used. In conditions of fairly uniform population density along the whole route, with some concentration around stops or stations, the feeder trip length is equal to about one-quarter of the average spacing between stops.

For a given set of speeds, acceleration rates and trip lengths, the expression thus derived can be simplified to contain only one unknown quantity – the average stop spacing. If this were very small, total trip time would be high, since each passenger's journey on the major mode would be interrupted by numerous intermediate stops. On the other hand, if stop spacing were very wide, feeder trip times would lengthen, outweighing the benefits of a faster 'line-haul' section. By differentiating the expression, as shown in the Appendix, the spacing which minimizes total time can be calculated.

Figure 5.1 shows such a case, for an average line-haul trip length of 5 km, walking as the feeder mode (at 1.0 metre/second), and a vehicle with an acceleration rate of 1.0 metres/second/second and steady speed of 12 metres/second. Trip time is minimized at a stop spacing about 550 metres. By substituting different values for each variable, trade-offs between them can be illustrated:

1   If acceleration and/or retardation rates are increased, optimal stop spacing will narrow (i.e. an intermediate stop imposes a smaller time penalty).

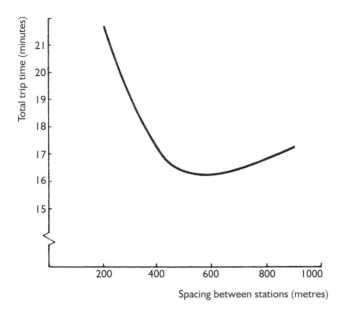

Figure 5.1 Optimal stop spacing to minimize total travel time

2   If steady running speed attained after acceleration increases, optimal spacing
    will widen (i.e. an intermediate stop will impose a greater time penalty).
3   If the speed of the feeder mode is increased, optimal spacing will widen.
4   If stop dwell time is reduced, optimal spacing will narrow (as for 1).

Many examples of these effects can be quoted. Replacement of walking or bus as
feeder mode to an urban rail system by park-and-ride substantially increases feeder
trip speed, and hence optimal spacing becomes wider. Urban rail systems of the
1970s in the USA, such as the Lindenwold Line in Philadelphia, and BART in
California, illustrate this trend.

    Where a more comprehensive local service is being provided, with most users
gaining access on foot, then additional stations may be created, and the resultant
delay to through-passengers offset by using higher acceleration stock, as on the
Docklands Light Railway in London. Where additional local stations have been
built in areas served by diesel multiple units, as in West Yorkshire, there is a greater
effect of journey times being increased as a result of the lower acceleration of
such stock.

    The argument presented above has been solely in terms of minimizing passenger
journey time. In practice, there will be a trade-off between this and costs incurred
by the operator. While simple roadside stops for buses or light rail incur very low
capital costs, those for underground railways will be much higher, tending to
encourage a wider spacing than on passenger waiting time criteria alone. In

addition, each stop will incur energy costs (as argued in Chapters 3 and 4), and by extending round trip running time, may increase the number of vehicles and crews needed to maintain a given service frequency. The overall economic optimal spacing will thus be somewhat greater than suggested by passenger journey time alone, especially for heavy rail systems.

Most urban flows are concentrated on the central area and hence loadings on buses or trains will be heaviest on the inner sections of radial routes. The penalty imposed by an additional intermediate stop to existing occupants will thus be greater, the closer to the centre it is located. On the other hand, density of population in the catchment area may be much greater. When additions of this sort on existing networks are being evaluated, each must be considered on its own merits, to establish the overall trade-off in passenger time. One illustration is the stop at Turnham Green on the western section of the Piccadilly Line of the London Underground, on the otherwise non-stop section between Hammersmith and Acton Town, for which the parallel District Line provides a local stopping service. Local residents' pressure for the Piccadilly to serve Turnham Green at all times of day (in addition to the present late evening/Sunday service) has met the response from London Underground that time losses to through passengers would offset such benefits.

Given the higher traffic densities on the inner sections of radial routes, limited-stop operation may be justified, with outer suburban services running non-stop through the inner suburbs – apart from selected interchanges – and a parallel local stopping service offered. This can be seen on most rail corridors into London, for example. In the case of bus services, limited-stop operation may be introduced to give an equivalent effect, as in the 'Timesaver' services in the West Midlands. Limited-stop operation may also be sometimes justified on high-density inter-suburban corridors, as on the Uxbridge Road in west London.

Access distances to the network

For the vast majority of local public transport services, walking is the access mode, representing about 75 per cent of Underground station access for example.[2] The maximum convenient walk thus determines spacing between stops and between routes. For urban bus services, a typical upper limit of about 500 metres may be taken. Normally about 95 per cent of the urban population is within this distance of the nearest stop. Table 5.2 indicates the distribution.

Note that the figures in Table 5.2 are national averages, including rural areas (although influenced by the high percentage of population in urban areas). Somewhat better accessibility is found in large urban areas – for example, in London and other major conurbations about 90 per cent of residents are within 6 minutes' walk of a bus stop. For rail, much greater variation is found – in London 60 per cent are within 13 minutes' walk of a rail or Underground station, but only 16 per cent in other metropolitan built-up areas.

A walking distance to a bus stop of about 500 metres also emerged from theoretical studies as part of the Runcorn New Town Master Plan. It corresponds to about 5 minutes' walk for the average adult, but can take up to twice as long for

Table 5.2 Percentage of population within walking time shown

	To nearest bus stop	To nearest rail* station
0–6 minutes	87	7
7–13 minutes	10	12
14–26 minutes	2	22
27 minutes or more	1	59

Source: 'Transport Statistics Bulletin SB(00)22: National Travel Survey 1997–9 update', tables 5.6 and 5.7.
Note: * Including Underground and light rail.

someone with a pushchair or an elderly person. Passengers will also tend to walk to a stop in the 'right' direction of travel, and not necessarily the closest one.

From this, one can suggest that different network densities may be appropriate for different types of passenger. Peak school and work journeys can be handled on fairly widely spaced routes largely on main roads, offering high frequency and/or using large vehicles. At off-peak times, users may be much more sensitive to walking distances. The development of 'hail and ride' operation – picking up and setting down at any safe point, usually off main roads, and generally associated with minibus operation – has provided such a facility, of particular benefit to those with heavy shopping or the elderly. It tends to be used more on the homeward journey than the outward trip, for which fixed stops still provide an easily understood point, at which information can also be displayed.

In the case of railways, a wider stop spacing is adopted. Although acceleration/retardation rates may be higher than for buses, intermediate stops incur a greater penalty, owing to higher running speeds, and higher energy consumption (see Chapter 4). The capital and operating costs of stations are high, especially if requiring underground construction and/or staff on duty. A spacing of about 1,000 metres is typical of U-Bahn networks, falling toward 500 metres in city centres, and somewhat lower on light rail. Rail station spacing is also affected by the extent to which that mode is expected to provide a general local service, largely accessible on foot (older parts of the Paris Metro, for example), or be supplemented by parallel buses for local movement (as is generally the case in London).

To a large extent, a wider rail station spacing is accepted by passengers (partly reflecting the emphasis on work journeys). The average line-haul trip by rail tends to be greater than that by bus, and hence a longer feeder trip will be acceptable within the minimization of total trip time described above. A walking catchment radius up to about one kilometre has been observed in the London area, and even in the case of the light rail system in Sheffield, although the probability of being willing to do so tends to fall off as distance increases.[3] Such estimates have formed the basis for planning housing densities in Stockholm, in which the innermost zone around a station is reserved for the highest densities, the outermost for single-family dwellings.

The other main element in total journey time is waiting. This is affected mainly by service frequency and reliability. Its impact on demand may be incorporated through use of a 'service elasticity' as described in Chapter 2. Use of smaller vehicles clearly enables higher frequencies to be offered, but at a higher cost per passenger. Waiting time may also be reduced by bus priority measures, as described in Chapter 3, and its perceived effect by better information systems, as mentioned in Chapters 3 and 4.

There are, however, two trade-offs between waiting time and network density outlined above. First, a wider spacing between routes and/or stops will give a greater density of traffic at each, and hence a higher frequency, for a given vehicle size, may be justified. Second, development of limited-stop services may help to reduce in-vehicle time, but increase waiting time through the lower frequency offered at intermediate points.

Route length and headway

For purposes of illustration, this section is written largely in terms of bus operation, but similar considerations apply to railways.

After selection of route and frequency for a proposed service – the latter usually a function of peak demand (peak:interpeak service ratios are discussed further in Chapter 7) – a running time is derived from previous experience (many new routes are in fact a restructuring of old ones rather than totally new road mileage) or a sample of test runs. Where an existing section is incorporated, past data from Automatic Vehicle Monitoring (AVM) systems, as described in Chapter 3, may provide a much larger sample. The running time set should reflect conditions which vary by time of day and a desired level of reliability. Setting the mode or mean average time may result in many journeys not being able to cover the route within the scheduled time. Hence the return trip may also be late, and passenger waiting time greatly increased. It is far more realistic to assume a distribution of running times than a simple average, and set a proportion, such as 95 per cent, which the schedule should cover. This may result in apparent inefficiency, as many buses and crews will spend longer at the terminal than necessary, but will provide a better passenger service.

There are, however, limits even to this approach, where buses operate in traffic close to saturation flow conditions, in which marked fluctuations may occur in journey time even at the same location and period of the day, as shown in the recent study by Buchanan and Partners for the CPT.[4]

Variability in running time is much less of a problem for railways, being unaffected by general congestion, and in any case needing to plan train paths with much greater precision. However, slightly greater running time should be allowed at peak periods, owing to increased station dwell time, and delays at junctions. Rail timetables also allow a small 'recovery time' in addition to the scheduled running time, to allow for minor delays.

The number of vehicles and crews needed to work a service is equal to the round trip running time (sum of single-trip running times in each direction, plus layover at each end), divided by the proposed headway.

The following examples illustrate this:

1   The single trip is 30 minutes each way, and 5 minutes layover is allowed at each end: round-trip running time will be 70 minutes. If a 10-minute headway is operated, 70/10, or 7, buses will be needed. If a 15-minute headway were intended, then the number of buses estimated would be 4.66; in practice, 5. This wastage becomes more serious the wider the headway, and the shorter the round trip time. It may be possible to interwork two routes at a common terminus so that the combined round-trip time is an integer multiple of headway.

2   For example, if the 15-minute headway were desired on the above route, it could be linked with one having a round-trip time of 35 minutes (itself using 3 buses inefficiently, if also on a 15-minute headway). The combined round-trip time of 105 minutes divides by 15 to give exactly 7 buses. Alternatively, the original route could still be worked separately with a round-trip time increased to 75 minutes (i.e. fully using 5 buses), the extra time being used to increase layover (with reliability benefits mentioned above), or to extend a short distance without extra buses being required.

Another approach is to set the round trip time and number of vehicles, and then derive the headway.

3   If 5 buses work a route with 70 minutes round-trip time, a headway of 14 minutes could be offered. However, the 'clockface' headway (one giving the same departures past each hour) would be lost, making the service more difficult to follow for users and crews. Such an approach is only sensible where the headway is low enough for passengers to arrive at stops at random, rather than aiming for a specific departure (typically about 12 minutes or less).

The operator should aim to make best use of crew paid time. If drivers do no other work, then driving time per shift is to be maximized. This will be subject to legal constraints, under current UK domestic regulations for local services (those under 50 km) these being:

Maximum driving time before a break of at least 30 minutes	5 h: 30 min
Maximum driving time per day	10 h: 00 min
Minimum rest between shifts	10 h: 00 min

The last limit effectively imposes a maximum range between the start and end of driving (irrespective of the number of hours actually driven), if the same day's duty is to be repeated the following day, of 14 hours. Within the paid work shift, time must also be allowed for 'signing on' and 'signing off' as well as driving *per se*. In addition to 'straight' shifts of continuous work apart from the break(s), crews may also work 'split' or 'spreadover' shifts, i.e. in which two separate spells of driving are worked during the day, typically to cover the peak periods. Implications for costing of peak services are considered in Chapter 6. In future, more restrictive EU rules (already applying to longer services and non-scheduled work) may apply, together with the effect of the working time directive on total weekly working hours, including activities other than driving.

In rail operations, trade-union agreements, rather than legal limits, generally set the crew scheduling constraints. Split-shift working is not generally practised, for example, although adoption of 'flexible rostering' in recent years has enabled length of shift to be better matched to round trip running times, hence increasing driving time per shift.

Bus network planning methods

So far as rail operations are concerned, a fairly systematic planning approach is clearly required, owing to the high cost of infrastructure and rolling stock. Even a change in the pattern of service on an existing network involves planning a year ahead to fit in train paths, connections, etc.

In bus networks, much less formal planning may appear to be necessary, as little infrastructure is involved. In deregulated areas, only 42 days' notice of service withdrawal or change is required. For certain types of change, an *ad hoc* approach may well be appropriate. Apart from determination of the schedule for crewing purposes as described above, passenger reaction may be gauged largely by monitoring use of the service once introduced, by use of ticket sales data and simple on-vehicle surveys. For example, varying the number of journeys on an existing route may be handled in this way, although a simple vehicle-km elasticity can be used to make an initial estimate of likely patronage effects. This simple approach may also be applicable to new services directed at very specific markets, such as direct shoppers' services to a new superstore, or the 'commuter coach' services into London, or services funded by Rural Bus Grant (see also Chapter 8).

However, within a complex urban network, and/or where a radical restructuring of routes is taking place, such methods are not sufficient. Even on a simple, small-town network many possible combinations of cross-centre linking, and combined headways on common sections of route, may be feasible. A series of *ad hoc* changes may identify some of these, but is unlikely to produce an optimal pattern. The operator may wish to assess the likely demand for new routes which do not serve a single well-defined market, such as an all-day inter-suburb service. There may also be a wish to reassess running times over the network, and investigate the case for traffic management measures to assist buses.

Comprehensive land-use transportation studies (LUTS) of the type mentioned in Chapter 2 are not generally appropriate for this purpose. True, they give a picture of the main corridors of demand and market share by mode at one period, but they soon become out of date. Zone sizes are usually too large to assign passengers clearly to specific routes, and household surveys are based on too small a sample to give confidence in data for particular routes by time of day, etc. The LUTS approach is useful for major infrastructure planning, especially rail; but other methods are needed for detailed short-to-medium term planning.

Techniques have therefore been developed in which a special-purpose bus passenger survey is undertaken, permitting a much larger sample and smaller zone sizes than would be the case with household survey data in LUTS. On-bus ticket sales/validation data may also be analysed to give a breakdown for a larger sample of trips, albeit not necessarily to the same degree of detail (for example, ultimate origins and destinations, and journey purposes are not available from such a source). A comprehensive origin-destination matrix may thus be assembled, from which alternative network patterns may be tested.

Perhaps the most widely used such system is the VIPS package, developed initially in Sweden and now applied in a number of countries. Transport for London use a simplified approach with some parallels in their area-by-area redesign of the bus system. Both methods involve similar initial stages:

1   The identification of network to be studied, not necessarily the whole network of one operator, but typically one focusing upon a market town or city centre, or part of a complex network within a large conurbation (such as that based on Wandsworth within London, recast in 1991).
2   Assessment of existing services in the area, including running times, frequency, peak vehicle requirement, etc.
3   Extensive on-vehicle surveys to obtain a detailed picture of existing bus users, with exact origin and destination, extent of linked trips, journey purpose, etc. Patterns for different periods of the day are observed, as those in the peak may differ radically from shopping periods, or late evening. A sample covering all scheduled bus journeys within a short period (such as one week) is usually taken, and a high response rate obtained with simple self-completion forms, collected on-vehicle. The current survey adopted for this purpose in London is known as BODS ('Bus Origin Destination Surveys').
4   This may be supplemented by additional background data, on market composition by age, sex, car availability, etc. This may be derived through the on-vehicle surveys, but generally a much smaller sample suffices. Household surveys may be used to collect attitude data, and trips by other modes.

The existing and proposed networks are represented in computer form. A route network analysis (RNA) is then undertaken, in which zone-to-zone links are assessed in terms of journey time, frequency, and extent of interchange. In VIPS, a direct demand model is calibrated for zone-to-zone flows, based on zonal data (such as population, workplaces, as one would find in LUTS), and public transport service characteristics. The manual and computer-generated networks are developed, and evaluated using the RNA. Alternative cross-centre linkages and frequencies may then be evaluated. In the network planning by TfL, a simplified approach has been adopted, in which the existing demand is taken as the base, and variations which would result from changes in frequency and interchange (applying established elasticities and interchange penalties) are calculated, rather than modelling total demand as such.

In both methods the planned network is then assessed by local management and may be subject to public consultation with local authorities and user groups (this last aspect has virtually disappeared following deregulation in Britain, except in

London where a different approach is adopted in any case, and some consultation is required by statute). A preferred network is then chosen, and detailed scheduling work completed. Introduction of the new network is usually marked by extensive publicity, and sometimes adoption of a new fleet name or local marketing title.

Both systems enable a better matching of supply with demand, and hence either a better level of service without extra resources being required, or savings without substantial losses of traffic and revenue. Better crew and vehicle utilization (especially in terms of passengers carried) is obtained.

Outside London, following deregulation, comprehensive network planning was largely abandoned. Operators made individual service changes, exploiting opportunities such as the higher frequencies permitted by minibus conversion. However, while this produced specific local innovations of value, the acute instability in the network was probably a major factor in loss of ridership. Competing behaviour by different operators in the same area does not necessarily produce an optimal overall network. Resources are likely to be concentrated on busier routes at busier times, often increasing frequency where it is already good, and giving little ridership growth in consequence. The separate provision of commercial and tendered services also has the consequence of fragmenting network planning. There is strong evidence that many service changes in the late 1980s were made, not in consequence of changes in passenger behaviour, or perceived opportunities to influence it, but in reaction to competing changes made by other operators.

In recent years, a more stable network has developed and a more mature approach taken by operators. In a number of cases this has taken the form of concentrating resources on a trunk urban network, offering high frequencies such that passengers would not need to consult a timetable (at least for Monday–Saturday daytime frequencies), supplemented by a network of less frequent services to maintain accessibility. In effect, it is assumed that most passengers would make the trade-off in favour of a greater walking distance to a more frequent and convenient service. The Brighton & Hove network focuses a high proportion of its demand on separately branded high frequency trunk routes. FirstGroup has adopted a policy of simplified urban networks, commencing with the 'Overground' network in Glasgow, marketed in a similar fashion to the London Underground, with encouraging results in ridership.

As indicated in Chapter 10, the overall impact of the approach taken in London has been much more positive than the post-deregulation experience elsewhere, especially in the metropolitan areas. However, some scope still remains for making the centralized system more sensitive to local service improvement opportunities.

Interchange

Within an all-bus network some interchange will occur owing to the problem of dispersed demand for which through services cannot be offered. Although the majority of passenger trips are undertaken without interchange, and may be increased through techniques such as VIPS, there will always be some trips involving interchange, commonly including hospital visits, those to friends and relatives and home-to-work journeys where the workplace is outside the central area or not large enough to be served by a special route. As populations become more dispersed, these trips will become relatively more important, even though public transport has a small share in these markets. The NTS indicates that about 10 per cent of bus journeys outside London involve interchange to a second bus. Within London, a higher ratio is found, although in some cases this results from passengers holding travelcards or passes taking the first bus to arrive and then interchanging en route, rather than waiting for a less frequent through service (see also Chapter 7).

Within larger cities, the proportion of bus trips involving bus-to-bus interchange grows, especially where separate services are required in the central area. Where rail networks are provided, some bus-to-rail interchange may occur spontaneously to save time, and may be encouraged by through-ticketing, clear information, etc. Interchange between urban and long-distance modes is also important.

In modelling of flows using generalized cost as a measure of deterrence (see Chapter 2), interchange may be represented by a time penalty (i.e. over and above observed interchange time) of about 5 minutes (a range from about 2 to 10 minutes). However, this is highly dependent upon ease of interchange, type of passenger, etc. Systems such as Stockholm and Hamburg have succeeded in stimulating high levels of public transport use, despite the high proportion of interchange (generally bus/rail) involved. The high proportion of passengers using travelcards clearly assists in this, and the very rapid take-up of London's travelcard from May 1983 (in a network with a high proportion of interchange) also illustrates its attractiveness to users in such circumstances. Some 70 per cent of London bus travellers now use travelcards, bus passes, or concessionary passes. This makes it easier to plan networks with a higher element of interchange (for example, shortening very long routes to offer improved reliability on each section) than in cases where the majority of passengers would incur a financial penalty under a cash-paid fare system.

Interchanges themselves form another criterion for station location, especially where a new rail route is added to an existing network: on London's Victoria Line all stations but one are interchanges with other rail routes.

If interchange penalties can be minimized, then systematic substitution of line-haul rapid transit for existing through bus services can be envisaged. Slow, unreliable and costly bus operation on inner sections of congested radial roads can be replaced by reserved-track rapid transit, being less labour-intensive and of higher quality. The outer sections of bus routes are then converted to rail feeders. The cost aspects of such a process are illustrated as a break-even chart in Figure 5.2. So far as the operator is concerned, the fixed-cost element may have been met largely by central or local government grants (whose justification would also have rested on estimated time savings to users, increased traffic, etc.).

The main example of such an integrated network in Britain prior to local bus deregulation was that in Tyne and Wear, where the Metro was opened in stages from 1980 to 1984. Buses were converted to feeder services through purpose-built interchanges such as those at Regent Centre and Heworth. Overall, the system proved successful in retaining a high level of public transport use despite

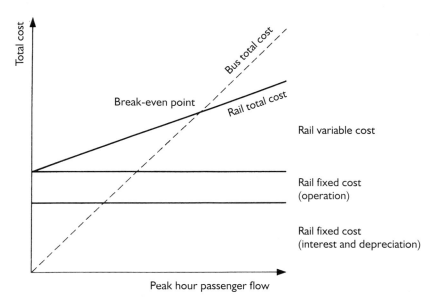

Figure 5.2 Break-even chart for bus and rail services in an urban corridor

other adverse trends. However, there were problems when all bus passengers were required to transfer to rail, if the rail journey leg was short. This is the case at Gateshead, where bus/rail interchange occurred within 1.5 km of the centre of Newcastle, and through bus services were offered once again after deregulation. However, many of the other bus feeder services to metro interchanges have been retained since deregulation, and even some of those at Gateshead reintroduced.

Elsewhere in Britain parts of conurbations have bus/rail integration of this sort where convenient interchanges can be made onto railways with good central-area penetration (e.g. the Birmingham–Longbridge corridor, or the role of purpose-built interchanges at Bury and Altrincham, which now serve the Manchester Metrolink). In other major European cities integrated bus/tram/rail networks are the norm. Typically, through bus services are provided within a radius of about 5 km of the centre, with an outer bus network feeding rail interchanges: this is the pattern in Paris, for example.

Non-central area trips

Some trips of this type are handled along existing radial corridors into the central area, their origins and destinations both being within the same corridor – for example, to a suburban shopping centre on a main road, or a school similarly sited. A tendency for households to relocate outwards along the same corridor assists this. Linking of radial routes across a city centre can also assist, as can easy interchange within the central area between radial routes. However, congestion within the centre can deter the former, since unreliability would thus spread more extensively through the network.

In many cases, however, use of radial routes for suburb-to-suburb trips would be highly inconvenient, and specialized services will be needed. Since these will generally be of low frequency (typically half-hourly or worse outside the very largest cities), adherence to schedule is essential, and timetabled connections between such services (and radials) essential. The Canadian concept of the 'timed transfer focal point', at which a number of services converge on a centre at fixed intervals, takes this one step further. In a small town, this approach can be applied to the whole network.

Within suburban areas, it is helpful if land uses such as office employment, shops, health centres, etc. can be concentrated at nodes which also have public transport interchanges, such as the 'Centrewest' development at Hammersmith.

Park and ride (P&R)

As well as being a competitor, the private car can also be used as a feeder mode to public transport – generally rail in large cities. It is particularly important in low-density suburbs of large cities, where local bus services are thin, and much housing beyond walking distance to the station, yet the railway is an attractive mode for the radial trip to the city centre. Some spontaneous development has occurred – for example, on Sheffield Supertram – but to an increasing extent P&R is being encouraged through provision by transport operators or local authorities of car parks at stations. Many of these are former railway goods yards, especially around London, not ideally shaped or sited. However, new sites have also been developed, and for long-distance travel specialized 'Parkway' stations such as Bristol (Great Western, London–Cardiff main line) and Warwick (Chiltern Line, Birmingham–London), have been built almost exclusively for this mode. The relative importance of P&R *vis-à-vis* other feeder modes in shown in the interchange study of London Transport: typically, about 75–80 per cent of Underground station users arrive on foot.[5] Within the 'middle ring' of suburbs (travelcard zones 3–4) bus plays a significant role, but further out into low density suburbs car-based P&R becomes the main motorized feeder mode, representing about 10 to 25 per cent of all feeder trips. It plays an even greater role in feeding London commuter services of privatized TOCs, in which the bus role is often very marginal.

At present, about 12,000 P&R spaces are provided at Underground stations, run through private sector contractors, and charged separately from Underground travel. (Is there scope for a common smart card?) West Midlands PTE (Centro) provides about 4,700 spaces, mostly free – and Strathclyde likewise charges at very few of its stations (except on the Underground line), providing about 4,000 spaces. On the Tyne and Wear Metro a rural station is provided largely for P&R use – Callerton on the Airport line. When parking charges were dropped in 1995 use more than doubled, extra rail passenger revenue offsetting lost parking charges.

In some other instances, P&R plays a very small role as a rail feeder. For example, very little planned P&R provision has been made on recent light rail systems in Britain, apart from two sites on Sheffield Supertram.

Motorists tend to 'railhead', i.e. drive fairly close in to the city centre, before transferring to rail, rather than driving to the nearest station. This tends to reduce public transport revenue without corresponding changes in cost. If the point of transfer can be placed as far as possible from the central area along a rail route, the financial position of the operator will generally improve, and fewer problems of on-street parking and traffic congestion will be caused by cars in inner areas.

A certain amount of time (or cost) saving is usually required to offset the perceived interchange penalty. Unless there are significant physical or price restraints, voluntary diversion is unlikely for trips of less than about 6 km. Generally speaking, one would not expect significant P&R demand within cities of less than about 500,000 people, as most trips would be under this length, and rail or rapid transit systems are not provided. Within Britain, most rail P&R use is found in London and the metropolitan areas.

There are, however, some exceptions. Where parking is very limited, as in some older cities, or at certain periods, such as the Saturdays leading up to Christmas, bus park and ride may be attractive. Many towns run pre-Christmas P&R bus services to supplementary car parks, or Saturday-only services for shoppers. Recently, there has been a major growth in services operating six days per week. In Oxford, where the historic city centre imposes limits on road space and parking, and buses enjoy very good access through priority measures, all-day P&R services were established in 1974: about 3,800 parking spaces are now provided at four sites, with plans to expand to 5,000. Bus park and ride has also expanded in similar historic cities, such as Cambridge and York. The other bus-based schemes with over 3,000 spaces are Bristol, Chester and Nottingham.[6] Some schemes have been financed through the Transport Supplementary Grant (TSG), and government support has also been evident in allocation of credit approvals for P&R schemes. The more comprehensive five-year Local Transport Plans (LTPs) with their associated funding permit a longer-term approach to be taken, and many further P&R proposals are found within them.

A feature of bus-based P&R is that the services are usually operated quite separately from the conventional public network (whereas rail P&R utilizes existing scheduled services, even where new stations are provided primarily for that purpose). A much better 'image' than conventional bus services is thus provided, often associated with strongly differentiated marketing, new low-floor vehicles, and simple fare structures (either a flat rate return per person, or per car load). In consequence, they may sometimes attract passengers who would otherwise use 'conventional' bus services and are located within walking distance of the P&R site (fares may also be lower, since many P&R services are supported by local authorities on corridors otherwise served commercially). There is thus a diversion of some conventional bus use to P&R service (probably in the order of 5 to 10 per cent of P&R ridership in the short run), in addition to the car users *per se*. In the longer run, a higher proportion of former bus users may be found, although a good deal of this effect would in any case be attributable to rising car ownership over time.

In addition to the effect of reduced congestion, P&R will also provide energy savings, although it should be borne in mind that car fuel consumption per vehicle-km will be higher for the short feeder trip to the P&R site, due to the 'cold start' effect.

The viability of a dedicated bus P&R service will depend on the site size provided. If a reasonably attractive daytime frequency is to be provided (about every 10 minutes or better) then the park must have sufficient capacity to provide for both peak and off-peak use. This probably implies around 400–500 spaces for a commercially viable operation. Where smaller parks are provided (as at Winchester) they may fill up during the morning peak, resulting in a highly-peaked demand for the bus service, and require local authority support for operating costs as well as site provision.

Oxford now offers an example in which almost all the bus service operation is registered commercially by the operator, the local authority role being primarily in site provision.

There is growing interest in providing sites adjacent to motorways, or at a greater distance from town centres, to maximize benefits of diverting cars from congested corridors. A P&R site for 500 vehicles opened in Fife at the north end of the Forth Bridge with a service to Edinburgh in late 2000, for example. One of the Cambridge sites is adjacent to the M11 motorway.

In addition to examples already quoted, some small resorts in scenic areas may wish to restrain summer visitors' cars for environmental reasons. One example is St Ives in Cornwall, where a P&R scheme was set up in 1978 on the branch line from St Erth, used by several hundred cars per day.

There is a danger of some increase in car vehicle kilometres occurring where users divert to a P&R site, rather than it being along the corridor by which they would normally approach the central area. Parkhurst[7] has suggested that this may offset the benefits usually attributed to P&R in terms of traffic congestion and reduced energy use, although a study by Atkins[8] suggests the effects are relatively small.

Bus-based P&R clearly will have the greatest attraction when accompanied by bus priority measures on the approach roads to the city centre, and priority within the central area. Oxford, Cambridge and Exeter offer examples. Use of busways gives further scope – a P&R site is provided at the northern end of the Scott Hall Road corridor in Leeds. Perhaps the most radical scheme currently in progress is the planned busway from Hoole, north-east of Chester (on the M53), running over a former rail route, which will provide a dedicated service for a site with 1,200 spaces.

The future of park-and-ride has four aspects:

1   A means of enabling existing car trips originating in low-density, or poorly served areas, to transfer to public transport without the need to provide additional feeder services.

2 Catering for further dispersal of the population by creating railheads or bus-served sites through which trips can be channelled. For example, the intercity station at Stevenage serves the north Hertfordshire area.
3 A means of enabling restrictions on car use in town centres, for traffic congestion or environmental reasons, to be implemented, while permitting commercial viability to be maintained. This is the major factor in historic towns such as York. Demand from dispersed origins may be concentrated at one or a few points.
4 On new suburban rail routes or guided busways, the optimal spacing between stations could increase if a high proportion of feeder trips were by car.

A variant on P&R is 'kiss and ride' in which the commuter is driven to the station by their partner, so that all-day parking is not required. In new interchanges, short-stay parking areas specifically for this purpose may be designated. Its pattern of use is often asymmetric – for example, a lift to the station in the morning, but not the evening, when a feeder bus may be used instead.

Public transport in low-density situations

Variations in traffic level are handled mainly by changing service frequency. Network density may also be varied by not running some routes at certain periods, and/or a simplified network at certain periods such as evenings and Sundays. This reaches its extreme (in urban areas) in skeletal all-night bus networks operated in some cities. Limited-stop services may be confined to busier periods only, their vehicles augmenting intermediate stopping services at other times. These problems are, of course, particularly acute in rural areas, considered separately in Chapter 8.

Where a mixture of minibus and full-size operation is found in the same network, minibuses and single-deckers may be deployed to cover almost all evening and Sunday work, thus enabling a similar route structure to be offered throughout the week, but at lower cost. The smaller vehicles may also be particularly appreciated in terms of passenger security when small loads are carried.

The alternative of less direct routeings offered at low-density periods (to combine traffic), or the absence of limited-stop workings, will of course result in longer journey times for some passengers, but these will be offset by a higher frequency than might otherwise be the case. Loadings are likely to be low, and higher scheduled speeds may be set when there is little traffic congestion.

The 'dial-a-ride' concept was introduced during the 1970s, offering variable routeing in defined area, responding to requests by phone, in writing (normally a 'standing order' for a regular trip), or on boarding the vehicle. Minibuses of about 16 seats were generally used. Telephone requests were handled by a radio control centre, sometimes making real-time use of computers to plan minimum-time routes. The very high unit cost per passenger which resulted made these services difficult to justify as general public services, and have all now been withdrawn, although a few similar services continue to operate elsewhere in Europe, where higher levels of support are generally given.

In Britain, the dial-a-ride concept has been adopted for specialized demands, notably many services for the disabled, using minibuses adapted to carry wheel-chairs. Examples include the local dial-a-ride networks within London, 'Ring and ride' in Manchester, and 'Readibus' in Reading. Despite the failure of dial-a-ride as a general purpose mode, there has been considerable expansion of radio-controlled single-hirer taxis. In some other countries taxis are used as planned substitutes for conventional buses at times of low demand, notably some evening/all-night services in West German cities. The legalization of shared-taxi operation in Britain since 1986 should have made this sort of mixed-mode operation much easier, but there has been little impact to date.

Recent developments in software have enabled more robust scheduling to be applied to flexible-routeing of services in real time, as may be seen through the 'SAMPLUS' trial projects in the European Union, and the development of new services in Britain. However, the extent to which such systems could enable commercially viable operation remains uncertain.

Conclusion

The process of matching supply to demand through design of the appropriate network structure has become much more systematic in recent years through the adoption of extensive passenger surveys with computer-assisted planning tech-niques. However, the pattern of land use has major effects on the ability of public transport to provide a good level of service, and public transport planners and operators should seek to influence it where change creates such opportunities.

Appendix: A technique for illustrating optimal interstation spacing

The components of total travel time are defined as on p. 83, the notation as:

L   average line-haul trip per passenger   (metres)
D   average interstation spacing   (metres)
S   station stop (dwell) time   (seconds)
A   distance covered by train or other vehicle in accelerating to
   normal running speed, and in retardation from normal running
   speed (dependent upon acceleration and deceleration rates,
   and running speed attained)   (metres)
B   time occupied in same process as (A)   (seconds)
V   steady running speed of train or vehicle   (metres/sec)
T   average feeder trip to stop or station   (metres)
   (as a working approximation, take T as equal to 0.25D)

A number of behavioural studies have suggested that passengers experience losses while walking and waiting equal to about twice the average valuation of travelling time. The component for feeder trip time could on this argument be multiplied by two if walking were the feeder mode. Waiting time is a function of service frequency and thus is not affected directly by spacing. It is therefore not considered in this calculation.

Total travel time = feeder trip time ($\times$ 2) + (number of intermediate station stops $\times$ station stop time) + (number of interstation runs $\times$ acceleration and deceleration time) + (number of inter-station runs $\times$ time on each run at steady speed)

$$= T \times 2/F + L \times S/D + L \times B/D + L(D{-}A)/(D \times V)$$

In the expression as shown, stop time at the station where the passenger boards the train or vehicle is included, since normally the passenger would arrive before the train or vehicle stopped. The values of A and B are calculated for given rates of acceleration and maximum running speed.

In this example the following values are assumed:

$$
\begin{aligned}
L &= 5{,}000 \text{ metres} \\
A &= 144 \text{ metres*} \\
B &= 24 \text{ seconds} \\
V &= 12 \text{ metres/second} \\
S &= 20 \text{ seconds} \\
T &= 0.25D \text{ metres} \\
F &= 1 \text{ metre/second}
\end{aligned}
$$

* Based on a constant acceleration/deceleration rate of 1.0 metres/second/second.

Inserting the values into the equation above we obtain:

Total time = $0.25D \times 2/1 + (5000 \times D) \times 20 + (5000/D) \times 24$
  $+ 5000(D\text{-}144)/(D \times 12)$
  = $160{,}000D^{-1} + 0.50D + 417$

Differentiating with respect to D we obtain:

$$dTT/dD = -160{,}000D^{-2} + 0.50$$

By setting the value of this expression equal to zero we can obtain the value of D for which time is minimized:

$$
\begin{aligned}
O &= -160{,}000D^{-2} + 0.50 \\
D &= 565.5 \text{ metres}
\end{aligned}
$$

The values inserted are typical of an urban railway fed entirely by walking trips, and station stop time is an average for sliding doors. In practice, a calculation of this type need not be made to within limits of less than about 100 metres, since curvature, location of entrances, etc. will affect site availability, and stations themselves are over 100 metres long.

In the case of bus operation, stop time can be represented as a constant, which for a one-man bus is about four seconds, plus a time per boarding passenger. The latter ranges from about two seconds on systems with simple fare scales and no change-giving up to about six seconds. The boarding time related to the number of passengers could be regarded as a constant total and only the four-second period be included in the optimal spacing calculation. In the long run, however, stop spacing will itself affect demand, and hence total delay caused by boarding passengers. (Widening the stop spacing would cut out some short trips, but encourage more long-distance ones, and vice versa.)

Notes

1   Sherlock, H. (1991) *Cities are Good for Us*, London, Paladin.
2   London Transport Planning 'Interchange in London: patterns of access and interchange at rail stations outside central London' (results also summarized in Willis, J. (1997) *Passenger interchange in London*, Public Transport International (UITP) pp. 4–8).
3   Transport Studies Unit, University College London, with W.S. Atkins [Sheffield] *Supertram Monitoring Study*. Final report for South Yorkshire Passenger Transport Executive and the Department of Transport, Environment and the Regions, January 2000.
4   Colin Buchanan and Partners. (2000) *The Factors Affecting Bus Reliability: Final Report*. Report to the Confederation of Passenger Transport, November 2000.
5   See note 2.
6   TAS Partnership 'Park and Ride Great Britain: a survey and report', revised and updated edition, December 2000. (A review of trends in bus-based park and ride, with inventory of all current urban areas and sites operated.)
7   Parkhurst, G. (2000) 'Influence of bus-based park and ride facilities on users' car traffic', *Transport Policy*, vol. 7, pp. 159–72.
8   W.S. Atkins Consultancy, (1998) *The Travel Effects of Park and Ride. Final Report*, August 1998.

6 Costing and cost allocation methods

The structure of costs: classification

The costs involved in a transport operation may be classified in three ways.

According to inputs

Groupings such as wages and salaries, other staff-related costs (National Insurance, pensions, etc.), energy, spares and materials, insurance, depreciation, rent and interest charges indicate the main inputs and their relative importance. For example, in countries such as Britain the staff-related costs comprise about 65 per cent of the total, but energy only about 10 per cent. This type of classification is useful in highlighting the importance of different inputs and hence likely future trends: thus change in real labour costs is likely to be the predominant factor in determining overall rates of change (in the absence of productivity change), rather than that in energy costs. However, this may differ in other countries, with energy costs forming a substantially higher proportion in developing countries, for example. Costs expressed in local currency will also be affected by changes in the exchange rate. For example, in a country with a falling exchange rate, oil prices (in dollars) will form a growing proportion of costs expressed in local currency. In the British case this factor applies to fuel, and also spares/new vehicles in view of the high import element now found.

According to the activity with the transport operation

For example, in analysing bus operators' costs, the following classification based on that by CIPFA (the Chartered Institute of Public Finance and Accountancy) has been found helpful:[1]

- Traffic operating costs.
- Drivers, conductors and supervisory staff, ticket equipment, uniforms, miscellaneous supplies.
- Fuel and power.
- Servicing, repairs and maintenance.

- Staff costs, materials and spares, maintenance of buildings, machinery, etc.
- Management, welfare and general.
- Administration, insurance, welfare and medical facilities, etc.
  (Interest, taxation and depreciation are treated separately.)

The advantage of this type of classification is that it highlights the relative importance of certain types of activity within the organization. Although similar in some respects to the 'input' classification above, it gives a more useful guide to where costs arise. For example, it can be shown that the cost structure for urban bus operators in Britain changed during the late 1970s as one-person-operation became widespread. Traffic operating costs were thus held down as conductors were lost, falling from 62 per cent of total operating costs in 1975–6 to 57 per cent in 1979–80, while servicing, repairs and maintenance rose from 23 per cent to 26 per cent of the total over the same period, as more complex rear-engined double-deckers replaced simpler front-engined types, and operators failed to reduce the scale of their workshops in line with falling fleet size.2 From deregulation in 1986, sharp reductions in labour costs were made, especially in maintenance and administrative staff, with smaller cuts in driving staff costs. This is consistent with the evidence for scope in cost reduction prior to 1986.

According to their basis of variation, and escapability over time

Table 6.1 shows the main elements identified in the CIPFA/NBC classification developed in the early 1970s. Note that variation by time is much more important than variation by distance, reflecting the major role of time-based labour costs in the total. 'Peak vehicle' based costs are those associated with all vehicles required to cover service at peak periods, not merely those used only at such times.

The examples in Table 6.1 have been drawn in terms of the bus industry. Comparable examples for railways would include train crews, track maintenance, signalling, terminals, and rolling stock maintenance. Variation of cost by traffic density would represent a major factor. For the bus and coach operator life is much simpler in that a public road network is used, to which a contribution may be made

Table 6.1 An example of the CIPFA bus cost structure

Category	Main components	Basis of variation
Variable costs	Crew wages, bus servicing	Time
	Fuel, tyres, third party insurance	Distance
Semi-variable costs	Bus maintenance	Time
	Depreciation and leasing	Peak vehicle
Fixed costs	Administration staff and welfare	Time
	Buildings and general	Peak vehicle
Interest on capital debt		Peak vehicle

Source: Derived from Appendix A of *Passenger Transport Operations*, Chartered Institute of Public Finance and Accountancy, London, 1974.

through annual vehicle duty and fuel duty, whereas the railways, in providing their own infrastructure also face the problem of allocating their costs to specific activities.

Interest and depreciation

In general, interest and depreciation are treated separately from the categories of operating cost described above. This is not to deny their importance, but to acknowledge their different nature, being often dependent upon accounting conventions and historic conditions as much as current operating methods.

INTEREST

Interest charges are often influenced by the capital structure of the business and historical factors rather than the current assets employed. Publicly owned businesses have generally been financed through fixed-interest loans, interest on which has been treated as a 'cost'. Conversely, a private company financed entirely through equity – or dividend – capital, would not incur such a 'cost', but be able to regard all its surplus after covering operating costs, depreciation and taxation, as 'profit'. Thus, in comparing profitability of businesses one should assess carefully their capital structure. In addition to bearing fixed interest, much of the capital in public sector operations was repayable, imposing a further cost burden on the operator that would not be faced with equity capital.

However, in a number of cases, the historic capital debt has been wholly written off. Transport for London and its subsidiaries have virtually no fixed-interest debt. For railways, interest charges on the current capital value of their assets could represent a very high charge indeed, and very few meet this requirement (the intention to do so for the Hong Kong Mass Transit Railway is virtually unique among urban systems). The requirement for Railtrack and ROSCOs to provide a return on their assets has greatly increased the apparent rail subsidy in Britain (no equivalent valuation is attached to the road network, funded purely out of current revenues). Within the bus industry in Britain, NBC and SBG were funded wholly from repayable fixed-interest debt. Since privatization, individual bus companies now have an element of equity capital, but in many cases (especially management buy-outs), a substantial proportion is in the form of borrowing. Since companies were often sold for more than their share of total NBC or SBG debt, in many cases they faced a similar or even higher debt burden than before.

The differences are shown in Table 6.2. This illustrates a notional bus company set up in 1992, running 20 vehicles. They were purchased at £60,000 each. The depot and office accommodation cost £150,000, giving a total initial investment of £1.35 m. Annual revenue from all sources (i.e. including concessionary fare compensation, tendered services, etc. as well as direct passenger income) is £2.0 m per annum, and operating costs (including administration, etc.) £1.7 m. Vehicles are depreciated over a 15-year life, but their current replacement cost is now £90,000 each. Hence, depreciation per vehicle is £4,000 per year (historic) or £6,000 (replacement). No depreciation is charged on the depot or offices.

Table 6.2 Effects of varying assumptions on vehicle replacement and capital structure, for a small bus company: £ million per annum

Case	A	B	C	D	E
Revenue	2.00	2.00	2.00	2.00	2.00
Operating costs	1.70	1.70	1.70	1.70	1.98
Surplus	0.30	0.30	0.30	0.30	0.02
Depreciation	0.08	0.12	0.08	0.12	–
Interest	–	–	0.16	0.16	–
'Profit'	0.22	0.18	0.08	0.02	0.02
Return on initial investment (%)	16.3	13.3	5.9	1.5	13.3

Notes
A   All capital as equity, historic depreciation.
B   All capital as equity, replacement depreciation.
C   All capital fixed-interest, historic depreciation.
D   All capital fixed-interest, replacement depreciation.
E   Fleet on operating lease. Only capital investment is that in depot (£0.15m), financed as equity.

If the company were financed entirely through equity capital, then all the operating surplus after subtracting depreciation would be regarded as 'profit'. If funded through fixed-interest borrowing (assumed here at 12 per cent per annum), then such charges would be deducted as a 'cost' before arriving at profits. Also shown is a case in which vehicles are supplied on an operating lease, at £14,000 per vehicle per annum. This is charged as an operating cost. The only assets of the company are then the depot and offices, represented by equity capital of £150,000. As can be seen, by varying these assumptions, the net 'profit' can range from £0.22m to £0.02m per annum, for the same operating performance. The rate of return on the initial investment ranges from 16.3 per cent to 1.5 per cent.

DEPRECIATION

This is the process of setting aside funds during the life of an asset, such that it can be replaced by an equivalent asset without additional capital being required. Transport operators generally use the straight line method, in which the assumed life of an asset is divided into its cost to give a sum set aside each year. For example, if a bus with 50 passenger spaces (seated and standing combined) costs £100,000 and has a life of 15 years, then the annual depreciation charge would be £100,000/15, or £6,667 per year. An alternative is the reducing-balance method, in which the same percentage of the initial cost is set aside each year. For example, at 20 per cent, £20,000 would be set aside in the first year, £16,000 (i.e. 20 per cent of £80,000) in the second, and so on. This method is appropriate to those assets which may depreciate more rapidly in the first few years of their lives, and be resold for further use elsewhere. However, even in the coach sector, to which this does apply, the straight-line method is generally preferred.

If there were no inflation, then the historic price of the asset would generally be sufficient as a basis for depreciation. However, the money thus set aside would clearly be inadequate for funding the replacement. Under such conditions, either additional capital must be raised to make up the difference (through equity or fixed-interest loans), or replacement cost depreciation adopted, in which the sum set aside each year is adjusted in the light of inflation, so that the final total is sufficient to replace the asset at current prices. This approach also formed part of the concept of 'Current Cost Accounting' (CCA). During the 1970s and early 1980s it was encouraged in the public sector – for example, in the National Bus Company – but was not generally followed in the private sector. It has now been largely dropped, in favour of reversion to the historic cost method. The effect of relying on historic cost depreciation is that only the monetary value of assets is retained, and a serious danger of failing to make necessary replacement investment will arise.

The lives used for depreciation purposes correspond roughly to those found in practice, but may vary according to accounting conventions, treatment of depreciation and profits in company taxation, leasing, etc. For buses and coaches 8 to 15 years is common, but for rail vehicles up to 30 to 40 years. Certain assets may not be depreciated at all – this is true of most infrastructure, such as embankments, bridges or tunnels (whether road or rail), where periodic heavy maintenance and occasional rebuilding is adopted rather than complete replacement (a major example of this is the Tyne and Wear Metro, which depreciates rolling stock and equipment, but not infrastructure as such). A critical point may be reached when a major structure needs replacing, the subsequent additional investment then raising the question of whether the route should be abandoned. From 1992–3, British Rail changed its accounting basis by charging to capital some costs previously treated as current, notably on track and infrastructure renewal. Subsequently, the shift to Railtrack under privatization involves more realistic provision for replacement of assets, included in the access charges made to the growth of leasing in recent years also raises complications. In 'operating leases' an annual charge is made by the lessor to the operating company (sometimes also including maintenance of the vehicle), and the assets are not shown on the balance sheet, nor in depreciation. In 'finance leases', the assets do appear on the balance sheet, and depreciation may be provided. This practice has been adopted to some degree in the bus and coach industry, and is the normal case in the railways following privatization, in which leasing companies (ROSCOs) take responsibility not only for the existing fleet, but the supply of all new stock is also likely to be on this basis, either through the leasing companies, or direct arrangements between rolling stock manufacturers and TOCs.

The effect of vehicle utilization

In view of the importance of depreciation, it can be seen that increasing vehicle utilization effectively lowers unit cost per kilometre, especially if replacement costing (or operating lease charges) are included. Certain other costs (such as depots and management) are also spread over a greater output.

In the local bus sector, scope for such expansion may be modest, although utilization has improved by around 10 per cent in recent years (to about 50–55,000 km per bus per year). However, in long-distance coach work, much larger variations are found, associated with length of route, speed and seasonality. For example, a standard specification coach (capital cost £135,000) is assumed to have fuel costs of 10p per km and driver costs of £7.00 per hour. The capital cost may be converted to an annualized figure by assuming straight line depreciation over the first eight years of the vehicle's life, with a residual value of one-third at the end of this period (i.e. annual depreciation is two-thirds of the initial capital cost, divided by eight), and assuming a 10 per cent return on capital invested is needed.

On this basis, cost per vehicle-km run falls from 75p at 50,000 km per year to 46p at 150,000. (NB this excludes management overhead and some incidental costs.) Cost per passenger-km at a 50 per cent load factor fall from 3.0p to 1.8p. If a high-specification coach costing £198,000 were used, then the respective unit cost per km run falls from 96p to 52p.

Cost allocation methods

From this point, the specific features of the bus and rail industries make it appropriate to discuss costing techniques separately.

Until the early 1970s, the general approach in the British bus industry was to estimate a total average cost per bus mile (now, km), by dividing total costs (all operating costs, and usually depreciation, and interest also) by miles run. Such an indicator is still produced (on a kilometre basis), and serves to describe trends. However, it is most unsatisfactory as a means of comparing costs between routes within a network, or between operators, since it is clear that most costs do not vary with distance, but with time. Demands for support to rural services made to county councils resulted in a questioning of cost allocation methods. This led to the formulation of the NBC/CIPFA system.

Standard unit costs for each cost centre – typically a depot – were derived for driver hours, fuel and tyre costs per vehicle mile, depreciation per peak vehicle, etc. Table 6.3 gives an example based on a fairly typical allocation of costs under the CIPFA system, where the cost centre is a single depot, running urban and rural services.

The grouping of costs in Table 6.3 slightly simplifies that in Table 6.1, by placing 'variable' and 'semi-variable' into one category, and grouping fixed costs at depot level (local administration, building maintenance, etc.) and a share of company costs (central administration, etc.), but enables the principal features of the CIPFA system and its underlying assumptions to be illustrated. Maintenance costs are treated on a distance basis.

For purposes of calculation, a bus life of 15 years is assumed. Depreciation is on a straight-line basis, at current replacement values. Hence, for vehicles now costing £100,000 each a sum of £6,667 per year per vehicle is needed. If 10 per cent return on capital invested is required, and the average value of each vehicle is £66,700, then each vehicle must generate £6,670 per annum for this purpose, a combined total of £13,337.

Table 6.3 Rural and urban cost allocation example: all units in £ except where stated

	Rural	*Urban*	*Weighted average*
Cost per driver hour	8	8	8
Distance-based variable cost/km	15p	27.7p	22p
Capital cost per bus (£ '000)	75	112.5	100
Annual contribution per bus to depreciation and profit margin	10,000	15,001	13,334
Peak vehicle requirement	14	28	42
Annual hours run per bus	2,500	2,500	2,500
Total hours run per year	35,000	70,000	105,000
Average speed (km/h)	27	16.5	20
Total km per year	945,000	1,155,000	2,100,000
Annual contribution per bus to depot fixed costs	5,952	5,952	5,952
Total cost per year:			
Time-based	280,000	560,000	840,000
Distance-based	141,750	320,250	462,000
Depreciation/profit margin	140,000	420,028	560,028
Depot fixed costs	83,333	166,666	249,990
Grand total	645,683	1,155,000	2,112,018
Cost per bus-km	68.3p	£1.27	£1.01
If revenue per bus-km	75.0p	£1.20	£1.01
Surplus per bus-km	6.7p	–6p	0

For the 42 vehicles based at the depot the total depreciation and charges and profit contribution would be £560,000. In addition, costs would be incurred of operating the depot itself (including management staff costs, and a return on capital invested in the depot and its equipment) plus a contribution to central company overhead costs. These elements are assumed to total £250,000 per annum.

Variable operating costs per bus-km are assumed to be 22p (covering fuel and distance-based maintenance costs), and costs per hour (mainly drivers) £8.00.

If each vehicle runs 50,000 km per year, total km run by the 42 vehicles based at the depot would be 2.1 million. At an average speed of 20 km/h (including layover), hours operated would be 105,000. Hence, on this basis, annual costs would become:

Time-based driver costs	$105,000 \times £8$	=	£840,000
Distance-based costs	$2.1m \times £0.22$	=	£462,000
Depreciation charges (replacement) and profit margin (10 per cent)	$42 \times £13,334$	=	£560,028
Fixed depot costs		=	£250,000
Total		=	£2,112,028
Total cost per bus-km run		=	£1.01
Total cost per bus-hour run		=	£20.11

The cost per bus-km is slightly above the 1999–2000 average in Britain of about 92p,[4] but does include replacement depreciation and a profit margin.

It should be noted that the marginal costs per bus-km are much lower than this, at around 62p (22p distance-based plus an average 40p per km time-based costs @ 20 km/h). In practice, the latter would vary according to time of day. If additional 'inter peak' services were operated within time already paid to drivers providing peak period services, then the driver cost could be almost zero. Conversely, if Sunday work cost £10.00 per hour, driver cost per km would be 50p at an average of 20 km/h.

If average revenue were 101p per bus-km, then the operation would cover all of its costs, including the profit margin. However, if rural services averaged a revenue of 75p per km they would appear to make a loss of 26p per km. Conversely, if urban services average a revenue of 121p per km, they would appear to make a profit of 20p per km.

In practice, the rural services would have lower unit costs, due to higher speeds. In addition, if smaller vehicles were used, depreciation and profit requirements would be correspondingly reduced. It is also the case that lower fuel and maintenance costs would be incurred per km for rural services, due to the mix of vehicle size and fewer stops per km.

Table 6.3 shows some illustrative figures. It is assumed that rural buses cost £75,000 each (with depreciation and profit contributions reduced pro rata) and urban vehicles £112,500 each. Direct distance-based costs are 15p per km for rural services, and 27.7p for urban. Annual vehicle utilization in terms of time remains unchanged (2,500 hours per vehicle) but average speed produces inverse changes in driver cost per km run.

The overall effect of such assumptions is to give a rural average cost of 68.3p per km, and urban of 127p. Hence, the profitability is now reversed, with rural services making a surplus of about 7p per km, and urban a loss of about 6p per km.

Clearly, the actual outcome will depend on the type of vehicle used. A similar contrast may also be drawn between minibuses and full-sized vehicles operating within the same area, in which cost would vary according to vehicle type.

Further variation may result from differing driver wage rates per hour, either by vehicle type (where thus differentiated) or region (for example, a depot in a remote rural region could recruit staff for a given size of bus at rate much lower than in a major conurbation).

Peak cost allocation

Another respect in which average unit costs are inappropriate is in peak/off-peak cost allocation. Not only are certain vehicles only used at peak times, making it appropriate to allocate their costs entirely to that period, but also the crew utilization on peak-only duties may be poor.

Suppose that, in addition to the urban operations shown in the initial data, 8 more buses operate at peak times only, each running some 3 hours per day, Monday to Friday, and covering 60 km per bus per day. Their drivers perform no other work, and result in time-based variable costs of £48.00 per working day (of which there are 250 per year). If we assume that 10 buses are owned in total to cover the peak-only operations (for purposes of depreciation and PVR costing), then these operations incur an annual cost of:

Drivers	$250 \times 8 \times 48 =$	£96,000
Depot costs @ £5,952 per bus	$5,952 \times 10 =$	£59,520
Annual deprec. and profit @ £15,001 per bus	$15,001 \times 10 =$	£150,010
Distance-based costs @ 27.7p per km	$27.7p \times 8 \times 60 \times 250 =$	£33,240
Total		£338,770

This gives a unit cost of £338,770/120,000, or £2.82, over twice the urban average. If the revenue from them was £1.21 per km, a loss of £1.61 per km would be incurred. This implies a much greater cross-subsidy from other traffic than in the urban–rural case above.

Although the assumed average revenue – at the same rate per km as over the day as a whole – may seem rather low for the peak-only services, one should bear in mind that they are often loaded in one direction only, and that much of the extra peak traffic in many towns is schoolchildren, who may pay substantially lower fares. Since deregulation, many operators have not run such journeys commercially, but only on contract to local authorities.

However, even if an average unit cost per driver-hour and per bus-km for the peak-only buses were derived, this could be a poor guide. One peak-only bus might be covered by a driver who also drives on all-day buses to cover the meal-break reliefs of their drivers, and in this case it would not be reasonable to allocate their whole shift to the peak. Conversely, an off-peak journey might be added to the service, covered by a driver currently employed for the peak only, within their guaranteed shift, hence with a very low avoidable cost.

The determination of cross-subsidy within a network by time period is highly dependent upon crew cost allocation, which in turn depends on the local working agreements (for example, whether split-shift duties are worked) and the level of output in each period from which change is proposed. These were examined in depth by Leeds University in a study for NBC.[5] A further review of the effects of different peak/off-peak costing assumptions is provided by Savage.[6]

Not only are some vehicles used only at this time, but many crews may be needed for the peak and not fully utilized at other times.

There are two main ways of looking at this. Either most costs are allocated the day's services as a whole, on a time and/or distance basis, with only the extra peak output costed wholly to the peak, or the peak output can be seen as the *raison d'être* of the service, with all the costs of providing it allocated initially to the peak (i.e. all vehicles, and a shift of crews), with extension of service to other parts of the day seen as an incremental cost. Neither can be seen as the only 'right' option, but whatever basis is selected should then be used consistently for calculation.

The first approach may be more appropriate where a fairly steady level of service is offered throughout the day, with some expansion at peaks. This is typical of many medium-sized towns. The minibus services introduced in such towns during the 1980s offer a case in which virtually no 'peak only' working is found (except where larger vehicles have been retained to provide separate journeys for peak school travel). The second would be appropriate where there is a very high peak, with which most costs are associated. For example, in rural areas the peak in demand associated with statutory provision for school travel often determines the number of buses operated, and other services can then be costed on an incremental basis. In large urban areas, rail services are geared very much to meeting the work journey peak, a very high share of their costs (rolling stock, train crews, scale of infrastructure, etc.) being associated with this. The extreme case is found in fully automated urban systems where, once peak capacity has been provided, the additional costs of off-peak service are confined to some energy and train maintenance costs, a very small proportion of the total.

A third approach to peak costing is to observe that some additional peak operation above a 'base' level of all-day service may be desirable in any case, to provide drivers to cover meal-break reliefs of 'straight shift' staff, and enable vehicles to be maintained largely during daytime hours. An optimal peak:inter-peak vehicle output ratio may be defined, dependent upon demand patterns, shift working practices, and vehicle maintenance procedures, typically around 1:2.[7] Only vehicles and crews needed above this level would then be attributable solely to the peak.

Rail cost allocation

The issue of rail cost allocation is considerably more complex than that in the bus and coach industry, and only a brief overview can be provided in the space available here.

Some costs incurred directly by TOCs – categories such train crew, diesel fuel, and rolling stock maintenance – correspond broadly to those found in the bus industry, with similar issues of allocation arising – for example, the costing of peak-only services. In addition, TOCs are responsible for the operation of most stations, incurring staffing and maintenance costs that are a function of the number and size of stations, rather than directly related to train movements. Overall, about 35 to 40 per cent of TOCs' total costs are of this form.

However, over half the total costs are not directly related to TOC operations as such, but access charges to Railtrack (covering provision of infrastructure, operation of signalling, and supply of electric traction current), and leasing charges for rolling stock. Typically, each corresponds to about 30 per cent of total costs, but varies between companies. For example, a low-density regional network may incur relatively low rolling stock leasing charges, but a high proportion of track access charges. Conversely, a London and South East intensive commuter operation will display a higher element of rolling stock leasing, due to greater train length, and a smaller share of track access, due to higher traffic density.

A number of approaches have been suggested in allocating infrastructure costs between different train types. For example, wear and tear on the track itself may be correlated with gross tonne-kilometres, but is also associated with the maximum axle-loads (usually greater for freight stock) and maximum speeds (usually greater for passenger services) over the section in question. Cost and complexity of signalling are determined by the headway between trains, mix of speeds (see Chapter 9), and safety requirements, usually much stricter for passenger traffic.

Comparing the attributed revenue with the allocated costs for such traffic often resulted in misleading choices. For example, a freight service sharing track with passenger trains might well fail to cover its share of allocated costs, yet withdrawing that service might bring about very little reduction in track or signalling costs. If the freight service covered at least its specifically attributable costs, then it could be worth retaining. Likewise, an off-peak passenger service might be improved at low marginal cost, making better use of existing track and train crews, yet appear not worthwhile owing to the higher share of track, signalling and terminal costs which it might attract.

In general, passenger traffic is regarded as the prime user of the system in Britain (reflecting the fact that it accounts for the majority of revenue, and justification for financial support). It thus represents the vast majority of Railtrack's income. However, where it is proposed that an existing freight line be used to carry a new local passenger service also, then the passenger service would by definition become the 'Prime User' of the track and signalling, and thus bear many costs now attributed to the freight sector. This could deter the reopening, even if the revenue and other benefits of the proposed passenger service exceeded the avoidable costs of its introduction.

It has been the general intention of central government since the mid-1970s that freight and long-distance passenger services should cover their costs (howsoever defined) from revenue, with the franchise support payments directed largely towards other passenger services. Within the first round of rail franchising, this is largely the case, with existing long-distance services either covering all costs from revenue or anticipating to do so within the franchise period, and many London and South–East franchises are similarly placed. Hence, the support will become increasingly concentrated on regional and PTE services. In practice, the privatization of freight operators was only made possible by provision of track access grants on the sale of Railfreight Distribution and Freightliner, and from 2001 freight charges to all operators have been halved.

In addition to the issues raised above, the question of 'opportunity cost' may also arise, i.e. competing operators over the same track may plan mutually inconsistent train paths, especially at peak times. Running a regular, high-frequency airport shuttle service may conflict with maximizing the total number of paths available for all types of train (see Chapter 9). Hence, the charges made to the airport service operator might be more than the share of train-km operated to reflect the displacement of other train paths.

The first phase of track access charging implemented by the Rail Regulator, running until April 2001, was based on a crude allocation, in which over 90 per cent of costs were classified as fixed, with an allocation to each named TOC. Under the revised structure from 2001 there is a greater variable element. However, there is little sign of the opportunity cost concept being incorporated, or transparency in costing for new 'open access' operations (in contrast to the published scale of charges in Germany, for example).

Statistical models of cost structures

In addition to the procedures for allocating cost categories to activities described above, statistical relationships can also be established between variables, and the resultant models used for purposes of allocation, or forecasting. In the latter role they may provide a quick method of estimating costs of proposed service changes without carrying out a detailed analysis from the start. Thus a regression model for bus costs, incorporating bus-km, bus-hours and peak vehicle requirement could be used to estimate total cost of alternative service provisions, prior to more detailed assessment of preferred options.

Modelling of costs has been used in rail systems to establish relationships between traffic density and unit costs (especially in track and signalling) and to test whether overall economies of scale by network size exist. Fairly strong relationships with traffic density may be found but an uncertain picture remains on the question of economies of scale by network size. These issues have been examined in the recent 'SORT-IT' study.[8] In some cases, there remains the danger that the variables included in the model themselves simply reflect judgements by engineers or accountants rather than fundamental relationships. For example, various standards of track maintenance are often set, associated with traffic density, based on engineers' judgement. These in turn will be associated with different levels of cost. A modeller would thus establish a relationship between costs and traffic density, but this may be a rather circular process.

Within the bus industry, a number of modelling exercises have been carried out to test whether economies of scale by fleet size exist. They have generally confirmed the earlier work, suggesting no economies of scale. Indeed, diseconomies may exist, although it is difficult to distinguish the effects of large fleet size from features of large conurbations such as greater traffic congestion and higher wage levels, the size of operator and size of city served often being correlated. As in the rail case, economies by route density may be found:[9] although bus operators do not incur the fixed costs of track applicable for rail, higher density permits larger vehicles and/or higher load factors to be thus obtained, reducing cost per passenger carried.

Notes

1   Chartered Institute of Public Finance and Accountancy (CIPFA), *Passenger Transport Operations*, London, 1974 (and peak/off-peak costing and revenue allocation supplement, 1979).
2   Higginson, M.P. and White, P.R. (1982) *The Efficiency of British Urban Bus Operators. Research Report No. 8*. Transport Studies Group, Polytechnic of Central London.
3   DETR Statistics Bulletin SB(00)26, table 30.
4   Ibid.
5   University of Leeds, Institute for Transport Studies and the National Bus Company, London. (1984) *Cross-subsidy in Urban Bus Operations*.

6 Savage, I. (1989) 'The analysis of bus costs and revenues by time period', *Transport Reviews*, Part 1 (Literature Review) vol. 8 (1988), pp. 283–99; Part 2 (Metholodogy Review), vol. 9, pp. 1–12.
7 Higginson, op. cit.
8 Shires, J., Preston, J., Borgnolo, C. and Ponti, M. (1999) 'Strategic organisation and regulation in transport, Interurban Travel' (SORT-IT) Deliverable 6.0, Appendix A, February 1999.
9 Windle, R.J. (1998) 'Transit Policy and the cost structure of urban bus transportation', in Dodgson, J.S. and Topham, N. (eds) *Bus Deregulation and Privatisation: An International Perspective*, Avebury, Aldershot, 1988.

References and suggested reading

Robbins, D.K. (Bournemouth University) *Performance Trends in the Bus and Coach Industry*. Lloyds Bowmaker, Corporate Finance Division, November 1997.
Transport Advisory Services (TAS) of Preston publish annual 'Bus Industry Monitor' and 'Rail Industry Monitor' reports, giving details of financial performance of all TOCs and major bus operators, and trends in the industries as a whole.
A general review of costing and pricing models, and their relationship with demand models, is provided in Kenneth A. Small, *Urban Transportation Economics*, Harwood Academic Publishers, Reading, Berks, 1992.

7 Pricing theory and practice

Basic concepts

Under commercial operation, a starting point in pricing policy is to establish links between prices and costs. An operator seeking to break even or make a small profit is taken as the initial case, with some simple average costing approaches described. However, provided that revenue at least exceeds the variable, or escapable, cost associated with a particular facility, it will be worth retaining, at any rate in the short-to-medium run. Simple average cost-price relationships should therefore be considered only as a guide to the principles involved.

The costs which an operator has to meet from passenger revenue will depend upon conditions already described in the 'costing' chapter. In addition to current operating costs, depreciation will have to be covered (historic, or preferably replacement), and interest charges (dependent very much upon the historic capital structure). Taxes and subsidies will also affect the 'total costs' as perceived by the operator. For example, in Britain local bus services receive a rebate of most fuel duty, but in other countries fuel may carry a high rate of tax. Where capital grants are given for new rolling stock (as in light rail systems in Britain), this may avoid the need to fund it from operating revenue.

The term 'revenue' may also be ambiguous. In addition to fares paid by passengers, this will also include income from advertising, work for outside bodies by engineering workshops, etc. Payments in compensation for concessionary fares offered to certain groups of passengers at the request of local authorities – the elderly, disabled, and in some cases children – are normally regarded by operators as 'revenue' rather than 'subsidy', especially as the aim of current policy is to ensure that the operator does not receive revenue totalling more than would have been obtained (after allowing for any specific extra costs) at the level of fares that would normally be set by the operator.

Thus, if one divides total revenue (as defined by the operator) by passenger trips or passenger-kilometres (km) to get an average unit revenue, this figure may overstate considerably the average cost as perceived by the passenger. An alternative measure, therefore, is to take passenger revenue net of concessionary fare compensation, and divide this by passenger volume – this approach has been used by the author for some years, and is also adopted in the recent UCL/TAS study.[1] Unit revenues will also be affected by the mix of traffic (standard adult cash fares, travelcards, off-peak fares, child fares, etc.), and, where graduated fare scales or zonal fares apply, by changes in trip length over time. Rather than talking of an 'average fare' (an almost meaningless concept), it is better to use the term 'average revenue per trip', which conveys the sense that revenue received will vary according to the mix of traffic as well as changes in fare scales initiated by the operator.

An alternative measure is to estimate a weighted fares index from a mix of current fare categories, as is done by the DTLR in its annual bus statistics. However, in some cases, notably London (with its high proportion of concessionary and travelcard use) this may give substantially different trends to those from the average revenue indicator.

Some simple average cost pricing approaches

Taking buses as an example, the simplest 'rule' for average cost pricing would be to set the fare equal to the average cost per passenger (pax) trip:

$$\text{Fare} = \frac{\text{Total cost}}{\text{Total pax trips}} \quad \text{or} \quad \frac{\text{Cost per bus trip}}{\text{pax carried per bus trip}}$$

The first version gives a flat fare over the whole system throughout the day, the second a fare which could vary according to the cost of running a bus under different conditions (for example, a higher cost in the peak) and passengers carried (for example, higher in the late evenings when poor loadings are found).

A pure flat fare as such is hardly ever found, lower rates usually applying for children or the elderly, but many systems in North America and Western Europe come close to it. In Britain, it is less common, but may be found in Newport (South Wales), together with services in small towns. Furthermore, the zonal bus fare structure in London is such that many users make trips within only one zone. The further simplification from January 2000 means that only two adult cash fares are now charged – 70p for any journey in the large outer zone (covering the great majority of trips), or £1 for journeys within the central area, or crossing its boundary – in effect most bus users perceive a flat fare, as do underground users in the central area. The simplification in January 2000 was cited as causing a passenger trip growth of about 2 per cent.[2] Adoption of a single flat fare for London bus has been proposed recently by Grayling and Glaister,[3] and is likely to be adopted in 2002.

Where a flat fare is charged each time a passenger boards a vehicle, the cost to someone making a linked trip becomes very high, increasing by the whole flat fare at each transfer. However, the simplicity of a flat fare system makes it easy to incorporate a transfer facility, by permitting unlimited transfers within a given period (such as one hour), the time of issue being printed on the ticket. In some cases, this can be superimposed on a graduated system for unlinked trips, albeit at a higher rate than that applied for short-distance trips.

Another approach, found in some North American systems, is to offer a ticket permitting one transfer on cancellation at a slightly higher price than the unlinked flat fare trip. Reliable operation is clearly essential for such systems, so that the connecting leg can be made within the period allowed by timetabled services.

A second simple rule would be to relate the fare to distance travelled, i.e.:

$$\text{Fare per km} = \frac{\text{Total cost}}{\text{Total pax-km}} \quad \text{or} \quad \frac{\text{Cost per vehicle-km}}{\text{Average passenger load}}$$

Under the first version, a common fare per kilometre would be set over the whole system, while under the second it would vary with costs and loadings – for example, a poorly loaded early-morning service would bear a high fare, a well-loaded inter-peak service, a low one. A low-density route would have a higher break-even fare than a trunk service (one might have expected such patterns to have emerged following competition under deregulation, but in practice they remain rare).

In practice, perfect graduation is not attainable. Although for railways station-to-station prices can be set, for bus services there are too many stops to make this practicable, and stops are grouped into fare stages, typically about one kilometre long. Fares are then set on a stage-to-stage basis, so that someone travelling from any point in Stage 1 to any point in Stage 4, for example, would pay a four-stage fare (as explained in Chapter 2, this can lead to an over-estimation of passenger-km on a network when derived from distance paid for, rather than directly observed).

Another typical feature of graduated fare scales, as shown in Figure 7.1, is that the fare is not in linear proportion to distance, but has an initial step, followed by an observed rate of increase thereafter. This can be represented (in some cases

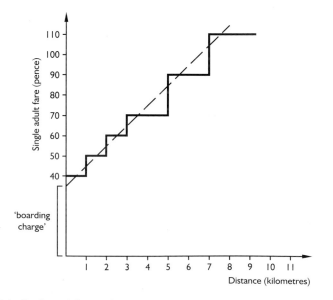

Figure 7.1 Graduated fare scales

explicitly) as a 'boarding charge', plus a rate per kilometre. The Dutch 'Strippen-kaart' prepaid ticketing system displays this feature, as a minimum of two strips must be cancelled on boarding the vehicle, then a further strip for each zone boundary crossed.

To some extent, this is a reflection of costs, as each passenger boarding incurs costs of ticket issue, and delay to the vehicle, but has often developed in a rather accidental fashion, as successive fare increases have caused a higher percentage to be applied to the lowest fares. The trip length distribution on urban bus services is such that relatively few trips are above 5–6 km, even in a large conurbation, and the need to distinguish various categories of longer trips becomes less important. Wider 'steps' in the fare scale are therefore applied as trip length increases.

Traditionally, the graduated scale has been considered a 'fair' reflection of costs, both by operators and passengers, yet it is evident that most costs are related to time, not distance, and that they will vary markedly by time of day, as described in Chapter 6. Nor, especially when passengers are charged in proportion to the distance travelled by the bus rather than the direct route to their destination (which may often be the case in rural areas), does the fare bear much relationship to perceived value of the trip.

Given the importance of time in determining costs, one could also set out a simple rule on a unit time cost, i.e.

$$\text{Fare per minute} = \frac{\text{Total cost}}{\text{Total pax-minutes}} \quad \text{or} \quad \frac{\text{Cost per vehicle-minute}}{\text{Average pax load}}$$

There is virtually no case of such policies being directly adopted by public transport operators, although charging by taxis sometimes incorporates this. The taper on graduated fares scales may have similar impact, the rate per passenger-km for longer trips reflecting the lower operating per vehicle-km on longer services at higher average speeds.

Peak costing

As indicated in the earlier discussion on costs, a major determinant of cost is the level of peak provision. Not only are some vehicles used only at this time, but many crews may be needed for the peak and not fully utilized at other times.

There are two main ways of looking at this. Either most costs are allocated to the day's services as a whole, on a time and/or distance basis, with only the extra peak output costed wholly to the peak, or the peak output can be seen as the *raison d'être* of the service, with all the costs of providing it allocated initially to the peak (i.e. all vehicle-based costs, and a shift of crews), with extension of service to other parts of the day seen as an incremental cost. Neither can be seen as the only 'right' option, but whatever basis is selected should then be used consistently for calculation.

The first approach may be more appropriate where a fairly steady level of service is offered throughout the day, with some expansion at peaks. This is typical of many medium-sized towns. The minibus services introduced in such towns during the 1980s offer a case in which virtually no 'peak only' working is found (except where larger vehicles have been retained to provide separate journeys for peak school travel). The second would be appropriate where there is a very high peak, with which most costs are associated. For example, in rural areas the peak in demand associated with statutory provision for school travel often determines the number of buses operated, and other services can then be costed on an incremental basis. In large urban areas, rail services are geared very much to meeting the work journey peak, a very high share of their costs (rolling stock, train crews, scale of infra-structure, etc.) being associated with this. The extreme case is found in fully automated urban systems where, once peak capacity has been provided, the additional costs of off-peak service are confined to some energy, train maintenance and some security supervision costs, a very small proportion of the total.

A third approach to peak costing is to observe that some additional peak operation above a 'base' level of all-day service may be desirable in any case, to provide drivers to cover meal-break reliefs of 'straight shift' staff, and enable vehicles to be maintained largely during daytime hours. An optimal peak:inter-peak vehicle output ratio may be defined, dependent upon demand patterns, shift working practices, and vehicle maintenance procedures, typically around 1:2.[4] Only vehicles and crews needed above this level would then be attributable solely to the peak. Figure 7.2 illustrates these three approaches.

Based on a simple assumption of a constant average revenue per single passenger trip over the whole day, the extent of cross-subsidy between different periods of the day may be estimated. An early attempt was the Market Analysis Project (MAP) study of the Hereford City network by NBC in 1976, using costing assumptions shown as (a) and (b) in Figure 7.2. On both, evening trips after 1800 made a large loss, but on assumption (a) other times of day generally covered their costs. On assumption (b), the morning peak made a loss (this being the more pronounced). If fares were to be varied around the existing average to reflect these costs (not allowing for elasticity effects), those in the inter-peak would be cut, and those in the evening increased by over 100 per cent.[5]

A subsequent study by Leeds University and the National Bus Company[6] examined four towns: Runcorn, Bridgend, Cheltenham, and, from Scottish Bus Group territory, Hawick. Cross-subsidy by time of day emerged very strongly. The inter-peak made a surplus, and early morning and evening services a loss, mainly due to poor loadings. The pattern for the peaks depended upon the costing assumptions employed (some five in all), being particularly sensitive to crew costs. It should be borne in mind, however, that the studies were based on the networks prior to MAP revised networks being introduced, which tended to reduce peak-only, and evening, vehicle output, thus reducing the extent of cross-subsidy. This study also showed that urban routes tended to be fairly close to break-even as a whole, and interurban routes made a surplus. These subsidized rural areas, often to a much greater extent than direct revenue support received from local authorities.

A more detailed examination of alternative networks and costing assumptions was carried out for the Cheltenham town network, showing route-by-route costing

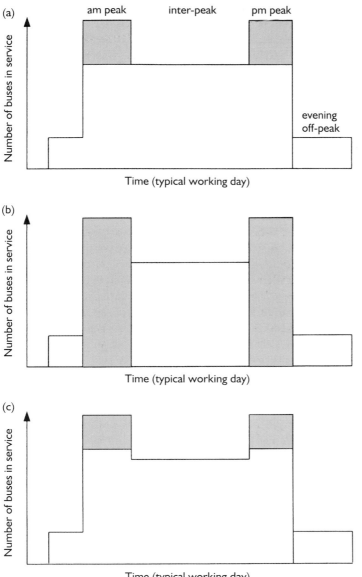

(a)

am peak   inter-peak   pm peak

Number of buses in service

evening
off-peak

Time (typical working day)

(b)

Number of buses in service

Time (typical working day)

(c)

Number of buses in service

Time (typical working day)

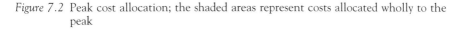

Figure 7.2 Peak cost allocation; the shaded areas represent costs allocated wholly to the peak

and cross-subsidy results to be robust under many assumptions, but time of day costing and cross-subsidy to be highly sensitive to any assumptions made. (Note that, although costing estimates for cross-subsidy purposes prior to deregulation became increasingly refined, crude assumptions continued to be made about revenue. Furthermore, the single passenger trip formed the basis of analysis. Further comment is made on these issues later in this chapter.)

The high cost of peak-only service provision generally means that it cannot cover its costs over the typical trip lengths found in local bus use. However, for longer journeys, this may be possible. The costs of putting a vehicle and crew into service for a peak-only return run are largely fixed, and increase only gradually with distance (the latter mainly fuel and maintenance costs). Figure 7.3 shows this case. The development of commuter coach services into London since the Transport Act 1980 illustrates the point well. With a 75 per cent load factor, an operator can break even if the journey is about 50 km or more each way. Shorter trips, or poorer load factors, may be viable if additional inter-peak work is found, such as tourist hire.[7] Likewise, long-distance commuter rail services into London may cover their costs even for peak-only workings.

Price elasticity

The elasticity of demand for a product (which may be defined very simply as the relationship between percentage change in units demanded – in this case trips – and percentage change in real price) will depend upon the degree of substitution by other products. In the case of local passenger transport, this takes six forms:

1   *Change of mode.* Although car driver/bus passenger comes first to mind, few perceive this choice. More likely, in the short run at least, are car passenger/bus passenger, and walk or cycle/bus passenger. Rail and bus, or coach, competition may be significant over longer distances, and rail may also be perceived as an alternative by the car driver more readily than is bus.
2   *Change of trip frequency.* Shopping, personal business and other non-work/ education trips can be varied in frequency in response to a fares change.

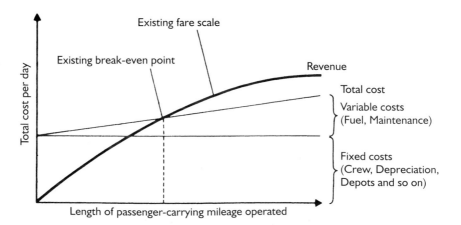

Figure 7.3 Break-even distance for peak-only operations

3 *Change in trip destination.* If fares rise, alternative destinations may be sought. For shopping trips, this substitution may occur quickly. For work trips, it may become apparent over the longer term, as home and/or workplace are relocated.

4 *Change in activity.* Some marginal activities may be changed, such as watching a video at home instead of seeing a film at the cinema.

5 *Shift in activities within the household.* Trips may be combined: for example, a working member picking up shopping on the way home, instead of someone else making a separate shopping trip.

6 A *shift between operators in the same mode, e.g. between competing bus companies.* This is identified as the 'operator' elasticity, in contrast to the 'market' elasticity, by Dargay and Hanly.[8] For a given sector, it will tend to be much higher, as the substitution is much easier than between modes, especially if both services operate at high frequency.

The above classification implies that demand for very short trips may be more elastic than long ones, since walking and cycling can be substituted easily. Some longer-than-average trips may also be more price sensitive, since locations can be substituted – for example, a local shopping centre for a regional one. We would expect off-peak travel to be more price sensitive, owing to the greater chance to vary trip frequency and location for the type of trip generally observed at such times. Long-run price elasticities would be expected to be higher than short-run, as more opportunities for substitution occur.

Evidence available largely supports such thinking. For urban bus travel an overall average elasticity of about –0.4 (changes in trips related to change in average revenue per trip) has been found remarkably robust, both in Britain and other countries.[9, 10] This is greater for trips of about 1.5 km or less where walking is easily substituted (around –0.7), and for bus trips over about 10 km. Elasticities are generally higher in small towns – associated with lower average trip lengths, a high proportion of non-work trips, and lesser constraints on car use.

Experience in Britain

Effects are illustrated in case studies on the Morpeth town service, and on the Morpeth–Newcastle route, in the mid-1970s,[11] the former displaying a high short-run elasticity (around –0.7) due to short trip length involved, the latter (an interurban route) an off-peak elasticity of about –1.0. Passengers with a car available also display higher elasticities.[12] Given the relatively large values found for very short trips, it is ironic that many bus operators in Britain adopt complex graduated fare scales, but none the less impose a very high fares per kilometre for the shortest trips, thus still deterring such trips much as a flat fare might do.

Another recent example arises from fares experiments by Stagecoach in the Manchester area in the mid-1990s.[13, 14] A local service within the conurbation, connecting a number of intermediate centres in a low-income area, experienced a short-run elasticity of about –1.0 following substantial reductions. This exceptionally high value was associated with short trip length, low incomes (perhaps making users more sensitive to price) and the fact that most of the route was paralleled by services of other operators, resulting in transfer between them.

Another Stagecoach service, an interurban route to Burnley, also displayed an elasticity of around –1.0, following a halving of the return fare, which affected both peak and off-peak demand. The presence of competing operators was very limited, and hence in this case the high elasticity would apply to the market as a whole. In both cases frequency increases (partly in response to the need to accommodate growing traffic) also affected ridership. Fares were subsequently increased from the very low levels offered at one stage, but with less effect, i.e. some of the additional traffic was retained, the low fare acting as a 'promotional' feature.

A further case of short-distance trips being more elastic is the one-stage fare offered by Travel West Midlands. Following adverse reaction to an increase, this was reduced back from 40p to 35p in February 2000. At about the same time First Manchester reduced its lowest fare from 45p to 40p – or by 11 per cent – trips subsequently rising by 11 per cent.[15]

An implication of variation in elasticity by trip length is that one might expect bus travel in more rural regions to display a greater elasticity than in larger urban areas, due to a mix of short trips within smaller towns and longer rural or interurban trips, both of which might be expected to have higher elasticities on the rationale outlined above. To some extent this is confirmed in Dargay and Hanly,[16] with rural counties showing higher average price elasticities than metropolitan counties, although with wide variation at the individual county level.

In looking at longer-term trends, it is essential to distinguish between 'money' and 'real' fare changes, i.e. adjusting money changes with respect to inflation (the RPI being generally used) to express changes in real terms.

The latest review of time-series evidence in Britain[17] confirms an average bus local trip price elasticity in the short run of about –0.4. Over the long run – up to about seven years – this rises gradually to about –0.9, e.g. if a real fares increase of say, 20 per cent, took place in one year, and fares were subsequently indexed to remain stable at this real level, demand would drop by 8 per cent in the short run, and 18 per cent in the long run. This effect may arise from two principal causes (which are not explicit in aggregate operator-derived data):

- the same individual becomes more responsive to the fare change over time as habits change, e.g. acquiring a car, or relocating to reduce length of the home to work trip;
- due to the marked 'turnover' effect in the local transport market, over the longer term, the individuals using the service or network will be largely replaced. The new users, not having the same habitual travel patterns, may be much more sensitive to levels of price and service quality.

Urban rail services display a somewhat different pattern. The work trip to the conurbation centre displays a low elasticity, probably around –0.15 to –0.20, since few alternatives may be available in the short run. However, a much higher long-run elasticity may be found. The introduction of commuter coaches may also increase the short-run elasticity, especially where the rail service is of relatively poor quality, and coach thus forms a more acceptable substitute.

Off-peak journeys on urban rail networks may be highly price sensitive, even in the short run, since many of them are for trips which can be relocated elsewhere (shopping in the conurbation centre, or in the suburbs), or generated by low fares (city-centre entertainment). Elasticities close to −1.0 (i.e. that at which total revenue is maintained when fares fall) may be observed. A very strong case may thus be made for offering cheap off-peak return fares, and perhaps even lower-priced evening returns, on urban rail services. For example, in February 2000 Tyne and Wear Metro introduced an evening one-day card priced at only £1.50, half the usual rate, valid from 1830.

Furthermore, if full account is taken of long-run interaction between transport costs, network structure and land use – including both home and work location decisions – an 'equilibrium' pattern may be determined, in which greater effects of fare changes are evident than in the short run. Mackett[18] indicates values of around −1.0 or greater for commuting from Hertfordshire to London. Models taking account of such interaction over entire urban areas likewise indicate higher values than those derived in the short to medium run by observing trends in one mode alone.

One can thus see a danger that, in the short run, the relatively inelastic nature of urban public transport demand encourages operators to raise fares as a means of increasing revenue, but in the long term such revenue gains are much smaller, and might even be negative.

In the long-distance market, even short-run elasticities are much greater – in the order of −1.0. This can be seen from the impacts on aggregate demand and revenue of sharp rises in real fares made by National Express in the period 1988–93.[19]

Combined with knowledge of cost structures, a clear case can thus be made within urban networks for lower fares during the inter-peak period, with higher fares at peaks. The evening period is less certain, since although costings suggest that a higher fare is needed to break even, this could also be a very price-sensitive market, at any rate for those trips originating from the home during this period (a considerable proportion of evening trips, especially in large cities, represents homeward journeys by those who have gone in to work or shop earlier in the day, as discussed in Chapter 2).

Some operators have shifted from a standard fare scale applying over the whole day to one differentiating by time period. For example, West Yorkshire PTE introduced a low maximum off-peak fare in 1981, which proved very successful in stimulating traffic. A much higher short-run elasticity than normally expected was found, around −0.85.[20] Evidence from price competition in Southend during 1992 also indicates a high sensitivity to the off-peak 'Summer Fares Bonanza' introduced by Thamesway (now a FirstGroup subsidiary, in competition with the then municipal operator), enabling total revenue to remain approximately constant.[21]

Other recent examples include the route-by-route branding and marketing adopted by Trent Buses, with specific fare level and structures for each (a policy which is more readily applied to their rural/interurban network than a complex network within an urban area), and maximum off-peak return fare of £1.40 introduced by FirstGroup within Scotland in January 2000, in the light of successful experience in the Glasgow area in 1999.[22]

A comprehensive review of elacticity values affecting public transport has been assembled by Hague Consulting.[23]

While in Britain there seems relatively little scope for differential pricing by vehicle quality, in some hotter countries premium fares are charged for air conditioning (for example, in Singapore and Hong Kong).

Note also that the concessionary fares for elderly and disabled, whose range was increased rapidly in the early 1970s (see Chapter 10) often act, in effect, as an off-peak fare, being confined to such periods. Their holders may account for 20 per cent or more of all trips on urban bus networks, and up to 50 per cent of the trips made at certain off-peak periods. Since the operators regard the compensation payments on their behalf as 'revenue', this income is attributed to the off-peak, contributing to the apparent cross-subsidy from the inter-peak to other times of day, although the fare perceived by the passenger – such as a half fare (the national minimum from 2001 under the Transport Act 2000) – may be a pretty close reflection of the actual average cost at such times.

Conversely, many peak bus users are schoolchildren who may be carried at half fare, or a low flat fare. Thus, revenue per passenger in the peak may be considerably lower than over the day as a whole. The cross-subsidy to the peak may be considerably greater than estimated from studies using a simple overall average revenue per trip, or the peak work journeys, at full adult fares, may cross-subsidize school trips during the same period.

The form of the demand curve, and its implications

The discussion on elasticities so far has been based on the form of demand curve generally applied by economists, as shown in Figure 7.4. A smoothly sloping concave curve is shown, with the price (in this case, fare per passenger trip) on the vertical axis, and volume (number of passenger trips) on the horizontal. The slope of the curve will depend on the elasticity value, being steeper as elasticity falls. That in Figure 7.4 represents a fairly high elasticity, as might be found for off-peak travel, or long-distance users. At an existing price (P1) a given volume of traffic will be found (V_1). However, some additional users could be attracted at a lower price (P_3), and if it were possible to discriminate so as to offer them this without loss of revenue from existing users, additional revenue could be attracted (the darker shaded area). Likewise, some of the existing users could still be retained at a higher price (P_2), owing to the consumer surplus they enjoy, and if it were possible to do so, additional revenue corresponding to the lighter shaded area could be obtained.

In practice, such clear discrimination is not possible, and a mixture of effects is likely, e.g. the higher price aimed at existing users willing to pay it would also hit some more price-sensitive users within the short distance urban market. It is generally impracticable to aim for discrimination of this sort with present pricing

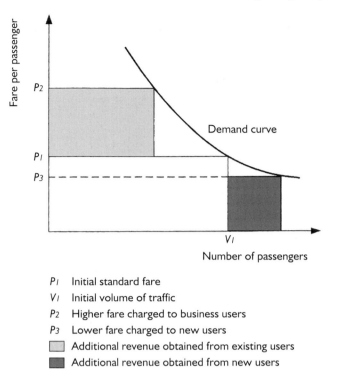

P*ı* Initial standard fare
V*ı* Initial volume of traffic
P₂ Higher fare charged to business users
P₃ Lower fare charged to new users
▢ Additional revenue obtained from existing users
▪ Additional revenue obtained from new users

Figure 7.4 A demand curve, and scope for price discrimination

systems, although some shift to peak/off-peak differential pricing may achieve part of the same effect, while mainly intended to reflect costs. Those travelling in the off-peak may be assumed to be more price-sensitive, and thus extra trips be stimulated from lower fares. Within the less price-sensitive peak there is often a need to raise fares in any case, simply to reflect costs, let alone discriminate by extracting a higher surplus of revenue over costs from such passengers. Scope for discriminatory pricing is generally much greater in the intercity sector, as outlined in Chapter 9.

Although a single elasticity value may be assumed at the existing price/volume level, this is likely to vary as prices change. One would expect elasticity to increase as price rose, since users would be more likely to seek substitutes for a product of given quality, and may experience budget constraints. Price would also rise as a proportion of generalized costs (for a given value of time). Likewise, if price fell, elasticity would be expected to fall. One simple assumption is that elasticity is proportional to price: thus, if the price rose by 50 per cent elasticity would increase by half. This is probably a rather extreme assumption, and for most price changes a constant elasticity may be assumed as a fair approximation, although the principle of elasticity varying with price remains valid. It should also be borne in mind that elasticities used in existing models are themselves derived from a range of past experience, and may only be valid within that range.

One may question, however, whether the traditional form of the demand curve is necessarily correct, or the most appropriate in all circumstances. As with much micro-economic theory, it assumes that consumer behaviour takes the form of many small incremental changes. Is this so, especially when modal choice is concerned? An alternative formulation is shown in Figure 7.5. Here, conventional scientific notation is followed, rather than that of economists. Thus, the causal (x) factor, price, is shown on the horizontal axis, the dependent (y) factor, quantity, on the vertical. Quantity is in turn represented as a probability of choosing between two options – for example, between rail (1) or car (0) – an approach analogous to that adopted in disaggregate mode choice modelling.

An individual, faced with the choice between two modes, will experience a critical threshold point at which the perceived advantages of the mode now used will be offset by a price increase, and a shift to the other mode take place. Thus a rail user with car available might shift back to car, despite problems of congestion and parking, at a certain price increase. The 'demand curve' for an individual would thus be represented by a discontinuity, from a probability of 1 to that of 0. In aggregate form, it is likely that this value would vary between individuals. If, for example, it were normally distributed, then an aggregate curve of the form in Figure 7.5 would result, the point of inflexion being at the average threshold value for the group.

This logic leads clearly to the S-shaped curve in Figure 7.5, in which elasticity is low at either extreme, but very high in the centre, in contrast to the constant, or gradually changing, value generally assumed.

Another feature of the traditional demand curve is that it is held (if only implicitly) to represent demand levels among one group of users at one point in

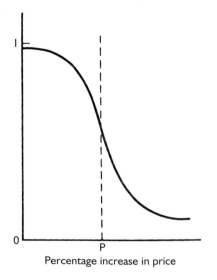

Percentage increase in price

Figure 7.5 An S-shaped demand curve, around a threshold value (P)

time, yet in practice aggregate elasticity values have been derived from observations over time. Given the high turnover in the market (Chapter 2), we are not observing behaviour of the same individuals.

This analysis is most appropriate for those demands where an 'all-or-nothing' change is likely, such as a shift in modal choice for the journey to work, or between different forms of public transport pricing, such as single cash fares and travelcard, described further below. For the cash-paid off-peak journey, given the quality of data available, there may be little difference in practice between the S-shaped and traditional demand curves, the latter continuing to be a valid approximation.

What product are we selling?

The structure of this chapter has so far largely followed the conventional assumptions made by transport economists. The supply of services is analysed in terms of output by route, and/or time of day, and the demand in the form of individual passenger trips. However, the passenger is concerned with getting from one activity to another, not with rides in vehicles. At the very least, we should consider the linked trip as the basis for analysis and pricing structures. Furthermore, relatively few users are making only an occasional one-way trip (taxi journeys are perhaps the main example of this): most normally make a return journey, based on the home. Even if return tickets are not sold, this should surely be the base for analysis.

Thus in considering cross-subsidy, comparison between different groups of users is certainly valid (off-peak shoppers and peak-only workers or schoolchildren, for example); but does it really make much sense to consider how far a worker on 'flexitime' travelling to work late morning and returning mid-evening is 'cross-subsidizing' one leg of his or her return journey from the other? In some cases, more complex trip chains (as defined in Chapter 2) may be the product purchased: for example, the ability to go from home to work, make some journeys within the city centre during the day, and a return home evening journey. On public transport systems, these are generally found in the larger cities, such as London.

Looking at private transport modes, the 'product' being purchased may be defined even more widely. Leaving aside an intrinsic benefit from purchase of a particular type of car, we see that the user is purchasing the use of a transport system (car, and road network), chiefly through a few large transactions (car purchase, annual maintenance check, insurance and tax disc), while costs varying with use (fuel, parking charges) account for a small proportion of the total. There is evidence for petrol price elasticities affecting car use, analogous to those for local bus travel: around –0.3 with respect to vehicle-km[24] – the elasticity of fuel consumption as such is somewhat greater, but offset by a shift to smaller vehicles in response to price increases so far as car vehicle-km is concerned. However, for local travel in the very short run, individual trips may be perceived as having a zero money cost.

Although various policy options exist to make more costs proportional to use, and place taxation of benefits on a similar footing, the greater part of car user costs are still likely to be invariant with distance in future.

Traditional selling of public transport, especially bus, has been based on a transaction for each single trip, heightening the perception of costs *vis-à-vis* another mode and also operationally cumbersome, especially on one-person-operated buses.

Some exceptions to this have applied for many years. The station-to-station rail season ticket provides a convenient form of prepayment, and gives unlimited travel between points specified during a defined period (week, quarter, etc.). On buses, a number of operators have offered multiride tickets, i.e. tickets prepaid for a given number of journeys, of fixed value, and cancelled on each trip. These reduce the number of transactions, and change perception of cost. There are few examples in Britain, the principal one being the 'Carnet' of flat-rate Zone 1 Underground tickets. However, such tickets have been widely used elsewhere in Europe for many years and form the basis of a nationwide system in The Netherlands (the 'Strippenkaart').

The travelcard concept

Overall development

The most important development has been the 'travelcard', used here as a generic term (and also as the trading name 'Travelcard', in London and the West Midlands): a season ticket or pass which permits unlimited use of a network, or zones thereof, usually for all public transport modes, during a defined period. The user is normally identified by a photocard, with a renewable portion indicating zones and period of validity. Such cards have been in use in German cities for many years, and in Edinburgh (Lothian Region) since the 1950s. However, their major growth began with the Stockholm monthly card introduced in 1970, followed by most other large cities in Europe, including West Midlands in 1972, Paris in 1975 and, rather late in the day, London in 1983.

The initial effect of such a card may be seen as giving a 'discount' (i.e. a lower average cost per trip) to existing travellers, especially those who make a great number of trips, and, where graduated fare systems apply, longer journeys. At the same time, new users may be attracted, especially from car, by the lower cost and convenience of the travelcard, and existing users are encouraged to make more trips, especially in the off-peak.

In common with traditional rail seasons, the travelcard has been criticized for the 'discount' given, which might be seen as inequitable and not reflecting the higher marginal costs of peak capacity. It is important to distinguish the question of a 'discount' given to frequent travellers through prepayment, and that given to peak travel as such. A travelcard price may be set so as to attract users now paying in cash – with benefits for the operator (in speeding boarding times, reducing operating costs, and cash flow), and the user's own convenience – while at the same time being priced to reflect peak costs (for example, a separate off-peak travelcard at lower price might be offered, as in the West Midlands, or cheap multiride tickets to off-peak users). Indeed, to regard any fare other than the full single cash rate as being offered at a 'discount' becomes unrealistic when, as in many European cities, the great majority of travellers are on some form of prepaid ticket, and the cash fare is in effect a penalty price (hence my preference for the term 'average revenue' rather than 'average fare', since the latter carries connotations of the cash single fare being the norm).

More important are the long-run, versus short-run, effects of the travelcard. Following an introductory phase at a low price, to gain market penetration, with operating benefits but revenue loss, the price may be later increased (while maintaining a differential with cash fares), taking advantage of the threshold price effect depicted in Figure 7.5, i.e. within a certain range (probably around 10 per cent on any one increase), relatively little traffic loss may be experienced, as the price change occurs along the relatively 'flat' part of the curve. Provided that the price increase is not around or above the threshold level, much of the traffic generated in the initial phase may be retained, with increased revenue.

There is also evidence of an underlying growth in the travelcard market over time, as the convenience of use becomes more widely appreciated. This can be seen in the Lothian Regional Transport case, where market penetration of the travelcard grew steadily during a period in which the relative price *vis-à-vis* cash fares was unchanged.[25]

These effects have been analysed with respect to the West Midlands and London, documented in more detail elsewhere.[26, 27] In the West Midlands, travelcard use grew rapidly from its introduction in 1972. After an initial price freeze, both real and money fares rose from 1975. Using a time-series demand model of the type discussed in Chapter 2, it can be shown that, for the same net revenue target, about 7 to 10 per cent more passengers were retained than might have been the case had cash-only fares applied. A cost-benefit analysis, including operating benefits (such as faster boarding times), and the cost of additional retained peak period capacity, also showed a net benefit. In 1984–5, the travelcard accounted for 31 per cent of all unlinked passenger trips, and the concessionary pass for free travel 24 per cent, leaving only 45 per cent paying cash on bus. Similar proportions were found in Tyne and Wear.

The London travelcard experience

The sequence of events in London was somewhat more complex. A traditional pattern of cash-based graduated bus fares applied until 1981, apart from the introduction of a bus pass (a bus-only travelcard) in 1974. On the Underground, a form of graduated fare was adopted for station-to-station singles, with route-specific season tickets also offered. In spring 1981 a flat fare was introduced for suburban bus routes, following successful results from earlier experiments. The latest shift to the two-zone structure in London for cash bus fares from January 2000 can be seen as an extension of this process.

This was soon followed by the then Greater London Council's 'Fares Fair' policy, in which bus and Underground fares were reduced by about 25 per cent in money terms in October 1981. A zonal structure, based on concentric zones around the central area, was also introduced, although bus and rail pricing remained separate.

LIVERPOOL JOHN MOORES UNIVERSITY
LEARNING SERVICES

Following a challenge to the legality of the 'Fares Fair' policy, a House of Lords appeal decision resulted in a 100 per cent cash fares increase in March 1982. However, the zonal structure was retained.

Following clarification of the legal position, a fares reduction was introduced in May 1983 (19 per cent on buses, 28 per cent on the Underground), together with the LT bus/Underground Travelcard, which effectively superseded most rail season tickets and much bus pass use (although a separate bus pass remained on sale). Growth in sales, and also in total travel on the system, was very rapid. Between December 1982 and December 1984, passenger-kilometres on the Underground rose by 44 per cent. This growth continued to a peak in 1988–9, in which year Underground passenger-kilometres were 72 per cent above the 1982 level, and bus passenger-kilometres some 13 per cent higher. Car commuting into the central area fell. The growth in both bus and Underground usage was much larger than would be expected through a simple application of traditional price elasticities. Work by London Transport[28] indicates that specific effects attributable to the travelcards as such (i.e. quite apart from its impact in reducing average cost per trip made) may be identified:

	Underground	Bus
Growth in passenger-kilometres	33 per cent	20 per cent
Growth in real revenue	16 per cent	4 per cent

Note that revenue also rose, albeit less rapidly than volume. In 1992–3 total bus revenue in London was 1 per cent higher than in 1985–6, compared with a drop of 14 per cent for the rest of Britain (despite the sharp fare rises in some metropolitan areas). This contrasts with the impact of 'across the board' fare reductions on traditional cash-based systems as a means of stimulating public transport use (such as the policy followed in South Yorkshire between 1976 and 1986). Applying a standard –0.3 elasticity, a 10 per cent real fares reduction would indeed stimulate bus use by about 3 per cent, but at a revenue loss of about 7 per cent (although on long-run elasticities a better picture would emerge, a trips growth of about 9 per cent with only a marginal net revenue loss).

New York was even later than London in adopting the travelcard, but the 'Metrocard' introduced in 1997 has resulted in rapid growth, especially in bus use, and subway use is now the highest since 1971.[29]

The LT analysis[30] also indicated differences between 'own mode' and 'conditional' fares elasticities, i.e. if the price of one public transport mode was raised while that of another remained constant, a significant switch of trips between the public transport modes would occur, as well as a net overall reduction in travel (the 'own mode' effect). If, however, prices were raised simultaneously (the 'conditional' elasticity) the effect would be limited to the net reduction in public transport use as whole. In the London case (in which a substantial proportion of public transport users would have a choice of modes), the 'own mode' elasticity for buses is estimated at –0.62, but the 'conditional' elasticity at –0.35 (corresponding figures for the Underground are –0.43 and –0.17 respectively). In other cities, such effects may be harder to distinguish, owing to the much more limited rail networks.

The convenience of a travelcard is particularly noticeable in a large city, in which many more opportunities are opened up by removing financial penalties of interchange. One large benefit, which cannot be quantified easily without good Origin and Destination (O&D) data, is the extent to which the same trip can be made more quickly, by optimal choice of route, and reduced waiting time. One estimate by Shon[31] evaluated such opportunities for a corridor in north-east London, equivalent to about 10p per trip at 1989 prices.

Elsewhere in Britain, travelcard market penetration prior to deregulation tended to be somewhat lower, especially in many smaller towns, where much less interchange occurs, and the card has not been promoted through an initial period of low price to gain market penetration. It is noteworthy, however, that some operators in the privatized, deregulated market have introduced their own travelcards, notably Stagecoach's 'Megarider', both in competition with other operators, but also in areas where little operator competition is evident, as a means of expanding the market. In some cases growth has been sufficient to maintain or increase revenues, even in the short run.[32]

More recent developments of the travelcard illustrate scope for differentiating by type of person and journey, to a degree that would be impracticable for single cash fares. They include:

- the weekend travelcard in London, giving lower rates for purchasing Saturday and Sunday travel together than separately;
- the family travelcard, also in London, in which a lower price is charged, with a small 'add on' per child, similar to the family railcard for longer-distance rail travel, and reflecting the economies of car sharing as the alternative mode;
- reduced rates for students (as distinct from concessionary fares required by local authority policy), notably the cards offered by Travel West Midlands, and major bus operators in Manchester, together with the 30 per cent discount offered in London since 1998. A rural area is now provided with a similar scheme, set up by First Red Bus and Devon County Council in the Barnstaple area, using smart card technology. An innovative approach has been adopted by Brighton Hove and District (part of the Go Ahead Group) in which those aged 16 upward are offered a discount from the full adult fare after ceasing to be eligible for the child fare automatically. By holding a card, they can continue to travel at child fares for several years, then being offered a period travelcard at gradually increasing prices. In 1999, some 85 per cent of 16-year-olds had bus ID cards, and 50 per cent took up the offer of a £20 annual card permitting continued travel at child rates.[33]

Is there a case for premium pricing?

Most urban public transport provision is priced according to distance, time, ticket type and user type, rather than directly reflecting service quality. In the long-distance sector, wide variations exist (first and standard class, for example), but they are largely unknown in the urban sector, except for the significant role played by taxis, which represent a much larger share of user expenditure than of trips made (see Chapter 2).

In many developing countries, for example, 'paratransit' services often operate at premium fares 100 per cent or more above standard rates. However, where there is little overcrowding, as in Britain, the evidence to support such imitation is very weak. Splitting the urban market by class of service requires accommodation to be provided in separate vehicles, hence effectively lowering the frequency of service to each user group (the past operation of first-class coaches on the Paris Metro being the only significant exception). Since waiting time is important, particularly to those with high values of time, the effect could easily be self-defeating.

It is sometimes suggested that a higher frequency of service could be justified at higher fares. Users with high values of time, in particular, might be willing to pay for the reduced waiting time thus incurred. However, the short-run average elasticity of demand with respect to service level (vehicle-kilometres) very rarely exceeds +0.4 (as in more successful minibus conversions, for example), and may be lower. It is thus of the same magnitude as that for fares. Hence, if a conversion to a higher-frequency service, with a pro rata increase in costs, generated extra demand, an attempt to 'price up' to reflect quality would simply be self-defeating.

For example, if a doubling of frequency (100 per cent bus-kilometre increase) took place on a +0.4 elasticity, demand and revenue would rise by 40 per cent, but costs by 100 per cent. If a premium fare of 100 per cent was introduced simultaneously on a –0.4 elasticity, demand would revert to its previous level. However, load factors would halve, as twice as many vehicle-kilometres were operated to serve the same demand. A similar argument applies also in the long run, since both fare and service level elasticities are of the same magnitude.

In practice, almost all minibus conversion in Britain has been based on the same fare levels as initially charged for full-size vehicles, the economic case resting on lower unit cost per vehicle-km of minibus services (for example, if minibus unit costs were 70 per cent of those of full-sized buses, a doubling of frequency would only entail an increase in total costs of 40 per cent. This would match the revenue growth resulting from a 40 per cent passenger increase, at the same fare level as charged before.) However, it would be true to say that some of the most extensive minibus service conversion occurred in parts of Britain which were charging fairly high real fares for low-frequency full-sized bus services (parts of the South West and South Wales, for example), and hence the minibus's higher frequency could be seen as giving better value in relation to fares already imposed.

Premium fares do apply to urban light rail schemes funded under Section 56 criteria, in which such fares are charged to reflect the improvement in service quality (as seen on the Manchester Metrolink, for example). Here, quality is reflected more in the overall image and speed of the service than frequency *per se*. However, the imposition of a premium fare makes it difficult to offer a reasonably-priced bus/rail through travelcard, and hence to maximize use of the public transport network as a whole.

An area for possible premium pricing yet to be fully explored is that of taxibus and shared taxi operations. Although legalized under the Transport Act 1985 they have had very little impact to date, yet could offer attractive services to fill a 'niche' market (for example, direct late evening services), at prices between those of conventional public transport and single-hirer taxis.

Fare collection methods

Approximate revenues per trip in Britain by mode as are follows:

Local bus journeys	65 pence
London Underground	£1.15
National railways	£3.50

(Derived from DETR Transport Statistics Bulletin SB (00)26 *A Bulletin of Public Transport Statistics*: GB 2000 edition, data for 1999–2000 from tables 4, 5, 10 and 11)

Then average revenue per trip is low, even for national railways (which includes long-distance trips within the average quoted above). Conversely, in the intercity sector with average revenue per trip of £10 upwards, a complex price structure is justified in terms of relatively large price elasticities (around –1.0), and the wide range of ticket types and service quality offered. This is often associated with pre-booking of capacity, notably through pricing policies such as 'Apex' fares. Increasingly sophisticated 'yield management' systems, pioneered by airlines, are now being applied to rail also.

For urban public transport use, the very low revenue per trip makes the present typical means of collecting revenue – cash transactions on the vehicle – very cumbersome, incurring direct operational costs (through slowing down a service, the majority of whose costs are time-based), and worsening service quality by extending boarding times, affecting both average speed and its variation (not only those paying in cash, but also those paying by other means are affected by such delays, both in extending in-vehicle travel time, and increasing waiting time at stops through more erratic running).

The user also requires information about the service (exact timetable, and/or frequency; likely in-vehicle time) in order to judge the door-to-door duration of a journey. Uncertainty may be increased by the need for information on timing and feasibility of connecting and/or return journeys, and need for fares information in order to produce the exact fare, or avoid penalties for overriding.

In contrast, the uncertainty faced by a user of alternative modes for short-distance urban trips is much less. For the shorter trips (up to about 2 km) walking and cycling are alternatives. Here, the user is involved in no cash transaction specific to the trip, and has no need to consult a timetable. If the alternative is the car, then again cash transactions are generally avoided (except where parking must be paid for), and no timetable information is needed, although some uncertainty about travel times under congested conditions may apply. The first Chartered

Institute of Transport working party report on the bus industry, in reviewing market research evidence, noted that 'Finding accurate information can be time-consuming and deters the casual user. People who have to use buses will persevere, others will not. . . . Attention was drawn to difficulty in paying for fares if passengers were expected to have the right change'.[34]

It could be argued that road pricing, if introduced, will impose a need for car users to incur a transaction for each trip made. However, any money transactions will be made electronically at regular intervals, rather than physically handled for each trip.

If we can reduce the information needs of the bus user, we can thus reduce the uncertainty about use of this mode. Real-time information systems and electronic ticketing technology can then be used to provide assistance and reassurance, rather than adding complexity to the process. This can be achieved by reducing the need for timetable information (through high frequency, and reliability), together with the need for cash transactions and fare information (by using simple off-bus systems).

From the user's point of view, possession of a travelcard also reduces the need for information. Provided that zones and any other validity conditions are clearly understood, their use does not require information on specific fares for the journey being made, or to handle cash.

However, the travelcard in present form may be criticized in that checking for validity is often rudimentary, and management information is reduced. In principle, each occasion on which a travelcard or pass holder boards a bus may be recorded by the driver pressing a button on a electronic ticket machine (ETM), such as the 'Wayfarer'. This data is then recorded on a data module along with that for cash-paid fares, so that the number of pass holders boarding in each fare stage for each bus journey is recorded. In comparison with the data collected on cash-paid journeys no information on trip length is recorded, whereas for a cash-paid fare the maximum number of stages paid for is known. One might add, however, that in practice bus management rarely seems to use ETM data for detailed analysis, and the quality is often variable.

None the less, errors may occur in checking the validity of a travelcard or pass as a passenger is boarding, especially at peak times. Drivers may fail to manually record such boardings on their machines. The need for all pass holders to show their pass to the driver on boarding offsets some of the savings in boarding time that might otherwise be found if multiple entrances could be used, as common elsewhere in Europe (although on safety grounds, a single entry adjacent to the driver is to be preferred).

Some form of automation for the validation stage of travelcard use may thus be of assistance. Recent developments in contactless smart cards no longer require the user to pass the card through a device. Hence validity (by zone, card type, renewal date, etc.) may be checked automatically, and a record of boardings obtained. Unit costs of producing such cards are now acceptably low. The fundamental marketing concept of the travelcard is unchanged.

It has been argued that we should go one step further, to a smart card (or magnetic card) system in which the cost for each trip could be deducted for each occasion it is used, through re-encoding. Typically, a discount may be offered for such use *vis-à-vis* cash fares (e.g. £5.50 worth of travel for £5 card) – assuming that 'discount' is a meaningful term (see above). Travelcard holders making a much greater number of trips than the average might be asked to pay more. A further benefit may be that occasional users for whom travelcard is not worthwhile could be encouraged to switch to cashless payment through such a system.

A further factor encouraging such development is the apparent need to attribute trips and revenue collected in much greater detail than before, under deregulated systems, in which precise allocation of revenue between routes and operators becomes much more important from the viewpoint of separately owned and financed undertakings (although it is not a matter of interest to the passenger). Apportionment of revenue in proportion to passenger-km is also a requirement for the 'block exemption' from Competition Act conditions for joint ticketing (see Chapter 10).

Where a flat fare is deducted for each trip (e.g. for some types of concessionary fare in Britain), this adds little complexity or delay. This is the case in the largest bus fleet running with smart card fare collection, Seoul. However, incorporating fares graduated by journey length continues to cause difficulties. Technology is available which permits an inspector to check validity of a stored value card in terms of the journey length for which a deduction has been made on boarding the bus, and trials are taking place in Geneva of monitoring smart cards on bus exit. In some cases, a paper ticket may be issued (as on the Milton Keynes network), corresponding to the value of the smart card deduction made. However, at this level the basic benefits of off-bus systems – reducing boarding time – are being negated.

At this point it may be helpful to distinguish between 'journeys' and 'transactions'. The former are the trips made by users (defined either as single bus rides, or linked trips to the ultimate destination), the latter the handling of money. Under traditional cash-based systems these are the same. With travelcards, the transaction is recorded at the point of sale (such as a local shop): clearly, good records of this are needed to combat fraud. The journey is then recorded separately, perhaps through the driver actuating an ETM (see above), smart card validation, or through on-bus surveys estimating the overall volume of card or pass use.

The latter do not produce the apparent precision of ticket machine data, but may enable estimates of total use to be made within a high degree of accuracy. Such surveys may also enable data to be collected on exact origins and destinations of trips, trip purpose, etc. To what extent is it worthwhile installing a more sophisticated system in order to increase this degree of accuracy, in terms of the overall economic benefit obtained, especially from the user's point of view? In particular, where automatic validation is applied, then a record of the number of boardings is obtained. Sample surveys could then be used to determine average trip length and its distribution, without imposing more complex fare and ticketing systems on the passenger as such.

These issues currently arise in London, where a system of 'net cost contract agreements' has been favoured by central government, rather than the 'gross cost contracts' under which most tendering has taken place. While in theory, the net system gives incentives to operators, the much greater complexity incurred in terms of revenue allocation causes substantial administrative costs, and a shift back to gross cost tendering has occurred recently.

Experience since local bus deregulation

Deregulation of local bus services in 1986 was effectively preceded by removal of much of the fares control traditionally enforced by the Traffic Commissioners, following the Transport Act of 1980. However, price competition has been limited in practice. Apart from occasional 'fare wars', most competitive action has taken the form of variations in service level. Outside London, fares have generally risen in real terms (and not only in those metropolitan areas where they rose from a very low level after abolition of the metropolitan councils in April 1986). Most operators have also tended to retain a traditional graduated fare scale applied over the whole network, although more opportunity now exists to vary fares by time of day, and between routes according to traffic density, etc.

The explanation lies largely in the elasticities of demand already mentioned. Given the fairly small price elasticities for bus use in the short run (around –0.4), a fare reduction by a single operator would cause considerable revenue loss, unless very substantial transfers from other operators took place. Insofar as users typically board the first bus to arrive, only those with a low value of time would find it worthwhile waiting for a 'low fare' vehicle. For example, if existing operators charge 80p per trip, and the users' value of waiting time is 5p per minute, then a large differential would be needed.

If a new operator charged 60p per trip, then it would not be worth waiting more than 4 minutes for the lower fare buses. Given that timetable information is often poor, quite apart from variations in service reliability, most users will tend to board the first bus to arrive, even with this price differential of 25 per cent. Hence, the logical strategy for a new operator in most cases is to charge the existing fares. One implication might be that price competition would be most likely on corridors with very high frequency of service, where waiting for the 'cheaper' vehicle would be worthwhile – one example in the Wilmslow Road corridor in Manchester, with its large student market.

The role of travelcards outside London has tended to diminish. In some cases, these became the preserve of a single operator (since competition policy condones this practice, but initially required inter-operator travelcard price agreements to be submitted for approval).

Where competition has developed, operators have sometimes offered their own travelcards, but these carry the disadvantage that users cannot board the first bus to arrive. Hence, a shift back to cash fares may be seen. For example, a low proportion of off-bus ticketing developed in Oxford, following development of competing networks by two operators. Although each offers a travelcard, many users prefer to board the first bus to arrive, and hence pay in cash in order to retain this freedom.[35] While reducing waiting time, this has the unfortunate effect of increasing boarding times on the buses themselves, thus contributing to lower average speeds and greater variability.

Conclusion

The pricing of urban public transport is a function both of costs and of passenger demand characteristics. While a highly disaggregated approach – charging separately for each trip made – may, in theory, be appealing, the convenience and simplicity of systems such as the travelcard may enhance the quality of the public transport service as a whole, leading to higher utilization and higher revenues.

Notes

1 Dargay, J.M. and Hanly, M. (1999) *Bus Fare Elasticities* A report to the Department of the Environment, Transport and the Regions', ESRC Transport Studies Unit, University College London, December 1999.
2 *Transit*, 5 May 2000, p. 20.
3 Grayling, T. and Glaister, S. (2000) *A New Fares Contract for London*, Institute of Public Policy Research, London, January 2000.
4 Higginson, M.P. and White, P.R. (1982) *The Efficiency of British Urban Bus Operations*, (Chapter 7). Research Report No. 8, Transport Studies Group, Polytechnic of Central London.
5 National Bus Company. Data from the Hereford Market Analysis Project, as quoted in *Innovations in Rural Bus Services*, Eighth Report from the Select Committee on Nationalized Industries, Session 1977/78.
6 National Bus Company/Institute for Transport Studies, University of Leeds (1984). *Cross-subsidy in Urban Bus Operations*.
7 Robbins, D.K. and White, P.R. (1985) 'Combining scheduled commuter services with private hire, sightseeing and tour work: the London experience'. Proceedings of the 26th Annual Meeting of the Transportation Research Forum, Jacksonville, Florida, November, pp. 273–81.
8 Dargay, op. cit.
9 Ibid.
10 Goodwin, P.B. (1992) 'A review of new demand elasticities with special reference to short and long run effects of price changes', *Journal of Transport Economics and Policy*, May, pp. 155–69. (Fuller details of the examples discussed may be found in Goodwin, P.B., Oum, T.H., Waters, W.G. and Yong, J.S., *An Annotated Bibliography of Demand Elasticities*, Report 682, Transport Studies Unit, University of Oxford, July 1992).
11 Heels, P. and White, P.R. (1977) *Fare Elasticities on Interurban and Rural Bus Services*. Research Report No. 4, Transport Studies Group, Polytechnic of Central London.
12 Transport and Road Research Laboratory (1980) *The Demand for Public Transport* Results of an International Collaborative Study.
13 Colson, B. (1996) 'UK bus deregulation: a qualified success with much still to offer customers and society at large', *Transport Reviews*, vol. 16, no. 4 (Oct–Dec).
14 White, P.R. (1997) 'What conclusions can be drawn about bus deregulation in Britain?', *Transport Reviews*, January–March 1997, pp. 1–16.
15 *Transit*, 10 March 2000, p. 2.
16 Dargay, op. cit.
17 Ibid.
18 Mackett, R.L. (1985) 'Modelling the impact of rail fares increases', *Transportation*, vol. 12, no. 4, May, pp. 293–312.

19   White, P.R. (2001) 'Regular interurban coach services in Europe', in Report of Round Table 114 (of the same title), Paris, 1999. European Conference of Ministers of Transport (published 2001).

20   Grimshaw, R.F. (1982) *The Effect of Maximum Off-peak Fares on Bus Patronage and Revenue*. Development Report D19. West Yorkshire Passenger Transport Executive, Leeds, December 1982.

21   Office of Fair Trading, *Thamesway Limited: The Operation of Local Bus Services Commencing in, Terminating in or Passing Through Southend-on-Sea* (an investigation under Section 3 of the Competition Act 1980), London, August 1993.

22   *Transit*, 28 January 2000, p. 3.

23   De Jong, G. (Hague Consulting) (2000) 'Elasticities from the TRACE project'. Paper at 'Think-up' workshop, Dresden, December 2000 (download from http://www.netr. fr/think-up)

24   Ibid.

25   White, P.R. (1981) 'Travelcard tickets in urban public Transport', *Journal of Transport Economics and Policy*, vol. XV, no. 1, January, pp. 17–34.

26   London Transport Planning Department (1993) *London Transport Traffic Trends 1971–90*, Research Report R273 London, February.

27   White, P.R. (1984) 'User response to price changes: application of the 'threshold' concept', *Transport Reviews*, vol. 4, no. 4, pp. 367–86.

28   See note 26.

29   *Tramways and Urban Transit*, February 2001, p. 71; see also Atefeh Riazi 'Fare collection in New York moves into the 21st century', *World Markets Series Business Briefing – Global Mass Transit Systems* (London, January 1999) pp. 146–50.

30   See note 26.

31   Shon, E. (1989) 'Evaluation of public transport fare integration in London', PhD thesis, Institute for Transport Studies, University of Leeds, 1989 (unpublished).

32   Stagecoach plc. *Annual Report for Year 1995/96*, pp. 10, 11.

33   *Transit*, 30 June 2000, p. 2.

34   Chartered Institute of Transport (1993) *Bus Routes to Success*. Report of a bus working party. London, June.

35   Heseltine, P.M. *et al.* (1992) *Transport Research Laboratory Contractor Report CR348*, Crowthorne.

References and suggested reading

Dargay, J.M. and Goodwin, P.B. (2001) 'Bus fares and subsidies in Britain: is the price right?', Chapter 5, in Grayling, T. (ed.) *Any more fares? Delivering Better Bus Services*, Institute of Public Policy Research, London, February.

York, I.O. (1995) *Passenger Reactions to Present and Alternative Travelcard Schemes*, TRL Report 142, 1995.

8 Rural public transport

Defining 'rural'

The term 'rural transport' appears to conjure up immediately an image based on remote rural areas of very low-density population, such as the Scottish Highlands or central Wales, in which low frequencies of service are found, 'unconventional' approaches such as the postbus are widely used, and high levels of financial support required. While such areas may characterize the extreme case, they are highly untypical. Concentration on such conditions as 'rural', and likewise those of the very large cities as 'urban', leads to a large and growing proportion of the population being ignored.

The 1991 Census showed that the population of England and Wales was then 51 million. Of this, Greater London accounted for 6.8 million (13 per cent), the metropolitan areas 11.1 million (22 per cent) and the 'shire' (non-metropolitan) counties 33.0 million (65 per cent). The 1991 national total was 3 per cent above that for 1981, being static in Greater London, but falling by 2 per cent in the mets. The shires increased by 5 per cent during the decade, with increases of up to 8 per cent in 'resort, port and retirement', and also in 'remoter, mainly rural' areas.[1] Some of the growth is, in effect, the suburban fringe of larger centres, but other growth is in free-standing settlements, as patterns of employment and population structure are changing.

Only the most remote rural areas continue to lose population in absolute terms, although the traditional rural occupations, such as those based on agriculture, continue to decline in numbers employed. In many regions, new residents have been attracted – either urban commuters, or those retiring to such areas. While this movement is mainly based on high car availability, it also has implications for public transport use. The traditional rural population, characterized by lower income and car ownership, may be displaced to towns. At the same time, those retiring to rural areas may subsequently become more dependent as their age makes car driving difficult. Working-age newcomers may make little use of rural public transport themselves, but may depend upon school buses to transport their children.

For purposes of analysing rural transport use in this chapter, the definition of 'rural' employed by the Office of National Statistics (ONS) and in the NTS will be used – all those resident in areas with a population outside those defined as 'urban' (i.e. a continuously built-up area with a population above a certain value). 'Small urban' areas are defined as those of 3,000 to 25,000 people, and hence 'rural' as all settlements below 3,000. Somewhat broader definitions have been adopted by other bodies, which are often more appropriate when defining patterns of public transport services. For example, the definition adopted for the 'Rural Transport Development Fund' (RTDF) under the Transport Act 1985 by the Rural Development Commission for funding innovations was that of areas containing population centres of less than 10,000. Thus, many small towns and some lower-density parts of metropolitan areas were included.

This is a realistic reflection of current network structures, in which village-to-town and town-to-town movements are often served by the same routes. Services within small towns are often very limited, and facilities may be provided largely by longer routes picking up local traffic. Even in larger towns, rural and urban services are often inter-mixed, being provided by the same operator and forming part of the same cost centre.

Under the greatly increased grants for rural services introduced in 1998 – the 'Rural Bus Subsidy Grant' (RBSG), and 'Rural Bus Challenge' – similar definitions are adopted (i.e. the 10,000 population criterion), and for RBSG a flat rate per head of population per annum (initially £5.50) was paid to the areas concerned in order to secure improved services. While this grant is received mainly by shire and unitary authorities, there are also some 'rural' areas thus defined within the PTE areas.

More broadly, the public transport activities of county councils and unitary authorities outside the metropolitan areas, and largely urban unitaries have often been equated with 'rural transport'. In this case, some larger settlements clearly are involved, but much of the expenditure on tendered services and even more so education transport by such authorities is within the rural part of their territory.

The great majority of scheduled public transport in 'rural' areas as defined above continues to be provided by so-called 'conventional' bus services, using full-sized vehicles. In addition, similar vehicles employed on school contract services play a major role. The 'unconventional' modes such as community minibuses, car lift-giving or postbuses still account for a very small share of the total rural public transport market, but as described below, may be very important in certain localized areas, or for particular functions, such as hospital visiting. Also important within rural regions are some limited-stop and cross-country bus and coach services, linking smaller towns with large cities, and those rail services which did not close during the 'Beeching' era of the 1960s and early 1970s. Often, traffic has been retained or increased, sometimes assisted by new stations and rolling stock.

It should also be borne in mind that certain 'unconventional' modes such as those operated under the Minibus Act 1977 (and, subsequently, the Public Passenger Vehicles Act 1981), and community transport groups like the disabled, are by no means confined to rural areas. Although treated for convenience within this chapter, they also play a significant role even within the largest urban areas for certain specialized requirements.

Public transport's market share and composition

As indicated in Chapter 2, the proportion of all motorized trips taken by public transport in rural areas is small, as one would expect from the low density of population, low level of service and high car ownership (all inter-related).

The 1997–9 NTS indicates (on the definition shown above) that rural residents travel about 14,800 kilometres per year (by all modes), some 35 per cent higher than the national average.[2] This is associated with a similar number of trips per year, but a much higher trip length. The difference is particularly marked for children, whose average trip to school at 12.7 km is over twice the national average. Between 1985/6 and 1997–9, the average total distance travelled by residents of rural areas and small towns grew substantially more than in larger urban areas.

As might be expected, very much higher car ownership levels are found in rural areas, with 39 per cent of households having two or more cars in 1998–99, and only about 16 per cent with no car (compared with about 17 per cent and 40 per cent respectively for London). Car driver licence holding is much higher in rural areas, comprising 81 per cent of adults compared with 70 per cent in Britain as a whole: the differences are more marked for women (73 per cent and 59 per cent respectively). An even higher proportion of total person kilometres than the national average is performed by car. However, due to the high absolute distance travelled by all modes, the average total distance per person travelled by public transport for rural residents is not as markedly lower as one might expect.

In 1997–9 the average rural resident made 28 bus stages per year, compared with the national average of 64, or in terms of distance travelled 287 km per year by local bus (compared with the national average of 395 km). For children, the differences were less marked – 53 stages per child per year in rural areas compared with a national average of 57, and a *higher* distance at 523 versus 348 km.[3]

The overall total distance by public transport modes in rural and urban areas thus does not differ as much as might be expected. However, the public transport use is geared much more to lower-frequency, longer trips, and to school and college travel.

Within the public transport market, education travel has a greater importance in rural areas than elsewhere, and shopping/personal business is typically the next most important function. The role for the adult journey to work is very limited (see Table 2.4) and scope for other personal and leisure travel is restricted by low frequencies, or absence of service, at times suitable for such trips. The overall demand is thus highly peaked towards education travel, especially when the role of contract and local education authority services is considered as well as scheduled public services. However, certain trips which may not be very substantial numerically may be vital to users, notably medical journeys. The ability to make these when required without access to cars is very important.

Another characteristic of the rural public transport market is the large proportion of passengers who are children, working-age women or pensioners, with very few working-age males. In contrast to the intercity market, and trips to the centre of large conurbations, there is little prospect of attracting car drivers to rural public transport, although one study of new interurban services introduced in Lincolnshire and Norfolk under RBSG did suggest a significant proportion of new bus users formerly made their journey by car.[4] However, many public transport users do come from car-owning households, especially for school and shopping trips.

Types of service provided

Local bus services fall into two main categories.

(i) Those between towns, or large villages and towns. Here, traffic densities may be sufficient to justify regular-headway services, up to hourly or better, and use of large vehicles. Those villages fortunate to be located on such routes enjoy a good level of service which their own population would not justify.

(ii) Those between smaller villages and the nearest town, which do not have any 'interurban' function, and experience low average load factors as traffic 'tails off' to the end of the route. Frequencies may range from several journeys per day down to once or twice a week.

NTS results for rural areas indicate that 74 per cent of residents live within 6 minutes' walk of a bus stop, and 87 per cent within 13 minutes. However, average frequencies are much lower, so that the proportion living within 13 minutes of an hourly service or better was only 42 per cent, compared with 87 per cent in all areas; none the less this represented a marked improvement from 35 per cent in 1985–6.[5] Under the Ten-Year Plan the government has set an aim of increasing to 48 per cent the proportion of the rural population within 10 minutes' walking distance to an hourly bus service or better.

The interurban type of service may be operated at a relatively low cost per bus km, owing to high average speeds attained (compared with urban services – see Chapter 6), especially where main roads are followed. Loadings benefit from the mixture of village-to-town and town-to-town traffic on the same route. There is a good chance that costs can be covered from revenue: indeed, such services may have cross-subsidized others, as indicated in the Leeds University/NBC cross-subsidy study (see Chapter 7). The second type suffers from poorer loads, and often high costs owing to lower speeds on minor roads. Cross-subsidy from profitable routes, and/or direct support from local authorities, will be required.

Both types of service have suffered a general decline in traffic as car ownership has risen, factors which have also reduced the ability to cross-subsidize. In general, evening and Sunday services have largely disappeared, except on the busiest routes. Daytime frequencies have also been reduced, especially on Saturdays, formerly the busiest day of the week in many areas. However, given a peak demand on Mondays to Fridays, largely for school travel (due to statutory provision, and, in some areas, shorter trips on public services), services at these times have continued, often with a daytime shopping service which can be added on at modest cost using the drivers and vehicles needed for the peak school facility. This can take the form of a combined service scheduled for both purposes, or the use of buses and crews justified for the education peak at marginal cost at other times (for example, on commercially registered market day shopping services). Under the RBSG substantial expansion of services has taken place, in some cases reintroducing evening and/or

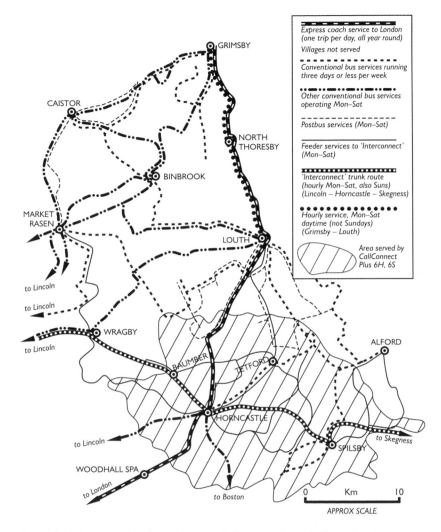

Figure 8.1 An example of a rural network from east Lincolnshire, showing a pattern of frequent trunk services between main towns, with less frequent secondary links and local routes. A noteworthy feature is the existence of two postbus services, and the 'Interconnect' network, established with Rural Bus Challenge funding in 1999. This provides an hourly trunk service with full-sized vehicles between Lincoln and Skegness via Horncastle and Spilsby, and local feeder services (mostly with minibuses) connecting at points such as Wragby, Horncastle and Spilsby. About half the trunk route journeys, and all journeys on some of the feeder routes, are operated with wheelchair-accessible vehicles.

Sunday facilities, as well as introducing entirely new routes, or strengthening daytime services.

An illustration of a network in a low-density area is shown in Figure 8.1, covering a north-east section of the shire county of Lincolnshire (roughly corresponding to East Lindsey District) and some adjoining areas, as at March 2001: for comparison, maps of the same area in 1969 and in 1985 are provided in earlier editions of this book.[6] The main towns around the area to which trips are attracted are Grimsby (population 95,000) to the north-east, and Lincoln (70,000), to the south-west. Market towns at Louth (12,000), Horncastle, Market Rasen, Caistor, Alford and Spilsby (all under 4,000) act as local centres.

It can be seen that wide disparities in service provision exist, as would be expected. In terms of Monday–Saturday daytime services, hourly frequencies are offered between Grimsby and Louth, and Lincoln, Horncastle, Spilsby and Skegness. The former is a long-established commercial service, the latter a doubling of the previous frequency introduced in 1998 under a Rural Bus Challenge project (now run mostly commercially). A National Express coach service from Grimsby to London once daily traverses the area via Louth and Horncastle. Other local services typically operate about five times per day or less. Local Sunday services are limited to the Skegness–Spilsby–Horncastle–Lincoln section. For many years a postbus service has served the area south of Louth. Conventional bus services are run by the former NBC subsidiary Lincolnshire Road Car, and locally based independents.

Following deregulation in 1986, the overall scale of service provision remained fairly similar to that before. Commercial attempts to provide taxi-bus services had a limited and short-lived impact, although with many changes of time-tables and operators. A surprisingly high proportion of services provided by Road Car and independents was commercially registered, tendered services comprising mainly the lowest-frequency routes and evening services between Grimsby and Louth.

The most dramatic changes have come about through the 'Interconnect' project initiated by Lincolnshire County Council under the Rural Bus Challenge in 1998. The strengthened Lincoln–Skegness trunk route now carries double the number of previous passengers. A network of minibus-operated feeder routes was established from Market Rasen, Louth, Alford and surrounding villages as shown in Figure 8.1, ranging from one to five trips per day. These connect at Wragby, Horncastle or Spilsby for Lincoln and Skegness with through ticketing offered. Many journeys are operated by wheelchair-accessible vehicles. From March 2001 these have been revised to incorporate flexible routeing in response to prior demand. 'Call Connect' services cover fixed routes with diversion to nearby villages on request (such as the Louth–Tetford–Horncastle service), while some low-frequency routes shown on the map have been replaced by 'Call Connect Plus', hourly loops whose route is determined wholly by demand, around Horncastle and Spilsby, run by 8-seater minibuses (the shaded area services 6H and 6S). Although most RBSG services in Britain are conventional fixed-route, examples of such flexible routeing may also be found elsewhere, such as the Dengle peninsula in Essex. However, the totally flexible pattern of 'Call Connect Plus' is almost unique.

The 'rural transport problem'

The general nature of the problem is clear: a low frequency of service, providing very limited access activities such as work, or entertainment. Even where a particular facility is served, such as shopping or education, the range of timings is limited: the length of stay in the market town for shopping may not suit all travellers, and statutory school contract buses usually give little opportunity for after-school activities.

Some would argue that the 'problem' is overstated, in that many people live voluntarily in rural areas, and car ownership is very high. However, even among car-owning households, a significant demand for educational travel, and some weekday shopping trips, may exist by public transport. Essential workers in rural areas may be on low incomes.

Furthermore, if we see the problem as that of access to facilities, rather than provision of particular levels of service, it is clear that more travel is now required to gain access to the same range of facilities, as village shops and schools have closed. Smaller towns have also suffered losses, notably of hospitals, making much longer journeys necessary. There is little evidence that mobile services – apart from libraries – have done much to offset these trends. They too, like local buses, have declined owing to high cost and low demand. They are more likely to serve larger villages, which in turn also tend to retain better bus services.[7]

There is also a 'problem' from the viewpoint of the bus or rail operator seeking to reduce deficits, or the degree of cross-subsidy, and the local authority seeking to contain the costs of providing statutory school transport (although savings will generally be made from closing of small village schools even when these are taken into account).

Although support payments per trip may be fairly high, overall support levels for rural public transport are fairly limited, especially in the case of bus services. Much support to rural bus services has been on a basis of supporting the services as such, rather than users. Yet high fares may also limit mobility of those without access to cars, as well as low service frequencies. This is particularly evident in regions where long distances to the nearest major centre are found – for example, around Inverness.[8] Concessionary fares often took the form of tokens, or a reduced-fare pass, rather than the free off-peak travel or low flat fare found in some urban areas. Some rural districts, notably in south-west England, did not give any concession to the elderly at all until the Transport Act of 2000 made a minimum half-fare scheme compulsory in all areas from June 2001. This may substantially improve mobility in some rural districts.

Improving 'conventional' public transport

First, one should examine the scope for improving the performance of existing bus and rail services. The bus industry, in particular, has devoted little attention to marketing or product quality.

Some general changes in recent years have applied to rural services as elsewhere – improved cost-allocation techniques, and locally based management being given a greater role. As illustrated in Chapter 6, more accurate costing highlights the extent to which rural costs may have been previously overstated by use of overall network averages. Higher speed and better fuel consumption produce significantly lower costs per bus-km.

The framework of the 1985 Transport Act led to a clearer demarcation between 'commercial' and 'tendered' services, although given the growing realization of lower unit costs for rural operation, a higher proportion of kilometres was registered commercially than might have been expected. Where entire routes are tendered, then, subject to local authority budgets, they may continue to be provided as part of an overall network. However, where a mix of tendered and commercial operation is found on the same route according to time of day or day of week, some difficulties in marketing and promotion may occur where different operators are involved as a result (for example, regarding inter-availability of return tickets).

Pricing policy has received little attention in rural areas. During the mid-1970s in particular it was noticeable that steep real fare increases were often applied. There is evidence that rural traffic may be somewhat more price elastic than in large urban areas, owing to the mix of trip purposes (other than school travel) and journey lengths: trips within small towns may be liable to walking and cycling substitution owing to their short length, and longer rural journeys to regional shopping centres may be reduced by less frequent travel and/or a shift to smaller centres. Pricing policy now displays more awareness of this, with cheap shopping returns now offered by many companies especially over longer distances. The elasticity in this market segment is close to −1.0, making overall real price increases undesirable when off-peak capacity is available.[9] The more recent study by Dargay and Hanly[10] confirms higher average elasticities for bus services in 'shire' counties than large urban areas.

The virtual decontrol of fares under the Transport Act 1980 was followed by greater variety in some rural areas. Operators are able to experiment easily, and standard fare scales over whole networks have become less important. However, this may have the consequence of increasing fares on low-density loss-making routes. While logical for the operator, this hits again those who already experience poor access.

Under the RBSG and Rural Challenge, substantial expansion of funding has been provided. It was recently increased further together with sums allocated via the Countryside Agency, rising from £155 m in 1998/9–2000/01 to £238 m in 2001/2–2003/4 for England. The initial funding was made available at fairly short notice in 1998, giving local authorities relatively little time to plan services or optimize the network thus provided. In practice, most expenditure was on expansion of relatively conventional bus services, either new routes, or augmenting frequencies over existing services. The funding was provided only for additional services, and its use for maintaining existing services was not permitted until recently. This had the odd effect that entirely new services were provided which in some cases were used by very small numbers of people, while some existing commercial services were 'deregistered' and other existing tendered services were discontinued due to constraints on other parts of local authority budgets.

Since April 2001 more flexibility has been introduced, permitting up to 20 per cent of RBSG to be spent on supporting existing bus services in England (greater flexibility already applied in Wales). It is also proposed to widen the eligibility criteria from a population of 10,000 to one of 25,000.

Putting these changes together, one can see a continued role for conventional bus operation on many of the busier rural routes, and even some very low-frequency routes where services can be interworked with school contracts. However, few areas will have an evening or Sunday service, and some low-density areas a very limited frequency indeed. In addition, certain types of trip will not be handled very well – visits to medical facilities (especially where not centrally located), and journeys by elderly and disabled who may have difficulty using conventional buses.

A much more flexible approach to the operation of rural railways is now evident in Britain. This has included not only a willingness to adopt single-track working, and simpler signalling methods, but also extensive replacement of manually worked level crossings by automatic barriers, in some cases with local authority assistance, as between Skegness and Boston in Lincolnshire. Adoption of 'paytrains' in the 1960s (in which the guard issues tickets as on a bus, replacing station booking offices) has been followed by general use of the 'open station' concept where booking offices remain, removing manned ticket barriers. During the late 1980s, most of the earlier diesel multiple unit stock was replaced by 'Sprinter' and 'Pacer' units, giving savings in maintenance and fuel costs, and in the case of Sprinters, an improvement in quality. The creation of the Regional sector as part of BR's reorganization from 1982 also encouraged a positive view of such services, with specific policies for their marketing and investment being developed at national level. Under rail franchising, further local initiatives have been introduced.

Alternative 'solutions' to the rural transport problem

Use of cars

The high level of car ownership and licensed drivers in rural areas means that many empty seats are available for those without access to cars – indeed, offers of lifts in such vehicles are one of the causes of decline in rural bus use. However, where public transport services are almost entirely lacking, or not available for specific activities (such as medical visits), lift giving can be organized systematically, through voluntary associations or local councils. This concept, generally known as social cars, developed on a limited scale in the late 1960s/early 1970s in some areas, and has become more widespread as bus services have declined, and the legality of payment became generally established under the Transport Act 1978. Prior to this, the only form of payment was that from a sponsoring agency to the car driver, usually on a flat rate mileage basis, with no offsetting fare received. Provided that the service is not being offered commercially, and only the car driver's costs covered, such charging is now generally adopted, reducing the net expenditure, and removing some of the aspects of 'charity' implied when a completely free service is offered.

Such schemes may be arranged through organizations such as the voluntary groups or through the local authority public transport co-ordinator. Local organizers are appointed, through whom bookings may be made, usually by telephone. They then seek to match volunteer drivers with trips requested. A fairly substantial pool of such volunteers is generally needed, to spread the commitment involved, and give a good chance of meeting specific requests.

In areas of very low population density, such schemes may serve most travel purposes. Elsewhere, bus services may continue to be used for many shopping trips, but the social car service acquires a more specialized role, such as taking patients and hospital visitors to medical centres – about two-thirds of the trips on the Shropshire scheme were for this purpose in the late 1970s, for example.[11] However, Root[12] has noted that interest in supplying car sharing diminished in an area of Oxfordshire between 1977 and the late 1990s.

Social car schemes may also be organized through other agencies, such as area health authorities, to meet the needs of outpatients and hospital visitors. However, some of these have since been merged with general-purpose schemes administered through the county council, as in the area shown in Figure 8.1.

Postbuses

The comprehensive facility offered by the Posts Office creates an opportunity for passenger service at low cost. Not only is mail collected six days per week from numerous points, but all addresses are served for deliveries. Postvan routes typically serve both purposes, running as loops based on market towns, where sorting centres are located. Two or three trips per day (less on Saturdays, and none on Sunday) can be provided with no additional staff or vehicles being needed, for the cost of running a minibus instead of a minivan, and marginally higher fuel and maintenance costs. The first postbuses appeared in the 1960s, but they extended rapidly during the 1970s, encouraged by availability of the New Bus Grant (at 50 per cent, offsetting entirely the difference in capital cost), and fuel-tax rebate for local services (likewise offsetting extra fuel cost). In some cases, no support at all from counties was required; in others a very low figure.

Introduction of postbuses has varied considerably according to local initiative. Over 100 are found in Scotland – in some cases using vehicles as small as estate cars or Land Rovers – but a smaller scatter in England and Wales. The topography of some parts of Scotland – with most settlement concentrated in narrow valleys – is more appropriate for postbus operation, and very low population densities in the Highlands encourage multipurpose operation.

By July 1992 some 170 postbus routes were in operation in Britain, with a plan to expand to 200: some 100,000 passengers were carried in 1991. A national postbus manager was appointed by the Royal Mail in 1992. However, the impact of postbuses has been less than initially expected. Elimination of the New Bus Grant increased costs incurred and stricter costing has also stimulated higher demands on county support. While small in total these may be high on a per-passenger basis, and in some cases have resulted in withdrawal of postbuses.

More recently, some expansion has taken place as part the RBSG, including cases of postbuses being operated primarily for passenger needs, rather than schedules determined wholly by collection and delivery of post.

In some other countries, postbuses play a much larger role, notably the well-known Swiss network.[13] However, much of the traffic on such systems is often between village post offices and sorting centres, rather than to/from private homes, and the network functions more like that of a large company – often cross-subsidized through other postal and telecommunication activities – rather than the type of postbus found in Britain.

Minibuses

Minibuses appear an obvious solution to rural transport problems, given the low demand and limited room for large vehicles on many routes. However, peak demands for school travel often require full-size vehicles, and a purely commercial minibus service (i.e. one with a paid driver) is unlikely to be justified in a rural area. The development of intensive minibus services from 1984 took place almost entirely in urban areas, relying on high utilization throughout the day. Notwithstanding a substantial number of medium-sized vehicles such as the van-derived minibuses (seating around 21–25 passengers) or 'midibuses' (such as the Dennis Dart), are used on rural services in preference to full-size vehicles. More recent models, such as the Optare Solo, also offer the convenience of low-floor access, and in some cases have been specified as a contract condition on new services. Low-floor access is reported as a major factor in the 15 per cent passenger growth found on the Perranporth-Lizard service of Truronian in Cornwall in 1998/9.

Use of the small minibus for flexibly routed services in Lincolnshire has already been mentioned – another example is the DoRis network around Midhurst in West Sussex. Minibuses also play a significant role in rural areas through voluntary or non-commercial activity, or their use on services for particular groups. Clearly, if the cost of a driver could be greatly reduced or even eliminated, the lower capital and running costs of minibuses could make them attractive for rural use. In 1976 the Eastern Counties company launched a service in Norfolk, using a 9-seat Ford Transit maintained and supplied by the company, but driven by local volunteer drivers, trained to PSV standards. Weekly shopping services were provided, and private hire and excursion work undertaken at weekends. A high proportion of costs could thus be covered from passenger revenue at conventional fare scales. A number of other areas adopted such schemes soon afterwards. Under the Transport Act 1978 they were removed from the requirement for drivers to have PSV licences (a questionable change), provided that the vehicle used had not more than 16 seats, and was operated on a non-profit-making basis. The term 'Community Bus' was applied in this Act, and has been adopted generally to describe such schemes. About thirty now operate, mainly in southern England. A fairly conventional pattern of local shopping services is provided, with weekend hire work (often greatly improving financial performance).

Many minibuses in rural areas are run through agencies for specific groups such as schools, churches, youth clubs, or voluntary bodies such as Age Concern. Their legal position in providing some form of regular service, but not as PSVs, was clarified in the Minibus Act 1977, under which permits are issued through county councils for each vehicle so operated. However, various inconsistencies remain in terms of the safety requirements for both vehicle and drivers in comparison to those imposed on bus operators.

The Transport Act 1985 'tidied up' some of the inconsistencies in various forms of minibus legislation (PSV, community bus and permit services), notably through providing for the issue of permits to organizations, rather than in respect of vehicles as such, but specification differences remain, with implications for passenger safety. Some 4,600 'small bus' permits (i.e. for vehicles up to 16 seats inclusive) were issued in the year 1992/3 – of which 1,553 were issued directly by area Traffic Commissioners, 1,535 through local authorities, and 1,518 by other designated bodies (which include local education authorities). In comparison, only 108 'large bus' permits (i.e. vehicles over 16 seats, used for non-profit-making purposes), and 8 community bus permits, were issued in the same year (the Traffic Commissioners being the sole issuing authority for these categories).[14]

Taxis play a limited role in rural areas, indeed prior the 1985 Act, many rural districts did not exercise their permissive powers to license them, making it difficult to trace their extent. Shared taxis were in any case not generally legalized until the 1985 Act, a by-product of which has been the requirement for all districts to introduce a taxi-licensing system. However, a shared taxi or hire car could clearly be a useful mode for rural travel where small numbers are found. Informal sharing occurs in any case.

Minibuses have also been used to develop combined-transport services, carrying different user groups, or passengers with goods. A notable example of a multi-purpose operation is the 'Border Courier' in the Peebles/Galashiels/Berwick area, in which a service is supported by health authorities and the local councils, carrying medical supplies to villages, as well as providing a general passenger service.

School buses

As mentioned at the start of this chapter, school buses play a major role in rural areas. These may be public services on which children are carried using season tickets, but in many cases special contract services are provided. In recent years, many have been registered as local services open to the public (qualifying for fuel duty rebate) although children form the vast majority of ridership. Vehicles and crews are normally hired from PSV operators, although some counties, notably Suffolk, Norfolk and West Sussex, operate their own fleets. Taxis and minibuses are also hired in by education authorities where smaller flows arise, or 'special needs' pupils are carried. Traditionally, there was little co-ordination between education departments hiring such vehicles, and co-ordinators responsible for public services, but the situation has greatly improved in recent years. Co-ordinators can also take into account the implications for school contracts of public service operations – for example, a market day shopping service may be provided at low cost, if the same operator has a school contract in the area.

Under the Transport Act 1980 councils running their own (non-PSV) school buses were able to receive permits for public services by such vehicles: these have been used in a few instances, generally to provide off-peak shopping services. However, another inconsistency in safety standards was created. Under the Transport Act 1985, counties are required to consider school and public services together, to obtain best value for money. This encouraged those authorities still handling school and public services separately to co-ordinate their planning.

However, there have also been some pressures to separate services once again, at least at peak school times. These have come about partly through the requirements that 'coaches' carrying school children should be fitted with seat belts, while 'local buses' performing the same function do not (there is little evidence of risk as a result, but demands may be generated by parents). There are also problems arising from mixing children with working age adults, generally due to the behaviour of children, but also some parental concerns.

A problem has also arisen from the increasingly specialized nature of coaches used by independent operators in rural areas. While the traditional Ford or Bedford lightweight vehicle could be downgraded to school contract work in later life, modern coaches tend to be to a much higher specification (high floor, toilets, etc.) and less suited to such work. One option is to specify brand new medium-standard coaches with high density seating (such as the Volvo B7/Plaxton Prima) which can take a large school peak load, but also be of acceptable standard for local excursion and hire work.

A further division between school and other work has been stimulated by adoption in some case of American-style 'Yellow bus' purpose-built vehicles, as operated in West Sussex and proposed on a more extensive scale by FirstGroup. These would provide dedicated school bus services, but be unsuitable for off-peak public use (especially due to their high floors) probably resulting in low utilization. Further consideration of the school transport issue is provided in Chapter 10.

A general split may thus emerge between some rural routes justifying a high-capacity bus used both by schoolchildren and other passengers, and other areas, where quite separate high-capacity school services may run, with services for the general public and/or at other times of day by small, flexibly routed minibuses.

Impact of the 1985 Transport Act and subsequent policies

At the time of its introduction, it was anticipated that the deregulation of local bus services under the 1985 Act would have particularly marked effects in rural areas, due to the pressure to eliminate cross-subsidy previously found, and removal of the comprehensive network planning role of local authorities in favour of a more limited role in 'filling gaps' in commercially registered networks. In acknowledgement of this, a special rural service grant was introduced, at a flat rate per bus mile run for the first four years after deregulation. A special fund to encourage innovative services, the Rural Transport Development Fund (RTDF) was also set up – now handled by the Countryside Agency in England – with parallel schemes in Wales and Scotland.

There is little comprehensive statistical data available on rural service levels and ridership since 1985. Although detailed information for English 'shire counties' is published (see further comment in Chapter 10), much of the operation therein is in fact within urban areas. Broadly speaking, a similar overall level of rural service has been maintained, as discussed in the Lincolnshire example. In some cases, a period of service expansion and competition on rural routes was followed by a return to a similar level of service to that applying before deregulation. A general review is provided by Astrop.[15]

One significant factor which helps to explain the relatively high level of conventional service retention since deregulation is the shift from national wage bargaining to local negotiations. In many rural areas, the wage levels paid by large operators were considerably above those applying in local labour markets. The expansion of service by smaller operators, notably for tendered work, has been followed by substantial reductions in operating costs by larger incumbents, in some cases enabling them to regain tendered services initially lost to smaller operators. This factor has undoubtedly been important in the area shown in Figure 8.1, for example.

The main problems arising from deregulation were to some extent much the same in rural areas as in the industry as a whole: lack of investment in fleet renewal and the instability in service provision associated with frequent changes in commercially registered services, and consequent changes in tendered services.

The impact of the RTDF was limited. Although many schemes were set up in various regions, their overall contribution is small. One possible factor is the tendency of central government to set up initiatives parallel to those already taking place within local authorities through transport co-ordinators.

The more recent expansion through the Rural Transport Fund has already been mentioned. A more stable network is now in evidence, and with the ability to use such funds to support existing services as well as entirely new operations, a more rational allocation of expenditure may be attained. Together with the bus strategies produced in Local Transport Plans, there may be scope for a return to more systematic planning of rural network provision, using indicators of need and service provision first developed after the Transport Act 1978. Suggestions for changes have been put forward by Transport 2000 and the Council for the Protection of Rural England.[16]

Descriptions of methods developed to assess provision and need are provided by Burley and Snell in respect of Kent.[17] Subsequently, an assessment for mid-Wales has been made by Moyes.[18]

Perhaps the most critical problem is that of access to medical facilities. The continued shift to centralization into very large hospitals may be less evident now, but rural GPs continue to disappear, being replaced by group practices. Location of these in the centre of market towns, where local bus routes give good access may help, perhaps reducing the need for reliance on voluntary car schemes. Greater flexibility in opening hours, so that the morning surgery were held after work/school journeys arrive in town, would also help. Similar flexibility in shopping hours, and those of other facilities could be applied.

The question of interurban travel should not be ignored. As stressed at the start of this chapter, rural transport is not only a question of getting to the nearest market town, but also of getting to regional centres, being able to make visits to hospitals, friends and relatives, and go on holiday. These trips are occasional but none the less important. Further scope may exist for upgrading existing interurban stage bus services with higher-quality vehicles (as recently adopted by the Stagecoach Group, for example). However, some lower-density express coach services have been lost as a result of operators concentrating mainly on trunk routes after deregulation under the 1980 Act.

One must also return to the question of the role of the car. It clearly remains dominant. However, as the recent comprehensive review by Gray[19] has shown, rural dwellers do not, on the whole, spend much more on travel than others. Higher car dependence and distance travelled per person per annum are offset by factors such as better fuel consumption in less congested conditions. Overall, the proportion of household expenditure on transport (all modes combined), differs little between rural areas (18.1 per cent) and the national average (16.7 per cent), although some low-density pockets within rural areas may display higher figures. While increased fuel prices would obviously affect a small group of low-income motorists, their overall impact has perhaps been exaggerated.

A wider role for rural transport policy may become evident following the creation of a government department with specific responsibility for rural affairs in June 2001.

Notes

1 OPCS (Office of Population Censuses and Surveys). Monitor PPJ 91/1, October 1992.
2 Except where otherwise cited, data from the 1997–9 NTS is taken from *Travel in Urban and Rural Areas of Great Britain. Personal Travel Factsheet 11*, DETR, London, March 2001.
3 Derived from table 3.6 in DETR Statistics Bulletin SB (00) 26.
4 Wright, S. (1999) Research dissertation, MSc Transport Planning & Management, University of Westminster (unpublished).
5 Derived from table 5.6 in DETR Statistics Bulletin SB (00) 22.
6 White, P.R. (1976 and 1986) *Public Transport* (first and second editions): map in Chapter 8.
7 Moseley, M. and Packman, J. (1983) *Mobile Services in Rural Areas*. School of Environmental Science, University of East Anglia, Norwich.
8 Stanley, P.A., Farrington, J.H. and MacKenzie, R.P. (1981) *Public Transport Provision and Access to Facilities in East Ross, and the Black Isle*, Department of Geography, University of Aberdeen.
9 Heels, P. and White, P.R. (1977) *Fare Elasticities on Interurban and Rural Bus Services*. Research Report No. 4, Transport Studies Group, Polytechnic of Central London.
10 Dargay, J. and Hanly, M. (1999) *Bus fare Elasticities: A New Report to the Department of the Environment, Transport and the Regions*, ESRC Transport Studies Unit, University College London, December.
11 Fearnside, K. (1980) 'Experience of lift-giving schemes in Shropshire' Polytechnic of Central London Rural Transport Seminar, pp. 44–74.

12 Root, A. (2000) 'Rural transport after the deregulation of buses', in Bill Bradshaw and Helen Lawton Smith (eds) *Privatization and Deregulation of Transport* (proceedings of a conference at Hertford College Oxford, July 1997), Macmillan.

13 Holding, D. (1983) 'The Swiss post-bus system – a comparison with British rural operation', Polytechnic of Central London Rural Transport Seminar.

14 Department of Transport (1993) *Annual Reports of the Traffic Commissioners 1992–93*, London. Appendix 4.

15 Astrop, A. (1993) *The Trend in Rural Bus Services Since Deregulation*, Transport Research Laboratory Report PR21, Crowthorne, Berks.

16 Transport 2000 and Council for the Protection of Rural England. (2000) The Rural Thoroughbred: Buses in the Countryside, London.

17 Burley, R. and Snell, J. (1983) 'A method of identifying rural bus needs in Kent', Polytechnic of Central London Rural Transport Seminar, pp. 3–23.

18 Moyes, A. (1989) *The Need for Public Transport in mid-Wales: Normative Approaches and their Implications*, Rural Surveys Research Unit Monograph No. 2, Department of Geography, University College of Wales, Aberystwyth.

19 Gray, D. (Robert Gordon University, Aberdeen) (2001) *Rural Transport: an Overview of Key Issues*, Commission for Integrated Transport, May.

References and suggested reading

Lowe, P. (2000) 'Labour's rural policy', *Town & Country Planning*, May, pp. 143–5.

Lucas, K., Grosvenor, T., and Simpson, R. 'Transport, the environment and social exclusion'. Joseph Rowntree Foundation, York 2001 (Lincolnshire rural case study, pp 26–29).

Rural Development Commission (1996) *Country Lifelines – Good Practice in Rural Transport*, London, March.

Solomon, J. *et al.* (2000) *Social Exclusion and the Provision and Availability of Public Transport*, Report by Transport Research and Consultancy (University of North London) for DETR, July (London).

9 Intercity public transport

Introduction

It is in the intercity, or long-distance, sector that the highest quality of public transport service can be found, and the most extensive use of public transport by those with cars available for the journey in question. On many routes improved quality of service has stimulated an increase in total patronage, despite rising car ownership. Another contrast with the short-distance market is that productivity has risen sharply, as vehicle size and speed have increased. Commercially viable opportunities for investment are also more numerous.

A combination of greater vehicle size and higher average speed has produced large increases in productivity of vehicle and crew. For example, in domestic air transport, if an 80-seat turboprop is replaced by a 200-seat jet with an airport-to-airport average speed 50 per cent higher, seat-km per flight hour rises by 375 per cent. However, growing congestion around busy airports has offset some of the speed advantages that might have been expected from faster aircraft (likewise, express coach productivity is constrained by the application of the 100 kph EU limit and growing road congestion). Conversely, rail may have more scope for speed increases. While there have not been any marked changes in seating capacity (around 400 per train), increases in average speed from about 100 to around 140 kph together with much quicker turnround of stock at terminals have improved utilization dramatically. Further scope through high speed running is outlined in this chapter.

The present long-distance market in Britain

As described in Chapter 2, the National Travel Survey (NTS) gives a comprehensive sample of travel by residents of Britain. As in the case of local movement, the NTS provides a valuable data source. Within it, 'long distance' is identified as all trips over 50 miles (80 km). Such trips occur infrequently over the population as a whole, and hence in addition to the one-week travel diary, data on such trips for the preceding three weeks have also been collected since the start of 1992, giving more robust results. Table 9.1 uses this source to show composition of the current market.

Table 9.1 Modal split of long-distance journeys in Britain 1992–9 (percentages)

Distance (km)	Car	Bus & coach	Rail	Air	Total
80–120	86	4	8	–	98
121–240	84	6	8	–	98
241–402	80	7	11	1	98
403–563	69	12	13	4	98
564 & over	46	10	20	23	98
Total	83	6	9	1	98

Source:
Derived from DETR Statistics Bulletin SB (00) 02, table 3.9.

Notes
NTS data has been converted from miles (as reported by respondents) to kilometres, and categories for 75–100, and 100–150 miles, combined. Percentages do not sum to 100, due to rounding, and also the existence of a 2 per cent 'other' category in all distance bands. Data refer only to trips made by residents sampled within Britain and for journeys both commencing and terminating within Britain. Hence, it excludes travel within Britain by visitors from other countries, and journeys within Britain forming parts of journeys with an origin/destination outside Britain.

From Table 9.1 it can be seen that car is the dominant mode over all distances, except those above 564 kilometres. This is the only category in which domestic air services play a substantial role, and broadly corresponds to the trunk routes between South East England and Scotland (London to Glasgow, Edinburgh, etc.). The rail share averages about 9 per cent, being highest for the longest distances, where the speed and convenience of this mode are likely to offset the access/egress trip factors that otherwise favour car where it is available. Rail also has a fairly strong share in the 80–120 km band (8 per cent), probably associated with substantial commuting in the London region.

The overall bus and coach share is 6 per cent, but it is not far short of rail in some cases, notably for 403–563 km.

The same source[1] also indicates journey purposes for longer-distance trips (taking all modes together). Averaged over all distance categories they are:

Commuting (home to work travel)	14%
Business	17%
'Other essential'	12%
Visiting friends at private home	24%
Holiday	14%
Day trip	9%
Other leisure	9%

'Other essential' comprises education, shopping, personal business and escort travel. 'Holiday' may be distinguished from 'day trip' by an overnight stay being involved.

The shares for business and visiting friends at home vary little by distance. As might be expected, 'commuting' is greater for the shortest distances (under 160 km), and 'day trip' travel likewise (12 per cent of trips of 80 to 120 km). 'Holiday' grows with trip length and comprises 40 per cent of all trips over 403 km.

A general implication is that the long-distance market will generally display higher price elasticities than local movement, due to the optional nature of most of the trips being made, not only in their purpose, but also frequency. Hence, in calibrating modal choice models (such as those through stated preference techniques), the option of not travelling, or travelling less frequently, must also be considered thoroughly, as well as modal shift *per se*. If this is not the case, then an understatement of price elasticity may occur.

The optional nature of the market may also make it more sensitive to other quality factors such as speed, in-vehicle comfort, etc. than intraurban or local demand.

Recent trends in the market indicate a fairly stable express coach sector, but rapid growth (of about 5 per cent per annum in the last four years) for the rail and domestic air modes.

The most obvious market segmentation is that between the commuting/ business/'essential' trips and other purposes, insofar as the former category will tend to be more time-sensitive and less price-sensitive. Time is important both in the sense of the duration of journeys (especially where commuting or business return trips are completed in the same day) and timing (scheduling) of trips, insofar as users may have relatively little flexibility, notably in making outward journeys during the morning peak. The duration of activities may also be unpredictable (for example, the length of a business meeting), making frequency an important factor (i.e. even for wider service intervals an assumption that passenger waiting time may average half the headway may not be unreasonable).

Conversely, the large element of leisure, visiting friends, and holiday trips may be much more flexible in the timing of their trips, and perhaps somewhat less sensitive to journey duration (although day trips will still be constrained).

For the operators, cost is highly sensitive to vehicle utilization, the capital invested being spread over a greater output. Crews may also be scheduled more efficiently where operation is not confined to peak periods. These factors apply seasonally, as well as by time of day and day of week.

The long-distance market thus offers a case in which scope for segmentation is probably greater than in the public transport market as a whole, given the ability of users to change the timing and even destination of their trips. The higher price elasticities will enable pricing to be used, even in the short run, as a much more effective means of influencing demand patterns than for local movement.

It can also be regarded as a case in which entirely separate provision of services for different user groups can be contemplated more readily than in the local and intraurban market. For example, within rail systems, first and standard class accommodation differs in comfort and price. Entirely separate modes may be provided, whose cost to the user reflects cost of provision and journey time savings. This is already evident in the choice offered of rail or air between major city-pairs. In countries which permit competing express coach networks, such as Britain, a third mode is also available. To these may be added permutations such as 'low cost' airlines (notably 'easyJet') offering journey times similar to other airlines, but much lower prices associated with different levels of passenger service.

The 1997–9 NTS indicates that only 2.7 per cent of all journeys over 1.6 km in length were 'long', i.e. over 80 km. However, these obviously represent a much larger percentage of all kilometres travelled. In absolute terms, these 'long' trips averaged about twenty-one per person per year (i.e. about one return trip every five weeks), of which about seventeen were by car driver, one by bus or coach and two by rail.[2]

The ratio of car driver to car passenger trips implies an average occupancy of about 1.75 for 'long' journeys: this is consistent with the higher occupancy for non-work travel (see Chapter 2), and perhaps a greater tendency to share fuel costs which may be more readily perceived for long-distance journeys. Tickets such as the 'family railcard' can be seen as one response to this by public transport operators.

We can also derive variations in travel by person type from the NTS. Taking all modes and journey purposes together, the average distance travelled per person in 1997–9 within Britain was 10,960 km, but notably higher for working age males (about 14,500 km).[3] This was associated with higher levels of commuting and business travel in particular, implying a greater tendency to make 'long' journeys. Men typically make more trips than women, associated mainly with business travel. Those aged 65 or over make markedly fewer trips. Students are also among the 'economically inactive' groups, yet have a high long-distance trip rate, especially for 'visiting friends and relatives' (VFR). Another critical factor is car ownership: those from households with cars available make substantially more long-distance trips per year than those without. However, these differences are also correlated with variations in income, economic activity and area of residence.

Although the much higher total trip rates made by those with cars available are, naturally, associated mainly with car use, it is important to note that the average rail trip rate by both car-owning, and non-car-owning households is similar. The absolute level of rail use does not necessarily fall with rising car ownership, unlike the urban bus market.

In addition to collecting a larger sample of long-distance trips, the NTS since 1992 has also asked respondents to classify origin and destination to county level. While the sample size is still rather small for estimating county-to-county trips, this data can be aggregated at regional level. Table 9.2 indicates the approximate variations in modal shares by rail and coach for major corridors to/from the London and South East region. The balance of trips (not shown directly) is largely by car, with a small element of domestic air travel as indicated. The car share can be seen to fall as journey length increases. For example, cars take about 80 per cent of movement to/from the East Midlands, but about 60 per cent to/from the Northern region, and 20 per cent of the travel to/from Scotland.

The difference is represented by a growth in rail share, and, for the longest trips, air. Thus, for Scottish traffic, the air share rises to 46 per cent. If business traffic alone is considered, air became predominant in the market to Scotland. Coach travel (including tour and private hire, as well as scheduled express services) took only about 8 per cent of the long-distance market, although this is higher on certain corridors, notably to/from Yorkshire and Humberside.

Table 9.2 Coach and rail shares of the land passenger transport market in Britain: flows to and from the South East Region, or Heathrow Airport

Region	Trips to/from South East Region, over 100 miles		Trips to/from Heathrow, excluding air interline	
	Coach	Rail	Coach	Rail
Scotland	10 [5]	24 (air 46)	32	48
Northern	9 [5]	25 (air 7)	25	40
Yorks & Humberside	11 [4]	14	25	30
North Western	8 [4]	23	20	26
East Midlands	8 [3]	12	16	14
East Anglia	5 [1]	10	24	11
West Midlands	9 [5]	10	27	7
Wales	7 [3]	14	32	17
South West	7 [4]	14	30	10
Total (weighted average)	8 [3]	13	26 [18]	14

Notes
Underlining indicates coach share higher than rail.
Flows for trips to/from South East Region 1992–6 are derived from special tabulations from 1992–6 NTS. The percentage of coach traffic on scheduled express services is shown in square brackets, e.g. [3]. The total sample size (all modes) is 9,624, and of coach journeys, 738 [of which 334 scheduled express]. Flows to/from Heathrow are derived from special tabulations from the CAA survey 1996 (coach sample approx 3,800; rail 2,040).

Rail takes a higher share of the market to/from cities, in contrast to larger regions which car accessibility would be better. As Wardman and Tyler (2000) have shown, trip rates by rail fall rapidly as distance from a station increases, with an elasticity of about –0.50.[4] As population moves outward from traditional cities, rail accessibility is thus worsened, and 'city-centre-to-city centre' journey times – important though they be for business traffic – may not be the major factor they were once considered. Feeder journeys by local public transport may be particularly slow *vis-à-vis* the trunk journey.

Table 9.2 also shows land-based travel to/from Heathrow airport from the CAA survey for 1996. The greater share by public transport is partly accounted for by the fact that both British and foreign travellers are included, the latter generally having much lower car access. In addition, coach displays a much higher share than in the domestic long-distance market as a whole, due to the development of extensive direct services to major airports such as Heathrow, considered in greater detail later in this chapter.

Current patterns and recent trends within each mode

Domestic air services

Domestic air services within Britain fill two main roles:

1   Travel wholly within Britain – for example, from Newcastle to London – in competition with land-based modes such as rail. Air's role will depend on

relative door-to-door journey times and costs. Such trips made by British residents are captured in the NTS data, as shown in Tables 9.1 and 9.2.

2   'Interline' traffic, in which domestic routes serve as feeders/distributors to/from international routes through major airports such as Heathrow. This forms a large element in some of the shorter domestic routes (such as Manchester–London), which is included in operator-reported data, but not the NTS. While growth of more direct international services (such as Paris) from airports outside the London region has reduced some of the need for the 'interline' function, this is offset to some extent by continued growth in travel to widely dispersed international destinations as yet served by very few British airports outside the South East.

Since 1989, the total domestic air market has grown sharply, as one might expect from its status as a faster, high-quality mode, whose demand will be particularly responsive to real income growth. In addition, growth has accelerated recently due to the impact of 'low cost' airlines, notably 'easyJet', competing much more directly with rail (and even coach) markets than previously. Conversely, there has been little gain in average speeds since jets were in use on trunk routes throughout the period, and congestion at major airports has grown. Service improvements have come about more through gains in frequency and a wider range of direct services.

Table 9.3 shows trends in total passenger numbers and passenger-km since 1989. The market was hit by the impact of recession in the early 1990s, but a rapid spurt of growth then followed in the mid to late 1990s. Within the total shown, scheduled traffic represents the great majority, and non-scheduled only about 1 per cent of both trips and passenger-km. This very low market share (*vis-à-vis* international air travel from Britain) is partly as a result of effective surface

Table 9.3 Domestic air traffic in Britain 1989–99

Year	Passenger trips (m)	Passenger-km (m)
1989	12.6	4,900
1990	13.1	5,200
1991	12.0	4,800
1992	12.0	4,800
1993	12.4	5,100
1994	13.3	5,500
1995	14.3	5,900
1996	15.3	6,800
1997	16.2	6,800
1998	16.9	7,000
1999	17.4	7,300

Source: Table 7.3 sections (b) and (c), Transport Statistics Great Britain 2000 edition, TSO, London, October 2000.

Notes
Data include non-scheduled traffic (see text).
Data cover only British-owned airlines (see text).

competition in the leisure market, especially for family groups. The pricing flexibility enjoyed within Britain reduces the need for non-scheduled services, since a variety of low scheduled fares is available on routes with a leisure component. There is also relatively little package holiday or inclusive tour movement within Britain, typically associated with the non-scheduled sector. Although most of the scheduled trips are by British-owned airlines, Ryanair carries a significant number of trips within Britain – 0.34 million in 1999 – in addition to the total shown in Table 9.3.

Passenger trips grew by 38 per cent between 1989 and 1999. Passenger-km grew by a somewhat greater 49 per cent, as average trip length rose from about 390 to 420 km. This was probably associated with some loss of the shorter routes to London, and above-average growth on longer routes such as London to Belfast and Aberdeen.

However, the domestic market in terms of passenger-km is very small compared with international traffic handled by British-owned airlines, some 240,000 million in 1999 (albeit in terms of trips it is the third largest after Spain and the USA).

While there are a very large number of domestic air services, some operated with very small aircraft, the market is dominated by the routes to or from London airports, and cross-water routes. There are four distinct groupings:

1 Domestic trunk routes between Heathrow and Edinburgh (1.5 million passengers), Glasgow (1.4 m), Belfast (1.1 m), and Manchester (1.1 m): a total of 5.0 m trips in 1999,[5] or 28 per cent of all domestic passengers. They are significantly denser than any other routes. Their share rises to 38 per cent if parallel routes to/from Gatwick are included. In addition, passengers from London City, Luton and Stansted airports have grown rapidly in recent years. For example, between London and Glasgow and Prestwick, in 1999, 55 per cent of all trips were to/from Heathrow, 13 per cent Gatwick, 1 per cent London City, 13 per cent Luton and 17 per cent Stansted (similar shares were found for Edinburgh). The last two are associated mainly with low-cost carriers, such as 'easyJet' (at Luton), or Ryanair and 'go' (at Stansted).

2 Other London-based routes are more numerous but carry substantially lower volumes of traffic than the four trunks. Nevertheless, taking all the Heathrow and Gatwick routes together, including the trunks, they generated 9.3 million trips (52 per cent of all domestic air traffic). Luton accounted for a further 1.3 m and Stansted 1.4 m, their joint total comprising 15 per cent of all domestic trips and exceeding the share of Gatwick. They have also grown rapidly in terms of Anglo-Irish traffic, on which low-cost services emerged prior to those within mainland Britain.

3 Cross-water routes offer a case where air has a particularly large time advantage over surface modes. While several of the London routes, notably those to Belfast, Channel Islands and the Isle of Man involve such crossings, there are also several important routes not involving London. Most of these are from islands to the nearest airport on the mainland, or from Belfast to major cities. Flows between Britain and the Irish Republic comprise a similar market. The

combined total for all British cross-water routes in 1999 was 6.14 million (about 35 per cent of the national total), of which 1.76 million were between London area airports and Belfast airports.

4   Finally, it is noticeable that while there are many cross-country air services between points within mainland Britain, other than the London region, comprising about 10 per cent of the domestic market, their individual traffic levels are generally very low. Only five carried more than 100,000 passengers in 1999 (Manchester to Edinburgh, Glasgow and Aberdeen; Birmingham to Glasgow and Edinburgh). Some other routes have also grown rapidly, notably Bristol to Edinburgh which did not exist in 1989 but carried 99,000 in 1999. Most such services are from airports in the English regions to points in Scotland.

Liberalization of the domestic air network produced substantial competition on the trunk routes from the early 1980s onward, firstly in the form of BMI British Midland competing with British Airways, mainly for the business market, and more recently in low-cost carriers from Luton and Stansted which have encouraged leisure air travel as well as taking some of the business market. On non-trunk routes, liberalization has led to a rapid increase in their range, but most are business-oriented, using small regional jet aircraft that require high fares to break-even. The extent to which the recent expansion of supply has stimulated growth in the total market, over and above trends that might be expected, remains uncertain. As a broad generalization, Dennis and Graham[6] have suggested about 50 per cent of the low-cost carriers' traffic is newly generated, and 50 per cent diverted from other airlines or modes.

Journey purposes and passenger mix

While domestic air traffic was predominantly for business purposes, the share attributable to leisure and other purposes has grown steadily. For example, at Heathrow in 1997,[7] some 49 per cent of the domestic air trips were for business, and 51 per cent other purposes. A higher business share was found at Manchester, at 62 per cent, but lower at Gatwick, 41 per cent. There are routes such as those to the Channel Islands where leisure traffic clearly predominates.

Travel by non-UK residents also forms a significant part of the total volume on domestic routes, notably those to/from Heathrow, on which it formed 28 per cent of all trips in 1997. These trips are also omitted from data collected in the NTS.

As mentioned above, a striking feature of the domestic network in Britain is the role of 'interline' traffic, that is passengers using such services in order to transfer to international or, less frequently, domestic services, notably at Heathrow and Gatwick.

On average such interline passengers probably represent about a third of traffic on routes to/from London and on some it may rise to over half, especially from places with a limited range of their own international services or strong rail competition for the purely domestic market. For example, on Aberdeen–Heathrow services in 1996, 36 per cent were flying on to other destinations from Heathrow, and likewise for Edinburgh–Heathrow services the proportion was 39 per cent. On Manchester–Heathrow in 1997 this proportion was even higher, at 71 per cent, and on Manchester–Gatwick 57 per cent. For Birmingham the proportion was 83 per cent in 1992–93 and at Leeds/Bradford 51 per cent.

This 'interline' traffic can also be identified in the inter-modal sense, with substantial use of rail and coach to travel by land to Heathrow from other regions (see Table 9.2, and further discussion below in connection with the coach market).

The importance of international interlining for domestic air passengers has policy implications. Displacement of domestic flights from Heathrow or Gatwick because of runway congestion thus adversely affects many regional airports' linkages to foreign destinations. A number of airports have now lost direct services to Heathrow, such as East Midlands, Humberside and Birmingham, making use of hubs elsewhere (such as Schiphol) an attractive alternative.

Pricing and competition

Typically, the 'economy' fare category is the most commonly used, followed by 'discount', the latter usually for leisure travel. In addition two carriers, BMI and British European, have a business class on domestic routes. An overall fares index is not readily available, but it would probably be fair to say that the fully flexible standard ticket has risen considerably faster than inflation, while average yield may have risen less rapidly due to the wider range of fares aimed at the leisure market, and business travellers willing to give some flexibility.

For many years, British Airways accounted for a very large part of the domestic air market, stemming from an era of regulation which protected the incumbent carriers to a far greater extent than today. Following a fall in the 1970s and 1980s, a fairly stable picture has emerged in recent years, when the franchised subsidiaries of BA (such as British Regional Airlines) are included along with BA's own direct operations. For example, the BA brand's share of all domestic passenger trips was 50 per cent in 1992, rising to 56 per cent in 1995 then falling to 51 per cent in 1999.[8]

Competition influences pricing through the presence of land-based competing modes where these offer sufficiently attractive journey times, and within the airline market as such, although as already mentioned, this is largely confined to a number of trunk routes.

Express coach

The deregulation of express-coach services under the Transport Act 1980 (described briefly in Chapter 1) had immediate and dramatic effects. Taking the trips on National Express network as an indicator, a steady decline from the mid-1970s was clear, with just over 9 million trips in 1980 itself. The early 1980s saw a rapid growth, peaking at about 15 million in 1985. However, a subsequent decline returned the total to about 10.5 million in 1992. A combination of higher

Table 9.4 Express coach travel in Britain
1989–99: trips on the National Express network
in England and Wales (millions, approximate)

Year	Trips
1989	13.9
1990	13.5
1991	12.0
1992	10.5
1993	9.8
1994	10.9
1995	11.0
1996	11.7
1997	12.0
1998	12.0
1999	12.6

Source: Data from National Express and technical press
reports.

frequencies on trunk routes, greater motorway running to raise speeds, and fare
reductions of about 50 per cent immediately upon deregulation, together with
increased public awareness of coach travel, explain much of the initial growth.

Table 9.4 shows approximate totals for the network in England and Wales from
1989 to 1999. Much of the drop in the early 1990s was probably due to a rapid
growth in the real fare levels charged by National Express. A subsequent reduction
has helped to restore some traffic growth, to a level of about 12–13 million
passengers per year.

Trends shown in Table 9.4 are for National Express (NE), providing an extensive
network in England and Wales. No data on scheduled express coach travel as a
whole have been published since 1984, when 17 million trips were recorded,[9] but
given the market share of about 80 per cent held by National Express in that year,
it would seem reasonable to regard its trends as an indicator for the express coach
sector as a whole. It is important to bear in mind that non-scheduled services form,
in aggregate, a market of similar scale to scheduled operations. These include day
excursions, extended tours and private hire. These are included on the overall bus
and coach shares in Table 9.1, and identified separately in Table 9.2.

From the first day of deregulation in October 1980 a rival consortium of
independent operators, British Coachways, introduced competing services on the
main trunk routes, but were unable to match the high frequency of service that
National were able to offer. National also 'saw off' the competition by cutting its
fares to the levels of British Coachways, in some cases by 50 per cent, notably on
trunk routes to London. A fuller description is provided by Robbins and White[10]
and a description of subsequent changes by White.[11]

Price reductions were also made on major cross-country routes and other
London-based services. National benefited from their greater number of sales
outlets, and access to coach stations, notably London Victoria. They were already

a nationally known name which could take advantage of the publicity given to coach travel as a whole, whereas British Coachways was not. The independent consortium gradually broke up, and ceased in January 1983.

Some independent competition has continued on a number of corridors, but no single operator has been able to establish a competing network as such. By early 2001 significant all-year-round competition was reduced primarily to the London–Bristol–Somerset, and London–Glasgow corridors. It is noteworthy that even the large rise in real fare levels on the National Express network of about 30 per cent between 1989 and 1993 generated very little new competing independent operation, none of which has survived.

Within the National Express network, the initial phase of low-fare competition against British Coachways was followed by a strategy of improving service quality, notably the 'Rapide' service standard offered to most towns from London, major cross-country routes, and airport feeder services. giving lower seating densities, refreshments, hostess service, toilets and video TV. This type of service had in fact been pioneered by independents in the autumn of 1980.

The largest single source of traffic growth was probably rail, and some of the coach growth of the early 1980s may simply have represented a recapture of traffic lost to rail in the late 1970s, when BR was able to introduce a range of pricing innovations aimed at traditional coach users such as students and the elderly, which coach operators could not match initially. Visiting friends and relatives is by far the most important journey purpose, about half the total. Shopping/personal business, and holidays (with the obvious seasonal variation) are also significant. However, despite the service quality improvements, very few firms' business trips have been attracted to coach.

At coach deregulation in 1980, National Express was the trading name for the network of coach services offered by regional bus and coach companies within the National Bus Company. National Express was subsequently set up as a separate company, and as part of the NBC privatization, it was privatized through a management buy-out in 1988. After a subsequent change of ownership, it was floated as PLC in 1992. National Express owns very few vehicles directly, the vast majority of vehicles in its white livery being contracted-in from other operators, on a distance-based rate. From the passengers' point of view, a single network is offered.

A somewhat different pattern applied in Scotland. At the time of deregulation, the Scottish Bus Group (SBG) traditionally operated trunk routes between London and major Scottish cities, while other cities in England were connected by joint National Express/SBG routes. SBG subsequently placed the trunk routes between London and Scotland, and within Scotland, under the 'Citylink' company, which played a similar role to National Express in England and Wales. It was established as a separate organization in 1982 and, like National Express, came to contract in from a wider range of operators.

Citylink was privatized through a management buy-out in 1990 but in 1993 Citylink was acquired by National, and services rationalized. National thus exercised a remarkable dominance in a deregulated market. However, following an investigation by the Monopolies and Mergers Commission into the outcome of the Citylink purchase[12], due to NE also obtaining the ScotRail franchise, NE was required to divest itself of Citylink. It was subsequently purchased by Metroline, now itself a subsidiary of the Singapore-based Delgro group.

In addition to growth on long-distance services, substantial expansion has been seen in coach operation at the regional level, notably between London and Oxford on the M40 (where two operators each run several times per hour), and in Northern Ireland, where Ulsterbus has expanded its 'Goldline' network. In the Irish Republic, the express network of Bus Eireann has expanded substantially, both paralleling and complementing the rail system.

In terms of competing directly with railways on trunk routes to London, the express coach is always likely to occupy a 'second best' role, offering a lower speed service at a lower price. The average value of time at which a user would trade-off coach and rail travel (i.e. the value below which coach would be favoured) is about £4 per hour for full-fare users (or about £3 for those on reduced fares), a similar value to that for local bus passengers' time used in evaluating bus priority measures. This contrasts with £25–£30 per hour as the value of time applicable to business travel for which domestic air and intercity rail represent the choice open.

However, there is one market sector in which coach can compete more successfully with rail, namely airport access. Following deregulation in 1980, many services along the M4 corridor were diverted to serve Heathrow airport. Subsequently direct links have been established to Heathrow and Gatwick from many parts of Britain, and similar links to other airports. Coach can offer the convenience of a through service, and is less affected by congestion than on routes into central London. By 1984, coach had already captured about 30 per cent of the land feeder market from the West Midlands and Wales to Heathrow, compared with about 5 per cent using the rail–air coach link via Reading.[13] Increased emphasis has been placed on the airport market by National Express. Today, from Bristol and South Wales, a higher frequency is offered to Heathrow airport than to central London.

The current share is shown in Table 9.2, and in recent years National Express has placed strong emphasis on developing this market, through its Airlinks subsidiary, both at the long-distance and regional level. As yet, rail services to Heathrow are limited to central London connections only.

Private car and road traffic

No specific long-distance data are available, but Table 9.5 shows trends in vehicular traffic (the great majority of which, 86 per cent, is by car) on major roads and motorways.

The overall growth between 1989 and 1999 was 42 per cent on motorways (slightly exaggerated by growth in the motorway network), and 21 per cent on non-built-up major roads. As in the case of air travel, there was a period of low growth in the early 1990s associated with the recession, and then a rapid increase correlated with economic growth in the late 1990s. It is noteworthy, however, that the most recent year's data (i.e. for 2000) show very little growth despite further economic growth, probably associated with higher real fuel prices.

Table 9.5 Motor vehicle traffic 1989–99 (thousand million vehicle-km)

Year	Non-built-up major roads	Motorways
1989	111.9	59.0
1990	114.8	61.6
1991	117.0	61.0
1992	117.0	61.5
1993	118.1	63.9
1994	119.9	66.7
1995	122.5	70.9
1996	125.8	73.7
1997	128.9	77.9
1998	131.8	81.3
1999	134.9	83.6

Source: Table 4.10, *Transport Statistics Great Britain* 2000 edition, TSO, London, October 2000.

Note: 'Non-built-up major roads' includes both 'trunk' and 'principal' categories, handling similar total volumes of traffic (65.9 and 68.9 thousand million vehicle-km respectively in 1999).

Railways

Overall trends

Table 9.6 shows trends in passenger-kilometres travelled on national railways since 1989–90. Following privatization, the former 'Intercity', 'Regional' and 'Network South East' sectors are no longer distinguished directly, although most of the twenty-five Train Operating Companies (TOCs) can be assigned to one of them (apart from Anglia which operates a mix of intercity and local services within one franchise).

The principal long-distance operators are Great North Eastern (GNER, serving the East Coast Main Line), Virgin West Coast (West Coast Main Line), Midland Main Line (MML, to the East Midlands and Sheffield), First Great Western (FGW, to South Wales and the South West), Virgin Cross-Country (the principal cross-country routes focusing on Birmingham) and the intercity element of Anglia (London–Norwich). However, substantial long-distance traffic is also handled by some of the regional franchises, notably Northern Spirit (from which a separate long-distance franchise is being created by the SRA), and ScotRail.

Long-distance traffic has recently grown at a similar rate to railways as a whole, or somewhat faster in the case of certain franchises, at around 5 per cent per annum from 1996. However, over the whole period since 1989/90, the long-distance operators' traffic grew somewhat less than the railways as a whole (2.3 per cent, compared with 14.0 per cent for the whole network): growth was considerably faster on the former Network South East franchises (accounting for over half the net growth) and regional railways.

For the railways as a whole, average revenue per passenger-kilometre has remained remarkably stable in this period (in part due to price regulation since privatization). At 1999–2000 prices it rose from about 8.0 p in 1989/90 to about

Table 9.6 Passenger travel on national railways 1989/90–1999/00 (million passenger-km)

Year	Whole network	Long-distance operators
1989/90	33,600	12,900
1990/91	33,200	12,700
1991/92	32,500	12,600
1992/93	31,700	12,200
1993/94	30,400	11,400
1994/95	28,700	10,700
1995/96	30,000	11,100
1996/97	32,100	n/a
1997/98	34,700	12,300
1998/99	36,300	12,600
1999/2000	38,300	13,200

Source: National Rail Trends 2000–01, quarter 3. Strategic Rail Authority March 2001, tables 1.1a, 1.1b and p. 24. Earlier Intercity sector data is from *Transport Statistics Great Britain* 1996 edition, table 5.11(a), HMSO London, September 1996.

Notes: Data under the 'long-distance operators' from 1997/98 comprises the franchises for Anglia (intercity services), GNER, FGW, MML, Virgin West Coast and Virgin Cross Country as described in the text. For the period up to 1995/96 inclusive, it comprises the former 'Inter City Sector' of British Rail, broadly the same services but also including Gatwick Express (which carries about 200 m passenger-km per year)

8.7 p in the period since 1994/5.[14] The average for the long-distance operators is very similar to this, although was previously lower (about 7.8 p in 1997/8, for example), possibly as a result of a more restrictive approach to 'Super Saver' fares (see below).

About 72 million trips and 13,200 million passenger-km were made in the most recent year on the six main long-distance franchises listed above, with a total revenue of about £1,160 m, giving an average trip length of 185 km, and an average revenue per trip of £16.10.

Major speed improvements were concentrated in the early 1980s, associated with entry into service of the 200 kph diesel High Speed Train (HST) on Great Western, MML and Cross Country. This was followed by the electrification of the GNER route in the late 1980s. At lower speeds, major quality improvements also took place in the regional sector, with the adoption of class 158 stock on 'express' cross-country routes. More recently the class 170 'turbo' stock has been used to augment frequencies on existing intercity routes and provide new services (such as Hull–London, an 'open access' operation by GB Railways).

A market analysis in the 1980s[15] indicated that some 43 per cent of the InterCity revenue could then be attributed to 'leisure' travel (comprising visiting friends and relatives; holidays; days out; and sport/recreation); 37 per cent to 'business' travel; and 20 per cent to 'personal non-discretionary' (commuting to/from work; personal business; and to/from college). Although the business revenue per trip was higher than average, it is by no means entirely first class – the same analysis showed that 39 per cent of business trips were by first class, the majority (61 per cent) by standard. Prideaux[16] identified about 15 million of the population as users of

InterCity, some 10 million of whom used it in any one year, and 750,000 'very frequently', suggesting a highly geared market. Users are predominantly young, and only about 20 per cent are travelling on business, the most common single reason for travel being 'visiting friends and relatives'.

Pricing policy and elasticities of demand

The long-distance market is characterized by substantially higher price and service quality elasticities than are found in the short-distance sector. This is associated with the predominance of non-business journeys, whose frequency and destination may be highly responsive to cost. Even markets assumed to be traditionally inelastic, such as commuting, and travel in course of work, are now considered to be more price sensitive than before, as the possibilities for substitution are explored in the medium-to-long term (for example, relocation of home or job, or stricter control of companies' travel budgets).

For the rail long-distance market the average price elasticity is around –1.0, but may be greater where strong coach or air competition is found.[17]

For non-business rail travel, elasticities of greater size than –1.0 may be assumed. Modelling work for 'non-season ticket' rail travel by DETR since 1978 indicates an aggregate elasticity of –1.1.[18] Experience of trends immediately after express coach deregulation in 1980, and the impact of substantial real price increases by National Express in the late 1980s, suggest an average price elasticity of around –1.0 for that mode also.[19] A strong case for price reductions to maximize revenue and/or traffic thus exists, provided that significant extra capacity costs are not incurred.

In both rail and coach modes, a similar pricing policy is now adopted, in which highest fares are generally charged for the busiest day(s) (Fridays, and peak summer Saturdays or public holidays), while lower rates are charged at other times of the week. In the case of rail, there is also a marked business travel/commuting peak on Mondays to Fridays. For example, 'Saver' fares generally apply throughout the week, except at peak periods on busier routes, while lower fares are not available on Fridays. Rail operators have extended their policies further, adopting some of the airline industry 'yield management' techniques. 'Apex' fares (pre-bookable capacity of which a limited amount is offered) are now available on most main routes. Within the business sector, the full first class fare has been augmented by service categories (whose brand name varies by operator), offering an improved quality of catering service in standard accommodation.

Following privatization, a much greater range of fares and product types is now offered, dependent upon the management policies of each franchise. However, the 'Saver' fare has been protected by regulation, now limited to an RPI-1 per cent annual increase. A marked tendency, especially in the case of Virgin companies, has been for 'SuperSaver' and other off-peak 'walk on' categories to be reduced in scope or eliminated, in favour of book-ahead categories, in line with airline practice. This does, however, effectively increase real prices for users requiring the 'walk on' facility they previously enjoyed. Given the predominance of cars over almost all trip lengths in Britain (see Table 9.1) this might affect rail's long-run competitive position, since car journeys are not thus constrained.

National Express adopts a similar policy: its standard fare is applicable all days, but the lower 'economy return' fare is not valid on Fridays or peak summer Saturdays. Substantial reductions on the normal fares, subject to pre-booking (currently seven days) are offered, known as 'Apex Returns'. This was aimed at maintaining the typical 30 per cent fare differential with railways, following the latter's Apex expansion (above). A discount 'coach card' gives reductions of about 30 per cent (except on 'Apex' fares) to those aged 60 upward, or between 16 and 25 in a similar fashion to railcards. Many NE routes to London now offer 'special' fares dependent upon the degree of rail and independent coach competition.

Demand is also sensitive to speed. Using data for specific modes, we can derive relationships with respect to in-vehicle speed. However, the user responds to door-to-door speed changes, which may be less marked when access and waiting time are taken into account. In-train speed elasticities of around +0.8, or journey time elasticities of around –0.9, may be applicable with respect to in-train journey times for rail services. These are likely to fall as speed increases, and access/waiting time accounts for a growing proportion of door-to-door travel time.

A further quantifiable element is frequency. Especially for short-distance travel, and business trips, this may be more important than speed. However, derivation of robust elasticity values is difficult, owing to the problem of separating cause and effect: does a high frequency service stimulate demand, or does its presence merely reflect the need to provide capacity to satisfy such a demand? For low-frequency services, around every two hours or wider intervals, high elasticities may be applicable,[20] but these will fall as frequency rises.

Much of the modelling work for railways has combined these effects into a generalized time elasticity, as reviewed by Wardman.[21] Typical values for intercity routes are around –0.9.

Although difficult to quantify, other factors may also be very important:

1   *Timing of journeys.* Especially where frequencies are low, the timing of specific journeys will be critical. For example, is a day return trip for a business meeting practicable, or is a Friday evening/Sunday afternoon timing offered for weekend visits?

2   *Interchange.* Although the time taken to interchange may be reflected in estimates of total door-to-door time, an additional inconvenience and uncertainty result, especially where inter-modal interchange occurs. Non-business journeys may be particularly sensitive to this. It may be worthwhile incurring additional operating costs to offer a through service, and in some cases passengers may choose a lower speed mode (for example, coach instead of rail) for this reason.

3   *Access to terminals.* Provision of adequate car parking, as at the 'parkway' stations (such as Bristol or Warwick), may be a major factor, together with feeder bus, underground and taxi services. Growing interest is being shown by

franchisees in measures such as improved station parking, shared taxi services, and improved bus feeders (such as those now provided to the West Coast Main Line).

4 *Comfort and convenience.* Quality and cleanliness of seating, decor, availability of toilets, etc.

5 *Reliability of service*, and helpfulness of staff.

6 *Ease of pre-booking tickets and seats*, and/or ability to do so on demand without substantial queuing time. This has been greatly assisted by the rapid development of Internet (web) booking.

Developments in technology

Rail

Although certain aspects of rail technology were discussed in the urban context in Chapter 4, many aspects of long-distance rail technology are largely unique to this context, and recent developments offer further prospects for improving rail's market share.

Motive power

Diesel power is the most widely used mode of traction, both in locomotive and multiple-unit form, but lower operating cost and improved performance may be attained by use of electric traction. References are made in Chapter 4 to urban systems. For long-distance routes the standard voltage now adopted is 25 kV (25,000 V), a.c., supplied via overhead catenary, at the standard industrial frequency of 50 cycles/second. However, the third rail d.c. system at 650–800 V, adopted on the former Southern Region, is also used for long-distance routes such as London–Bournemouth–Weymouth and, somewhat anachronistically, the current route connecting the Channel Tunnel with London. Due to the close spacing of sub-stations, this system is generally confined to urban networks, that south of London representing the cumulative extension of such a network.

Elsewhere in Britain, the 25 kV system covers the London (Euston)–West Midlands–North West–Glasgow and London (Kings Cross)–Newcastle–Edinburgh corridors, together with the London–Norwich route.

The benefits from electrification have to be set against the capital cost of sub-stations, overhead or third-rail traction supply, and modifications to existing structures and signalling which may be required, in comparison with diesel operation. Low-density routes thus cannot justify such investment. However, the proportion of electrification in Britain – whether in terms of route kilometerage, or passenger train kilometerage – is low in comparison with similar European countries, notably France.

The major benefits include lower maintenance costs of locomotives. Electric locomotive maintenance costs are one-third to one-half those of diesel. These stem mainly from the much greater mechanical simplicity of the electric locomotive.

Energy costs for an equivalent output may be lower than where diesel fuel is used. In many cases, this is the second main factor. The thermal efficiency of burning oil in a power station, or on a diesel locomotive, is in fact fairly similar (around 25–30 per cent), but the primary source for electricity can include many cheaper means, such as coal, hydro or nuclear generation. Use of regenerative braking – impractical with diesel – gives further gains.

The first two factors taken together may account for 75 per cent or more of the cost savings from electric traction. However, the substantial real fall in oil prices during the 1980s and 1990s offset the underlying trend increase that was previously assumed to apply, reducing the net savings from schemes such as the East Coast main line electrification. Rail privatization has also complicated matters, with a crude averaging of power charges made by Railtrack to train operators. Greater flexibility in use of rolling stock (especially where lessors may require scope for later use) also favours diesel rather than electric stock limited to certain routes. For the present, little significant expansion in the electric network in Britain is likely, although density of traffic on the existing network is likely to rise and speeds to increase (see below).

Control and signalling

Reference has been made already to the concept of block signalling in Chapter 4. The same principle has been in use on double-track long-distance lines for over a hundred years, but owing to the much wider range of speeds encountered and lower densities of traffic, multiple-aspect signalling is used to indicate a range of likely stopping distances. In more sophisticated systems, such as the TGV, a form of cab signalling may be used to provide a continuous indication of permitted speeds, replacing trackside signals.

The use of multiple-aspect colour light signalling has been associated with the replacement of manually operated boxes (one to each block section) by area control centres, in which track circuits (as described in Chapter 4) or axle counters are used to display the location of trains on a panel covering large areas. Substantial labour cost savings may also be made. As the reliability of computer hardware and software has improved, solid state interlocking (SSI) has replaced previous electro-mechanical systems.

In many areas, high labour costs are still incurred on low-density routes. The operation of level crossings has often remained manual, and only in the 1980s was a large-scale programme of conversion to automatic barrier operation carried out in Britain, although such methods have been commonplace in other European countries (such as The Netherlands) for many years. On single-track routes, several means of simplified signalling are provided, based on the general principle that only one train can occupy a section between two passing loops at one time. Former manual systems are now being replaced by systems in which authority to occupy a section of track is transmitted electronically. As in the case of area signalling schemes for main lines, savings are obtained in manpower, and more effective control obtained over a large area. Examples include low-density routes in Scotland and East Anglia.

Although in Britain single-track operation is still considered very much a feature of low-density routes, the lower signalling and track provision costs associated with it encouraged conversion of some medium-density double-track routes – such as parts of the Carlisle–Dumfries–Glasgow route – to single track operation, often associated with elimination of manual boxes which formerly controlled each double-track block section. In many other countries, much of the network is single track, often accommodating high densities of freight traffic, both in the developing world, and other European countries such as Sweden. Centralized Traffic Control (CTC), based on data from track circuits and radio contract with drivers, enables the best use to be made of route capacity over large areas.

It should be stressed that the description of rail signalling given above is necessarily a highly simplified one, the technology being a complex subject in its own right. Only those aspects immediately relevant to cost and capacity have been considered.

Capacity and flow

The basic characteristics are in principle the same as for urban railways described in Chapter 4. In general, minimum braking distances are greater, acceleration rates lower, and hence minimum headways somewhat wider. As a practical scheduled minimum headway between successive fast trains, a figure of 3–4, rather than 2, minutes may be taken.

A major difficulty arises when trains of different speeds and characteristics are mixed over a common route: Intercity passenger, freight and local passenger, for example. Although – dependent upon the length of block sections – trains of similar speed can follow each other at close headways, this is not practicable when different types are mixed. This may be illustrated by use of a time–distance diagram, in which distance along a specific route is shown on the vertical axis, and time on the horizontal. The path of the train is represented by a line whose angle of inclination to the horizontal increases with speed, and in which an intermediate stop is represented by a short horizontal line. The 'mix of speeds' problem may be alleviated by grouping trains of similar characteristics into 'flights', so that empty paths occur only when one batch of trains follows another.

Figure 9.1 shows the section of route between Birmingham New Street and Coventry, on which a basic half-hourly Virgin West Coast intercity service, calling intermediately at Birmingham International, shares the track with Central Trains locals, Silverlink semi-fast trains and some less frequent Virgin Cross Country intercity services. The evening peak period in the summer 2000 timetable is shown as an example, with six intercity or semi-fast trains, and three locals. 'Flighting' of intercity and semi-fasts is used to maximize capacity, but with an irregular service pattern. This route has been identified as a case for upgrading in Railtrack's Network Management Statement, and four-tracking much of it is proposed in phase 2 of the West Midland capacity study by the SRA, WMPTE and Railtrack.

The same concept may be applied to long-distance routes where speeds vary. For example, on the main line from Paddington, fast HST services are grouped

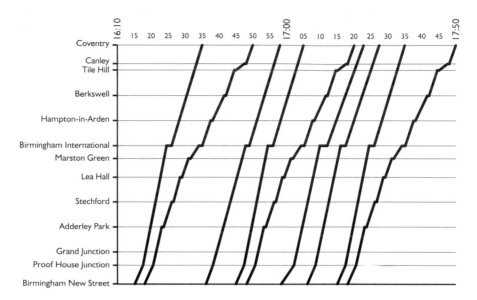

Figure 9.1 Time-distance graph of Birmingham-Coventry line. An example of the
capacity problems caused by 'mix of speed' operations. The Birmingham New
Street–Coventry line has only one track in each direction (apart from the
New Street–Grand Junction section and parallel platforms at Birmingham
International). Hence stopping trains cannot be overtaken by inter-city services.
A loss of capacity thus occurs when an intercity service is followed by a stopping
train, and vice versa. The route has been identified in Railtrack's Network
Management Statement as one for capacity upgrading. The pattern shown is
that applying in the evening peak from Birmingham, summer 2000 timetable.
(Original graph provided by Railtrack.)

within the same period in each hourly cycle. On the Euston–Rugby section of the
West Coast line, the basic all-day service is grouped into part of each hour, other
paths then being available for slower passenger trains, special workings, etc. In
the peak, a regular pattern, with an intermediate stop at Watford, is followed by
all trains.

A graphical timetable of the type shown in Figure 9.1 can be used for scheduling
purposes in several ways. On a single-track route, both directions of movement
can be superimposed (i.e. lines sloping in both directions: where they intersect,
passing loops will be necessary). On double-track routes, spacing between trains in
the same direction is constrained by block section length.

Track structure and route alignment

Conventional rail track is a flexible structure, in which the highly concentrated
train weight (axle loads of up to 25 tonnes – or even 30 on some US freight
lines) is distributed through rail and sleepers to the ballast (a layer of stone
chippings) to the sub-base, embankment, viaduct or tunnel structure. Flat-

bottomed, continuously welded rail (CWR) is fixed to concrete sleepers by steel track clips. Ballast cleaning, 'tamping' (placing of ballast correctly to support the sleepers), and rail replacement have been largely mechanized. At the ends of sections of CWR, overlapping tapered sections of rail have replaced the end-on joints, connected by 'fishplates' around which fractures were liable to develop.

In an attempt to reduce maintenance costs, some track is now constructed by use of a slip-form concrete paver, as for roads, forming a rigid base into which track clips are inserted. High capital cost results in it being confined to tunnels and other sections where reduced need for maintenance access is particularly useful.

Heavier axle loads are accommodated through use of larger cross-section rail, up to 60–70 kg/metre, although supporting structures, notably bridges, may continue to dictate axle-load limits.

A major constraint on alignment is the radii of curved sections. For a given speed, a minimum curvature will apply, and on open-country sections of many major routes (notably the East Coast main line) many curves have been realigned to permit higher limits. Use of super-elevation – raising the outer rail relative to the inner – also permits a higher speed for a given radius, but in practice, is restricted to a maximum of about 15 cm.

Besides curvature, the other main constraint on alignment is gradient. Ruling limits of about 1 in 70 (about 1.5 per cent) have been considered desirable on main lines, although on introduction of electrification, these have become less critical. The Paris–Lyon TGV route, used only by passenger trains, incorporates gradients as steep as 1 in 30 (about 3 per cent), making tunnels unnecessary, and requiring few major viaducts.

Rolling stock

The basic layout of long-distance passenger stock is that of two four-wheeled bogies supporting a body of about 20–23 metres. Lengths have gradually increased as lateral clearances have improved. An open-saloon plan with centre gangway gives a maximum capacity in standard class of about 72–76 passengers. Integral, all-steel construction is used to give a relatively low weight. As in the case of urban stock (Chapter 4) use of aluminium alloy extrusions can give further weight savings.

Most high-speed trains are locomotive-hauled, or with a power car at each end (the HST, TGV and Eurostar). On the main electrified routes (East and West Coast) push-pull operation now applies, the locomotive placed at one end of the train for both directions of movement, with movement in the 'reverse' direction controlled through a driving vehicle trailer (DVT).

High-speed conventional railways

A combination of track realignment, resignalling and new stock enables maximum speeds to be raised to about 160 km/h on many sections. Up to 200 km/h is found extensively in Britain, and other European systems. Uniquely for such speeds, much of the British network is based on the diesel High Speed Train (HST) technology and the newer class 180 'Atalante', rather than electric traction. However, the IC225 stock on the East Coast Main Line is electrically powered, and, as its title indicates, has potential for operation at up to 225 km/h if resignalling work is undertaken.

Apart from minor route realignment and resignalling, the upgrading to 200 km/h has not involved any new infrastructure, except for the diversionary route between Doncaster and York on the ECML, which was required in any case to by-pass the severe speed restriction at Selby.

Elsewhere, entirely new infrastructure has been built on a much larger scale, enabling conventional rail technology to attain much higher speeds. The Paris–Lyon TGV (Train à Grande Vitesse) route, opened fully in 1983, permits a maximum speed of 270 km/h (160 mph), and an average of about 200 km/h: 25 kV power cars at each end of the 12-car train give some 6,300 kW. Existing tracks give access to city centres and other routes for through-working. New construction has thus been confined to open country and, as mentioned above, use of the line by passenger trains only has enabled much steeper gradients to be accepted. A second route from Paris, the TGV Atlantique, opened in 1991 (with a maximum speed of 300 km/h) followed in 1993 by the 'TGV Nord' between Paris and Lille, connecting to the Channel Tunnel from its opening in May 1994, and subsequently with the 'Thalys' high-speed route into Belgium and The Netherlands. The TGV technology has also been employed for the Spanish high-speed service (AVE) between Madrid and Seville. Up to 330 kph is now possible with this technology.

The 'Shinkansen' network in Japan began in 1964 with the opening of the Tokaido Line between Tokyo and Osaka, relieving the heavily overloaded 1,067-mm gauge line between those cities. Subsequent extensions have taken this route to Hakata (1,100 km) and new routes north of Tokyo (Joetsu and Tohoku) were opened in 1983. Traffic densities are very high, but so are construction costs, owing to the mountainous terrain, and high population density in lowland areas. Adoption of standard gauge (1,435 mm) has limited the scale of the network, by making it necessary to build entirely separate routes, rather than utilizing through-running over existing tracks to reach city centres, for example. Penetration of Tokyo city has proved particularly costly. Further major extensions of the system are now unlikely.

New high-speed routes have also been built in Germany (served by the ICE train), albeit at extremely high cost, and have been proposed for several city-pairs in the USA. The French conditions, of low-density, relatively flat, rural regions between major traffic nodes may be largely unique.

Attention has thus shifted back to upgrading conventional technology. If existing curvatures and braking distances imposed by signalling can be negotiated at higher speeds, then little infrastructure investment will be needed. Given the limits to super-elevation of the track described above, the body of the train itself may be tilted further to increase maximum speed for a given radius. The tilt may be passive (pendular) or active (with a mechanism activated by lateral acceleration of the train). One abortive attempt was BR's Advanced Passenger Train (APT), tested extensively in the 1970s and early 1980s. Tilting suspension is, however, used successfully elsewhere, notably on the Swedish X2000, the Italian 'Pendolino', and also on the 1,067-mm gauge lines in Japan. In most cases, such tilting stock is used to raise relatively low speeds up to 160 or 200 km/h rather than match the very high speeds found on new main lines.

The 'Pendolino' concept is now being adopted for the Virgin network in Britain, both in electric form (West Coast Main Line) and the 'Super Voyager' diesel (for trunk cross-country routes). This will enable substantial improvements in average speed (rather than maximum speed) through permitting curves to be followed at higher speeds than at present. Coupled with resignalling and improved frequency the effect should be to dramatically increase passenger volume[22] – indeed, this will be essential if the financial targets for the franchises are to be met. Markedly higher service frequencies will be introduced, notably on the cross-country network through Birmingham.

New modes for high-speed movement

It has been suggested that a gap exists in the range of modes available, between high-speed conventional rail, and short-haul air services, in the speed range 300–600 km/h, for trips of about 400–500 km: for example, to give a timing of one hour from central London to central Manchester. In the late 1960s, physical separation of train and track was considered necessary to avoid effects of oscillation, although subsequent experience of the TGV has proved that higher speeds are possible on rail.

The first approach to this problem was to apply the hovercraft principle, in the form of the British 'Tracked Hovertrain' and French 'Aérotrain', but subsequently magnetic leviation ('Maglev') as been developed as a more efficient alternative. Maglev high-speed projects have continued to be tested in Japan and Germany, although commercial passenger operation still appears uncertain.

The current network structure and policy issues

Rail

A broadly stable network has operated in recent years, augmented by some re-opening of regional services (such as Worksop–Mansfield–Nottingham), which also contribute traffic to the national system. The range of through services offered over the existing infrastructure has widened (for example, through the Oxford–Didcot–Bristol service introduced after privatization) and further development is likely.

The major network infrastructure development at present is the construction of the Union Railways' high-speed link between St Pancras and the Channel Tunnel, also serving north and mid-Kent, The first phase is now well under construction (Ashford–north Kent) with the second (north Kent–Essex–St Pancras) following. This will supplant the current route on the third rail network, and reduce journey time from about 70 to 40 minutes.

The proposed East–West rail link, recreating rail connections between Cambridge, Bedford, Bletchley and Oxford may also greatly increase connectivity in this region of England.

The West Coast Main line handles the greatest concentration of traffic in Britain – about 6 million journeys per year on the London–Manchester trunk section – yet is currently limited to 175 km/h. The current upgrade should provide 200 kph over most sections. Entirely new high-speed routes paralleling large parts of the existing East Coast main line have also been proposed in the refranchising process.

Long-distance coach

The network has been re-oriented to provide fast high-frequency services (typically every two hours or better) between London and main centres, together with major cross-country services. 'Hub' interchanges are provided at London Victoria, Bristol, Birmingham and other centres. Victoria Coach Station, a subsidiary company of Transport for London, has been substantially upgraded, and is now open to all operators (albeit some independents continue to use on-street terminals in central London to avoid resultant costs). However, its location is not ideal, a site in the Paddington/Marylebone area being more logical in terms of the main flows now handled. Unfortunately, a hostile attitude toward coach terminals has been adopted by the local planning authority (Westminster) making such developments unlikely at present.

Further scope for express service improvement is curtailed by increasingly restrictive regulation on speed (although the safety rationale for this is unclear) to 100 kph maximum. This is exacerbated by the prohibition of coaches from the 'third' (fastest) lane on motorways. Together with the effects of road congestion, the overall average speed of express coach services is thus likely to diminish, worsening the competitive position *vis-à-vis* rail.

Air

As indicated above, a very substantial part of the domestic air network is focused on Heathrow and, to a lesser extent, Gatwick. Interlining traffic forms a major element. However, the wider access to Heathrow for international services since 1991, coupled with limited overall capacity, has meant that use of runway slots for low-density domestic flights becomes increasingly less attractive. Services from Liverpool, Humberside, Birmingham, East Midlands and Norwich have gone. While the major domestic trunk routes (from Manchester northwards) will continue to justify use of capacity at Heathrow, medium-distance services are being squeezed out. For direct access to London as such, rail offers a good alternative, but interlining passengers may find themselves suffering noticeably poorer access. In some other European countries, links to permit main-line rail services to serve major airports directly have been constructed (TGV services to Lyon Satolas, and Paris Charles de Gaulle; The Netherlands' services to Schiphol, etc.). However, the Heathrow Express provides a link only toward central London, with no west or north connection to the intercity network.

Notes

1 DETR Statistics Bulletin SB(00)02, table 4.3.
2 Derived from DETR Statistics Bulletin SB(00)22, tables 3.3 and 3.9.
3 Ibid., table 3.6.
4 Wardman, M. and Tyler, J. (2000) 'Rail network accessibility and the demand for inter-urban rail travel', *Transport Reviews*, vol. 20, No. 1 (January–March), pp. 3–24.
5 Where other sources are not shown, domestic air travel data are from CAA *UK Airlines 1999* statistics, table 1.12.
6 Dennis, N. and Graham, A. (2001) 'Airport environmental capacity and developments in airline operations', paper given at First International Conference on Environmental Capacity at Airports, Manchester Metropolitan University, April 2001.
7 Data on journey purpose, passenger mix and interline traffic proportions are from: table 62, Civil Aviation Authority report CAP678 *Passengers at Aberdeen, Edinburgh, Glasgow and Inverness Airports in 1996* (CAA, London, November 1997). table 60 of CAA report CAP690, *Passengers at Heathrow, Gatwick and Manchester airports in 1997.* tables 63 and 65 of CAP618.
8 Denton, N. and Dennis, N. 'Airline franchising in Europe: benefits and disbenefits to airlines and customers', *Journal of Air Transport Management*, Vol. 6 (2000), pp. 179–90.
9 Department of Transport, *Transport Statistics Great Britain 1976–86*, table 2.33, HMSO, London, 1987.
10 Robbins, D.K. and White, P.R., (1986) 'The experience of express coach deregulation in Great Britain', *Transportation*, vol. 13, pp. 339–64.
11 White, P.R., (2001) 'Regular interurban coach services in Europe', paper in report of ECMT Round Table 114 (of the same title), Paris, pp. 77–109.
12 Monopolies and Mergers Commission (1997) *National Express Group PLC and Scotrail Railways Ltd: A Report on the Merger Situation.* CM3773, TSO, London, December 1997.
13 Astill, D. and White, P.R., (1989) 'Express coach as an access mode to major airports', PTRC Summer Annual Meeting, September 1989, Seminar, D, pp. 13–20.
14 Where not stated otherwise, data on rail ridership are from 'National Rail Trends 2000–01, quarter 3', published by the Strategic Rail Authority in March 2001, tables 1.1, 1.1b, 1.2b, 1.3 and 1.3b.
15 *Modern Railways*, 'InterCity faces the future', January 1986, pp. 27–8.
16 Prideaux, J. (1989) 'How InterCity turned round', *Modern Railways*, August, pp. 404–8.
17 Wardman, M. (1993) *The Effect of Rail Journey Times and Improvements: Some Results and Lessons of British Experience Relevance to High-speed Rail Forecasting*, Institute of Transport Studies, University of Leeds, working paper 388.
18 Department of the Environment, the Regions and Transport (DETR) *Transport 2010: The Background Analysis* [evidence related to the ten-year plan for transport for the period to 2010]', TSO, London, July 2000, annex A.
19 White, op. cit., pp. 77–109.
20 Jones, D.E.S. and White, P.R., (1994) 'Modelling of cross-country rail services', *Journal of Transport Geography*, vol. 2 (1994), pp. 111–21.
21 See note 17.
22 Green, C. (2001) (Virgin Rail) 'Phoenix from the ashes', paper given to Institute of Logistics and Transport, London, February.

Reference

Rickard, J.M., 'Factors influencing long-distance rail passenger trip rates in Great Britain', *Journal of Transport Economics and Policy*, May 1988 (Vol. XXII), pp. 209–33.

10 Current policy issues in Britain

In this chapter some current policy issues in Britain are reviewed, in the light of recent and current central government policy. In the following chapter broader long-term issues are addressed, applicable also to many other countries.

Privatization

A strong theme since 1979 has been the privatization of the transport sector, as indicated in discussion of the organization of the industry in Chapter 1. This has taken place in several successive 'waves':

- some ancilliary activities, such as railway shipping interests and hotels, and the then National Freight Corporation, in the early 1980s;
- the principal state-owned ports (now Associated British Ports), airports (now BAA plc), and British Airways, in the mid-1980s;
- most of the bus and coach industry, initiated under the Transport Act 1985, a process which took place mainly between 1986 and 1994, leaving only about fifteen urban operators in local authority ownership;
- British Rail, mainly in the period 1995–7.

The principal remaining exceptions are air traffic control (in process of being partly privatized under the Transport Act 2000) and London Underground. In the latter case, operations will remain under direct public ownership, with infrastructure being placed on 30-year contracts to three 'infracos' under a 'Public Private Partnership' (PPP). Even in the traditionally wholly-public highway sector private funding is being used to provide new roads and major upgrading, under 'Design Build Finance Operate' (DBFO) contracts, and direct private sector projects such as the Birmingham North Relief Road (BNRR).

This process of privatization does not necessarily introduce any fundamental change in the role of public transport, which will depend on competition with the private car, and the attractiveness of its services in terms of price and quality to potential users. There is little reason to believe that users would respond differently to the service offered merely on the basis of ownership. The competitive position of public transport will also be affected by pricing and management of the role of the car, irrespective of ownership patterns.

Perhaps of greater consequence have been changes in operating costs and efficiency. In the case of the bus industry, discussed in further detail below, radical changes have been made, resulting in a reduction in real cost per bus-km of 48 per cent over the period between 1985–1986 (the last year before impacts of deregulation and privatization) and 1999–2000.[1] These are not necessarily wholly attributable to privatization, being stimulated by the degree of competition (discussed further below), changes in the labour market, and in average vehicle size. None the less, this sharp reduction has permitted a marked cut in public sector financial support to be absorbed while increasing profit margins and bus-kilometres run. In the case of the rail industry, net cost reduction has been less evident, the main impacts being in the savings attained (until autumn 2000) by Railtrack in maintenance and renewal, and the ability of train operating companies to reduce their unit operating costs sufficiently to absorb a small net subsidy reduction and increase train-kilometres operated.

The efficiency argument is less clear-cut in terms of capital spending. Scope for competitive bidding to undertake specified work already exists within the public sector, as well-established in road construction, for example. The concept of pushing privatization further, in terms of providing the finance, has been questioned insofar as private businesses in stable countries such as Britain normally require higher rates of return than would the state. This is evident both in the returns expected on equity capital, and the interest rates on borrowing. Hence, in order for the private sector to undertake a scheme at lower cost overall, large cost reductions would be needed in order to offset the higher cost of capital. A mixed outcome was evident from the first eight DBFO road schemes for example[2] (National Audit Office 1998), and while claims have been made of average savings of 17–20 per cent through PFI (Private Financing Initiative) schemes, these rest on projections of savings over a long period rather than outcomes directly observed to date.[3]

Insofar as the state often remains the ultimate source of funding, there is a danger that PFI or PPP schemes may incur greater costs in the long run than funding directly through state or local authority borrowing. In the short run, the need to provide capital is avoided, but over the whole project period the public sector generally provides a series of annual payments whose total may exceed the cost of funding schemes directly. Discounted cash flows, well-established in investment appraisal, may be used to compare the overall totals of such payments with the alternative of direct funding. At the time of writing a real rate of 6 per cent per annum (itself somewhat higher than the real cost of government borrowing) is used for evaluation purposes, and could be appropriate in making such comparisons.

Evidence submitted to an enquiry into the London Underground PPP proposal indicates that, based on a range of rates of return that typically might be required in the private and public sectors, private sector 'infracos' would have to undertake work at about 20 per cent less than through the public sector in order to offset these effects.[4] As an illustration of the cost of capital to even a large private sector business, the Rail Regulator's review of funding needed by Railtrack assumed that the company would incur an average cost of capital of about 8 per cent in real terms (this being prior to its recent difficulties), considerably higher than the public sector.[5]

Deregulation

The concepts of 'privatization' and 'deregulation' are often mixed together, and form part of the same economic philosophy. However, their application is not necessarily coincident, and separate effects may be adduced for each. For example, in the case of the express coach industry in Britain deregulation took place in October 1980 but the dominant operator, National Express, was not privatized until 1988. Local bus services outside London and Northern Ireland were deregulated in October 1986, but the privatization of the majority of operators was spread over the following nine years. Hence, somewhat clearer 'before' and 'after' periods can be observed in analysing the deregulation process than in privatization impacts.

As indicated in Chapter 1, several elements of deregulation may be distinguished. Price controls may be removed prior to quantity control (for example, they effectively ceased in the early 1980s in local buses, prior to deregulation in 1986), or the process may be simultaneous (as in the case of express coaching in 1980). In a few cases, strict controls remain – for example, specified fare scales for taxi services – even where quantity limits have been removed or never applied (as in the case of London taxis). Rail privatization in Britain has been associated with a greater degree of regulation than before, in terms of controlling overall price levels, and specifying minimum service patterns.

Perhaps the most obvious exception to removal of quantity control is the continuation of limits on the numbers of taxis in many towns, still permitted under the Transport Act 1985 where a case can be made on the grounds of 'no significant unmet demand'. It is difficult to see how this can be sustained in the long run, although in the short run some gradual adjustment might be needed where existing taxi licence plate holders have bought in to the market at a price determined by artificial scarcity.

Competition policy

Deregulation will generally result in an increased degree of competition, as new entrants take the opportunity to compete with incumbents. Increased competition may be particularly valuable in stimulating more efficient operating methods, as newcomers devise more efficient means of providing similar (or better) services. Such competition can be seen as 'in the market' (i.e. direct competition between operators on the same routes) for 'for the market' (in which competitive bidding helps to produce efficiency gains – for example, in the process of tendering for bus services in London, or the franchising of passenger rail services).

While some competition may emerge spontaneously, the full benefits would not necessarily occur in the absence of measures to enable new entrants to compete effectively. A large incumbent may, for example, reduce prices to levels below cost in order to drive off a newcomer, or run additional services timed just before a newcomer's in order to deter entry. One could also see a newcomer's tactics as potentially 'unfair', for example, by introducing new local bus services which simply duplicate existing routes, operating at similar fares but running just ahead of the incumbent's services.

Express coach deregulation under the Transport Act 1980 was accompanied by relatively few measures to ensure competition. For example, the principal coach station, London Victoria, remained under the ownership of National Express until the latter's privatization. Local bus deregulation under the 1985 Act reversed the previous emphasis toward co-ordination and integration, by applying the Fair Trading Act 1973 and the Competition Act 1980, from which the industry had previously been exempt. In the early years of deregulation this had a particularly marked effect on discouraging co-ordination between operators (such as joint ticketing or timetabling), but may have been less effective than intended in deterring anti-competitive practices – for example, following enquiries by the Office of Fair Trading or the Monopolies Commission, the offender was merely required to desist from such actions, rather than penalties as such being imposed.

Much stronger powers are now held under the Competition Act 1998 which have resulted, for example, in a 'dawn raid' on bus companies' offices in West Yorkshire to obtain documents. At the same time, uncertainty has been created regarding the acceptable degree of co-operation between operators, and hence potential conflicts with the government's policies in the Transport Act 2000. These have been partly resolved by a 'block exemption' announced by the Office of Fair Trading in February 2001[6] which permits joint ticketing between bus operators for travelcards, inter-available returns and 'add on' bus/rail tickets. However, standardization of single and return cash fares would still be seen as anti-competitive. The position of joint timetabling (for example, two operators of hourly services running a joint 30-minute headway) remains uncertain. Ironically, it may be easier to ensure co-ordination by operators within the same area merging completely, thus creating a network on which a common fare structure can apply, than for two separately owned operators to co-ordinate fares and/or timetables.

A contrast may be seen with the rail industry which, while subject to some aspects of competition policy, is generally encouraged to practise co-operation between operators. Inter-available single and return tickets at common prices remain over the whole network, with additional cheaper offers being operator-specific. Co-ordinated timetabling (in part due to technical constraints) remains, and has been encouraged in recent changes (for example, to provide common headways between expanded Virgin Cross-Country services and parallel sections on London-based routes, such as York to Edinburgh).[7]

The main issue to be resolved in competition policy applied to public transport is the degree to which competition within the public transport market is more important than that between public and private transport. In the local bus industry, for example, the short-run competition is much more likely to be within the existing public transport users' market, few of whom have cars available. In the long run, however, this market continues to decline as car ownership grows. If such competition takes the form of stimulating new higher-quality services then it may also make bus services more attractive to car users in the longer term. However, competition could also take the form of a fragmented network in which passengers are unable to get the full potential benefits due to lack of co-ordinated timetabling and ticketing. If, due to poor average loads, operators are unable to generate sufficient profit to replace their assets then longer-term quality may decline. Such a system would be unattractive both to those with cars available, and so-called 'captive' users.

Hence, one may argue that it is the outcome, in terms of service quality and efficiency, that matters rather than the degree of competition *per se*.

Experience in the bus industry

Since deregulation of the industry in 1986, an overall decline in ridership has continued outside London, but with marked local fluctuations and some cases of growth.

Comparative regional trends are shown in Table 10.1.

'Metropolitans' comprise the six major conurbations outside London within England covered by the PTEs, and 'shires' the rest of England after excluding London and the metropolitan areas. Figures for Wales and Scotland cover all areas within those countries.

A fuller discussion of these trends is provided elsewhere.[8] Essentially, some decline would be expected due to rising car ownership and some other negative factors, such as greater dispersal of land use. Real fares have generally risen, despite expectations that competition would bring about reductions. Fare rises were particularly evident in the metropolitan areas, largely as a result of previous support through local authorities being eliminated (hence, this effect is associated with government policy, but not deregulation or privatization as such).

However, a positive impact on ridership would have been expected due to the growth in bus-kilometres run. In the short run, the effect appears to have been rather limited, apart from cases such as high-frequency minibus conversion (see Chapter 2). Nevertheless, in the longer run the increased bus-km may have offset

Table 10.1 Trends in local bus ridership and kilometres operated since deregulation: percentage changes, 1985/6 to 1999/2000 inclusive

Area	Passenger trips	Bus kilometres
London	+13.5	+33.7
Metropolitans	−43.9	+14.3
English 'shires'	−20.1	+29.3
Scotland	−35.8	+27.0
Wales	−31.9	+24.2
Great Britain	−24.1	+25.1
All deregulated areas	−33.8	+23.8

Source: Derived from tables 10 and 12 in DETR Statistics Bulletin SB(00)26

at least some of the effects of the real fares increases, consistent with the evidence regarding higher values for long-run elasticities. NTS data show that annual distances travelled by bus for members of non-car-owning households have remained fairly stable since 1985/6 (890 km in 1985/6, 900 km in 1997–9), suggesting such offsetting effects for this category, although the trip rate as such will have declined due to rising average trip length. However, distances travelled by bus by members of car-owning households continued to decline over the same period (for those in one-car households by 9 per cent, two or more by 15 per cent), indicating a growing relative dependence on the non-car owning sector for the bus industry.[9]

The impact of additional bus-kilometres on ridership will clearly depend on their incidence. Whereas a fare reduction provides direct benefits to existing passengers and will stimulate some increase in demand, additional bus-kilometres run could take many forms. If competing services simply duplicate existing well-served routes, the effect may be to split the market between operators, rather than stimulate overall growth. However, improvements at times when existing service levels are low may have greater impact, as may improvements to evening and Sunday services which widen the range of travel opportunities. A conflict may thus exist between short-run competition (which may tend to focus on the busier, relatively well-served periods and routes) and improving service availability overall.

Table 10.2 illustrates such a case, in which there are two routes of equal length. Existing operator A runs Route 1. New operator B has the option of starting its own new route, number 2, which would increase the total market by 50 passengers per hour. However, since Route 2 is of lower density, the passenger boadings per round trip are lower than for Route 1, at 25 versus 40. The average for the two routes together is thus 37.5 passengers per round trip. It will be tempting for operator B to run two buses per hour just ahead of operator A on Route 1, which already has a high frequency (10 buses per hour, a headway of 6 minutes). The impact on total ridership may be very small, and hence an existing market will be divided between two operators. The overall average load falls by 11.2 per cent from 37.5 to 33.3, although from the viewpoint of operator B it will increase from 25 to about

Table 10.2 Effects on ridership and bus loadings of vehicles being transferred from a low-frequency to high-frequency route

	Route 1	*Route 2*	*Total/average*
Initial case:	Operator A	Operator B	
Passengers/hr	400	50	450
Buses/hour	10	2	12
Passengers per bus round trip	40	25	37.5
After switch of operator B to Route 1:	Both operators		
Passengers/hr	400	0	400
Buses/hour	12	0	12
Passengers per bus round trip	33.3	–	33.3

33.3. An analogous argument may be applied to expanding evening/Sunday services versus adding to daytime frequencies.

The London case remains a striking exception, in which a much better ridership trend may be observed – a growth of 13 per cent since 1985/6 – despite real fares also increasing. A number of factors may apply:

- the larger than average growth in bus-km (34 per cent versus the national average of 21 per cent);
- the distribution of additional bus-km (mainly on lower density routes, and evening/Sunday periods);
- continued availability of comprehensive travelcards and a simple cash fares structure (see Chapter 7);
- in contrast to some other large urban areas, retention of free off-peak pensioner concessionary travel over the whole period;
- some factors specific to London in terms of almost stable car ownership levels since the early 1990s and constraints on car use through limited road space, and parking policies.

It does not follow that applying the London approach elsewhere would automatically result in similar results, but none the less the differences in performance are very striking. For example, the West Midlands conurbation has experienced some population growth (as has London), has retained a fairly comprehensive travelcard facility (through the dominance of one operator), has retained free off-peak pensioner concessionary travel, and displays broadly similar trends to London in real fares and service levels (26 per cent in the latter case), but none the less showed a decline of 28 per cent in bus trips between 1985/6 and 1999/2000.[10]

Outside London, some cases of much better trends than the average may also be observed. Notable examples include Oxford and Brighton, the former with two strong competing companies, the latter one dominant operator, both of which show substantial growth since the mid-1980s. Greater attention has been paid to marketing and service quality, and in both cases car use (if not ownership) is constrained by relatively high urban densities and limited town centre parking. Oxford, in particular, benefits from extensive bus priorities and a large park and ride scheme (see Chapter 5).

Current policy, under the Transport Act 2000, is to encourage greater emphasis on service quality and co-operation within the industry, rather than impose radical changes in structure or ownership. The 'quality partnership' approach (see Chapter 3) has been formalized, with legal powers to exclude operators not meeting the agreed criteria. However, fares and service levels cannot be specified in the partnership (except in Scotland). Hopefully, this will encourage operators and local authorities to take a longer-term view. 'Quality contracts' would give powers similar to those found in London, under which contracts with a local authority would replace the deregulated framework. However, it appears to be viewed both by the industry and government as something of a last resort in the event of other approaches not succeeding. There is thus a danger that few schemes will be introduced, and those possibly in untypical conditions, rather than the concept being tried out as, in effect, a large-scale experiment from which broader conclusions could be drawn.

Despite losses of ridership the bus industry has succeeded in improving its profitability from very low margins in the late 1980s, essentially through cutting costs faster than losses of ridership or revenue. In real terms, total operating costs (including depreciation) fell by 33 per cent between 1985/6 and 1998/9, despite growth in bus-kilometres run. This offset a drop of 4 per cent in revenue and of 78 per cent in support through local authorities, and still permitted profit margins to increase to an operating margin of about 14 per cent. Fuller details are provided elsewhere.[11] However, there are limits to relying on cost reductions as means of increasing profit margins, especially under the current labour market in which better wages and working conditions may have to be offered. To secure its longer-run profitability the industry needs to increase average loadings through improved service quality.

Rail privatization outcomes

As mentioned in Chapter 1, the structure of the railway industry in Britain, deriving from the Railways Act 1993, is one in which the system is in private ownership, apart from London Underground and two other urban systems. The broad split between infrastructure and operations derives from EU Regulation 91/440, but Britain went much further than other members in privatizing both aspects, and in further sub-dividing the system between twenty-five train operating companies. The term 'national railways' is sometimes used to describe the largely surface-based system formerly operated by BR.

Most parts of the rail business were privatized in the period 1995/7, and thus it is now possible to identify some of the main changes, and the extent to which privatization as such may have caused them.

A feature since a low point in demand trends in 1994/5 was the rapid growth in rail passenger travel, to levels exceeding the previous peak associated with the economic boom of the late 1980s. Between 1994/5 and 1999/2000 inclusive total passenger-km rose by about 33 per cent, but varying between sectors:[12]

Long-distance (including Gatwick Express)	25%
London and South East	36%
Regional	46%

Perhaps surprisingly, the long-distance operators actually showed the lowest percentage growth, while the highest (albeit from a lower base) was in the 'regional' sector, comprising all operators outside the main long-distance franchises and the London area. Modelling work by DETR has shown that the non-season ticket market growth can be explained very largely by growth of GDP (with an elasticity of about +2.0), real rail fares (an elasticity of about –1.0) and the volume of car traffic (likewise, about −1.0). On this basis, a very close fit can be seen between observed and expected values over a 20-year period since 1978, including the most recent growth phase.[13] In the case of season ticket travel, employment in major centres, notably London, is likely to be a major factor (in turn correlated with GDP growth).

Although some cases have occurred of the privatized operators stimulating ridership through improved marketing and service frequency (notably on the Anglia and Midland main lines), this does not appear to be a very significant factor at national level. A more direct consequence of rail privatization is probably the decision to 'cap' certain fares (such as Savers and season tickets) to rise no more rapidly than the retail price index (and, since 1999, on an 'RPI-1' formula). Previously, real price increases had been used by BR both to increase revenue in less elastic markets, and to curb demand growth where capacity constraints existed. Removing this effect was one factor in permitting traffic to rise in accordance with the GDP stimulus, offset only by the growth in car traffic. Assuming that similar trends continue, a growth of about 40 per cent over the next ten years should be feasible, even before impacts of developments such as improved services.

Since even the non-regulated fares are found in fairly elastic markets, the average revenue per passenger-km has remained almost unchanged in real terms since the mid-1990s. Hence, real revenue has grown in the same proportion as passenger volume.

When franchises were awarded in the first round of bidding under OPRAF, it was evident that sharp reductions in the payment required (and, in some cases, offer of a premium to be paid to the state) were committed. In practice, most operators were able to absorb these reductions due to the growth in passenger revenue, reduced access charges to Railtrack (following a decision by the Regulator in 1995) and only a small part of the net reduction came from the operators cutting their own costs (in practice, the main impact was to reduce unit costs somewhat further, enabling an increase in train-km run of about 10 per cent without increasing total costs).

Overall, train operating companies were able to remain profitable (a net internal profit was made by the BR passenger business in its last year, after receipt of budgeted support), although by 1999/2000 almost all the regional companies apart from ScotRail were making a loss. Some franchises have been renegotiated, with higher payments now being made to operators than originally envisaged.

One could thus see the impact of rail privatization up to 1999/2000 as much more positive than that of bus deregulation and privatization, since users had not, overall, experienced real fare increases, and volume growth had produced the ability to absorb large reductions in support from the state. Although the growth appears to be a function largely of external factors, the industry did at least avoid the negative impacts of instability and fragmentation that affected the bus industry, especially in the period immediately after deregulation in the late 1980s.

The Strategic Rail Authority (SRA) is now adopting a longer-term approach, with new (or extended) franchises for up to twenty years being awarded, compared with seven as the typical period in the first round. Operators will be able to take a broader view, and substantial investment commitments are implied in the bids accepted (whereas in the first round, operators made very little investment as such, leasing all of their rolling stock and paying access charges to Railtrack). The cash flow profiles of these longer bids are not currently available at the time of writing.

Against this fairly positive picture, major problems have emerged since the crash at Hatfield in October 2000. Following identification of rail fragmentation as the cause, Railtrack immediately imposed extensive speed restrictions and temporary closures on many parts of the network. Extensive disruption to services, with loss of passenger volume and revenue, then followed, although recovery (except in the intercity sector) was evident by April 2001. Large compensation payments are being made by Railtrack to operators, but Railtrack itself faces large deficits.

A further review of access charges by the Regulator in 2000 resulted in reversal of the previous trend toward reducing them in real terms. Total payments to Railtrack (a mix of access charges to operators and government grants) rise by about 35 per cent in 2001/2 and then at 4–5 per cent per annum to 2005/6. To some extent, this may be due to factors which would have arisen in any case under continued state ownership, such as the need for a more realistic view of renewal costs, but some may be associated with the privatization process as such.

In terms of the structure, much public attention has been focused on the number of train operating companies and co-ordination between them. The current review by the SRA may slightly reduce their total as boundaries are adjusted. However, the main issue remains the vertical separation between Railtrack and the train operators. While this is to some extent inevitable under the EU framework, Britain has taken this approach much further than in other countries. There is also a problem related to the existence of a single monopoly provider, namely Railtrack, compared with the competitive bidding that occurs for the operating franchises. It is thus impossible for the state to have a ready-made 'comparator' business against which to assess Railtrack's performance and efficiency, or an alternative business able to take over in the event of severe difficulties.

A further possible development is the role of 'micro-franchising' which could be used for local lines in rural areas, for example.

The 1998 White Paper and the Transport Act 2000

The Labour government's Transport White Paper of 1998[14] marked a shift in policy aims, but not necessarily in the ownership and structure of the public transport industry. A greater emphasis was placed on the potential role of public transport, given growing importance attached to environmental issues and an acknowledgement that major road-building would not be a feasible option. This led to a wider role for public transport, both to improve mobility for those without cars (part of the 'social exclusion' issue) and to act as an alternative to some degree to extra road capacity being required. This latter effect is more marked on rail than for local buses, and even so would only accommodate a small part of the road traffic growth otherwise anticipated, much of which will have to be constrained by policies such as fuel taxation, road pricing, etc.

The 1998 White Paper was followed by the 'Ten Year Plan' in 2000, covering the period to 2010.[15] Much greater integration of forecasting and policy option assessment has been provided as described by Worsley.[16] Taking forecasts based on the likely effect of exogenous factors (such as GDP growth), these were then modified to allow for the effects of policy options, to produce policy-sensitive forecasts and targets for car, rail and bus use. This contrasted with the previous approach in the National Road Traffic Forecasts (NRTF) which were based largely on anticipated trends, with little effect allowed for policy options.

The combination of external factors and proposed policies for public transport has produced the anticipated outcomes shown in Table 10.3.[17]

'Baseline' figures referred to the expected outcome projecting exiting trends; 'plan' the outcome after policies set out in the plan are implemented.

The bus use figure is somewhat vaguer than the others, perhaps reflecting the low status of this mode, and represents a target or aspiration rather than the outcome of a policy-sensitive forecast as in the case of private car and rail use. Indeed, references to a possible 50 per cent growth in London and 10 per cent overall could at face value imply a net decrease elsewhere (due to the substantial proportion of national bus trips found in London), although this was presumably not the intention.

In the case of rail passengers, the implied average annual growth rate of about 4 per cent per annum is in line with that experienced from 1995/6, as a combination of GDP growth and restraint of real fares increases, although a sufficient increase in capacity is implicit in attaining such an outcome.

In the case of the bus figure, the modest growth could be attainable largely within existing capacity (even in the peak) but would require significant improvements in quality to increase ridership among the 'captive' groups and/or attract car users given the underlying growth in car use that might be expected during this period.

Subject to continuation of central government policy, a clearer framework is thus provided than for many years previously, in terms of national aims. These in turn inform targets set in Local Transport Plans (LTPs).

Concessionary fares

For many years, local authorities have provided concessionary fares to certain categories of passengers, typically the elderly and disabled. A rapid expansion of

Table 10.3 Percentage changes under the Ten Year Plan 2000–2010

Car: vehicle-km	+22 per cent baseline
	+17 per cent plan
	+13 per cent plan plus constant (rather than falling) motoring costs
Rail: passenger-km	+23 per cent baseline
	+51 per cent plan
Bus use	+10 per cent plan
Bus trips in London	+50 per cent plan

such schemes took place in the early 1970s, notably including the free off-peak travel schemes in London, the West Midlands and Merseyside which continue. Generally speaking, schemes were more generous in the larger metropolitan areas, and least of all in some rural districts.

Under the Transport Act 1985 a more consistent approach was adopted to operator compensation, and also to ensuring the availability of concessionary travel on all bus services within the same authority's area. The concept of compensating operators was also applied more strictly, being the net revenue forgone. This required calculation of the traffic generated by lower fares in estimating the net compensation required. However, the powers remained permissive (discretionary) rather than mandatory, and wide variations in policy continued.

Under the Transport Act 2000 and the corresponding Scottish Act a common minimum level of provision is required. In England this comprises a 50 per cent reduction on full standard adult fares for pensioners and disabled. In Scotland and Wales a more generous approach has been adopted: in the former, a half fare from April 2001 and free travel from April 2002; in the latter, free for pensioners from April 2001.

The Act also removed the previous power to make charges for the pass indicating validity for the concession, which is likely to increase take-up rates (albeit among those who may travel relatively little by public transport).

Authorities providing more generous schemes may continue to do so, and the 2000 Act also ensures continuation of the Greater London scheme. The constraint is generally that of expenditure incurred in relation to other local budget priorities. The Transport Act 2000 requirements came into effect in England from 1 June 2001.

Following local budgetary pressures, a number of authorities reduced the extent of more generous schemes in the 1980s and early 1990s, with free travel often replaced by a flat fare (for example in South Yorkshire, Tyne and Wear, and Edinburgh), although schemes in large metropolitan areas have continued to be more generous than elsewhere (typically, flat fares rather than half rate). This in turn reduced the volume of bus travel in such areas.

Generally speaking, if a concession is confined to off-peak periods, it may be assumed that no additional capacity costs are incurred as a result. Hence, the net effect on operator finances will depend on the share of total travel represented by concessionary users and the price elasticity. Typically, pensioner and disabled travel represents about 15 to 25 per cent of bus use, being higher in those areas where more generous levels are provided.

Local authorities remain free to specify concessionary travel for other categories, and in some cases child fares are treated in this form. (While operator commercial policy has traditionally offered half fares to children, the rationale for this is not always clear.) Particularly at peak times, additional child travel may incur substantial capacity costs, making the offer of lower fares more costly than at off-peak times when capacity is available. In these cases, compensation from the local authority to the operator could consider capacity costs, as well as additional trips and hence revenue produced by the concession *vis-à-vis* standard fares. There is, however, very little evidence regarding elasticities for child travel, either in respect of operator commercial policy or concessionary fare effects.

School travel

As indicated in Chapter 2, expenditure on 'statutory' school travel represents a large part of local authority spending, albeit not usually classified under 'transport' as such. This is additional to the question of child concessionary fares mentioned above, being the provision of free travel for those living above the specified distances (two miles under the age of eight, three miles eight and above). Costs have risen as the numbers of eligible children have increased, and exceptionally high costs (comprising about one-third of the total) are attributable to 'special needs' pupils.[18]

From the operator's viewpoint such peak-only demand may incur high costs for the reasons set out in Chapter 6. This may be reflected in contract prices charged to local authorities, or unwillingness to provide additional peak-only capacity commercially.

However, there is now growing concern at the congestion resulting from increased use of private cars to carry children to school at peak periods, now amounting to about 18 per cent of vehicle movements at 0850 during the morning peak during term-time.[19] This peak is often more concentrated than that for adult journeys to work, and may be associated with further increases in car mileage where the parent escorting the child makes a positioning run to/from home for each school trip (this does not, however, apply to all such movements, many morning school trips being combined with the adult's own journey to work). Growing dependence on car use may also have harmful effects on children's health and later independence.

An argument may thus be made for encouraging a shift from cars for the school trip, either to non-motorized modes for the shorter trips where it is safe to do so, or to public transport for longer journeys. A number of local initiatives are now in progress, notably the 'Safe Routes of School' concept. A comprehensive review of the issues from the parents' perspective is presented by Jones and Bradshaw.[20]

A trade-off thus exists between adding to public transport peak capacity, over and above statutory obligations for free travel, and reduced congestion benefits that may emerge. If, however, such capacity is not used at other times it may have very high costs, especially if using buses and coaches to standard specification. Two options may apply:

1   Use of lower-cost vehicles. There is a long tradition of using older buses and coaches no longer suited to intensive services. However, as mentioned in Chapter 8, these are often unsuitable for school work. Purpose-built vehicles may be more appropriate, and the American 'Yellow Bus' school vehicle has been proposed by FirstGroup in Britain partly for this reason. However, ensuring acceptable compatability with current design standards (such as Euro II and Euro III emission requirements) may be difficult, and with DDA requirements almost impossible.

2   Achieving better utilization of school buses by staggering school start and finishing times, so that, even while confined to school work, vehicles might attain two or three rather than just one loaded trip per peak period – this is understood to be the case in the USA. This would require co-ordination between schools within the same area (for example, for those taking older pupils to commence first, and youngest pupils last), but this may be difficult to attain where individual schools are given greater management autonomy.

At the time of writing, FirstGroup hope to establish a number of the 'Yellow Bus' initiatives in selected areas, and several authorities are also buying their own vehicles (both to American and British designs) as a means of containing costs.

An underlying issue remains that of the free travel distances dating back to the Education Act 1944. They are now generally seen as inappropriate given increased road traffic and safety concerns. One option might be to adopt a flat fare for all children, thus giving incentives to use non-motorized modes for short trips where safe to do so, while avoiding the arbitrary effects of a distance criterion. This could then be included in concessionary fares schemes, encouraging further integration of school and public transport.

The overall direction of policy

Within this chapter a number of major issues have been considered (within the space available a totally comprehensive review is not possible). Despite some shifts in policy following the election of a Labour government in 1997, a considerable degree of continuity with the previous Conservative administration can also be observed. Previous privatizations have not been reversed, and until about 1999, continuity was also evident in environmental policy related to transport (such as the 'fuel duty escalator' applicable to petrol and diesel fuel for road vehicles). The main changes in the period 1997–2001 might be seen as those of emphasis, with a greater degree of priority given to public transport, especially in longer-term planning. Greater co-ordination, rather than pursuit of deregulation and competition as such, could be seen as an aim.

The actual outcome has been more mixed, in part due to problems faced by public transport operators in improving quality to match the long-term policy aims. While rail use has grown very substantially, much of this growth can be seen as attributable to external factors rather than service quality. Likewise, on the London Underground poor service quality and peak overcrowding, resulting in part from low investment, have resulted in much public dissatisfaction. In bus operations, a more mixed picture is evident, with bus priorities, park and ride, and operators' initiatives helping to stimulate provision and use in some areas, together with wider impacts such those of low floor vehicles.

The ability to meet longer-term objectives which may imply a significant shift to public transport will also depend on policies adopted toward the role of the car (such as parking provision, road user charging, bus priority) and efforts to raise public transport service quality. Hopefully, the 'quality partnership' approach, possibly augmented by 'quality contracts' will enable bus operators to raise quality and attract car users. Assuming that some form of PPP scheme is agreed for London Underground, some improvement may likewise emerge in the longer term. On the surface rail system, significant improvements will emerge as work in progress is completed, notably the upgrading of the West Coast Main Line, and entry into service of new rolling stock.

Another element of government policy has been a greater attempt to integrate transport with other policy sectors, notably land-use planning (this issue is further examined in Chapter 11). Clearly, public transport's role is affected both by the average density of urban development, and location of activities with respect to the network. The framework developed by government through planning guidance (notably the revised version of PPG13 issued in 2001), and strengthening of local transport planning, should assist in this.

However, there have also been signs of a shift away from this approach, given the unpopularity of some measures (notably the 'fuel tax escalator'), and practical limits to constraining car use while public transport quality remains inadequate. The splitting up of the DETR following the general election in June 2001 may accelerate this trend.

Notes

1 DETR Statistics Bulletin SB (00) 26: *A Bulletin of Public Transport Statistics 1999/2000*, table 30.
2 National Audit Office (1998) *The Private Finance Initiative: The First Four Design, Build, Finance and Operate Roads Contracts*, TSO, London.
3 Arthur Andersen/London School of Economics (2000) *Value for Money Drivers in the Private Finance Initiative*, HM Treasury, London.
4 The Industrial Society (2000) The London Underground Public Private Partnership: *An Independent Review*, London, September. See table 1.
5 Office of the Rail Regulator (2000) Final conclusions of the periodic review of access charges for franchised passenger train services. Table 1.1.
6 Waterfront Conference Company (2001) Proceedings of a one-day conference 'Competition and Integration in Public Transport', London 7 February 2001. See presentation by John Vickers, Director General of Fair Trading (pp. 77–82).
7 Chris Green (Chief Executive, Virgin Trains) 'Phoenix from the Ashes: re-discovering the business-led railway', text of lecture to the Institute of Logistics and Transport, London, 13 February 2001, p. 19.
8 White, Peter, (2000) 'Experience in the UK bus and coach industry', Chapter 3, in Bill Bradshaw and Helen Lawton Smith (eds) *Privatization and Deregulation of Transport*, Macmillan, London, (Proceedings of a conference at Hertford College, Oxford, July 1997).
9 Derived from table 3.3 in DETR Statistics Bulletin SB(00)26.
10 From tables 16 and 18 in DETR Statistics Bulletin SB(00)26.
11 White, Peter, (2001) 'Local bus industry profitability and the role of longer-distance services', Chapter 9 in Tony Grayling (ed.) *Any More Fares? Delivering Better Bus Services*, Institute of Public Policy Research (IPPR), London, February 2001.
12 Data derived from SRA National Rail Trends Bulletin 2000–01, No. 3, table 1.1b and *Transport Statistics Great Britain* 1996 edition, table 5.11(a).
13 Transport 2000, *The Background Analysis* [evidence related to the ten-year transport plan for the period to 2010], DETR, London, July 2000, Annex A.

14 *A New Deal for Transport: Better for Everyone*, the government's White Paper on the Future of Transport, Cm3950. DETR, July 1998.
15 Transport 2010, *The 10 Year Plan*, DETR, July 2000.
16 Worsley, T. (2001) Presentation to a joint seminar of the Transport Planning Society and Transport Economists' Group on forecasting issues in the ten-year plan, 8 February 2001 (see report in *The Transport Economist*, forthcoming).
17 Transport 2000. The Background Analysis. TSO, London, July [forecasting issues in the Ten Year Plan] and 'Technical Report: Modelling using the National Road Traffic Forecasting framework for "Tackling Congestion and Pollution"' DETR 2000.
18 Sian Thornthwaite Consultants Ltd, 'School travel bulletin', Epsom, January 1999; and Sian Thornthwaite, *School Transport: The Comprehensive Guide*, TAS Partnership, Preston, 1994.
19 Dickson, Mark (2000) 'Characteristics of the education escort journey', in *Transport Trends* 2000 edition, TSO, March, pp. 47–54.
20 Jones, Peter and Bradshaw, Ruth, *The Family and the School Run: What Would Make a Real Difference?*, Transport Studies Group University of Westminster, and AA Foundation for Road Safety Research, 2000.

11 Policy in the long run

LIVERPOOL JOHN MOORES UNIVERSITY
Aldham Robarts L.R.C.
TEL. 0151 231 3701/3634

Within this chapter, issues affecting long-run policy and development of the public transport system are considered, such as the links with land-use planning, energy and environmental issues, and population trends. These are set in the context both of development within Britain and the European Union.

What is the role of 'planning'?

Within Britain, a shift back toward a 'planned' approach can be seen. As mentioned in Chapter 10, the ten-year plan adopted in 2000 involves making explicit forecasts (or setting targets), for both public transport and road traffic, the latter already well-established through the National Road Traffic Forecasts (NRTF). Long-term forecasts are required in the planning of major rail schemes, but at the same time, bus operations work on a very short timescale, often less than one year. While this reflects in part the degree of flexibility inherent in the technology of the modes concerned, it also reflects a different institutional framework.

Attitudes toward 'planning' became particularly polarized during the mid-1980s, but the early 1990s (under the Conservative government, prior to the General Election of 1997) had seen a shift back toward the realization of some need for a longer-term approach within the then Department of the Environment (DoE), especially through the rediscovery of links between transport and land use, and an awareness of the need to reduce travel as such.

It is desirable to distinguish three forms of planning:

1 Planning undertaken by a business, which often aims to anticipate and stimulate changes in the market as it changes. This thinking forms the basis of corporate plans and marketing strategies.
2 Planning in the sense of physical planning, mainly by local authorities, of land use, new infrastructure, etc.
3 'Planning' by central government, either of major pieces of infrastructure (such as motorways) or in the economy as a whole.

One alternative, clearly, would be to leave matters to 'the market'. Yet the 'market' itself does not produce new products. At the risk of sounding trite, one must stress that they come from people who are motivated to produce them and possess the technical abilities to do so. Some may be private businessmen, in the classic sense of the 'entrepreneur', who is motivated mainly by the prospect of profit. But others might be organizers of a voluntary project – such as a rural community bus scheme – whose motive is not profit. They also include local and central government, whose scale of organization permits them to make innovations which private business is not suited to undertake.

Examples of the type of innovation made by private business would include the commuter coach services into London since the Transport Act 1980. Innovation has come about through small-scale investment, and where this has proved profitable, further investment has occurred (although the majority of commuter coaches were initiated by operators then in public ownership, as part of NBC, or municipal enterprises, their behaviour was similar to that of private business in this sector). Examples of the innovation by public bodies include the travelcards in major cities, which only achieve substantial market penetration if valid for all or most of the network, and may require substantial public financial support, at least in their initial stages, to gain market penetration (see Chapter 7). Much of the technological innovation in public transport – for example, in real-time information systems, or smart cards – also rests on public bodies as the 'purchaser', although many competing businesses may offer rival products to meet this demand.

What is happening is that new products (whether provided by the public or private sectors) are being tested in 'the market' to establish whether they are successful. The criteria of success may simply be a commercial profit (as in commuter coaching), or achieving some wider benefits measured through social cost-benefit analysis. Clearly, an achievement aim must be set before a product is introduced, if unsuccessful products are not to be maintained unwisely.

The major role of 'planning', therefore, may be seen as the devising of these new products, or projects, so that they can be implemented successfully. It must therefore include a substantial element of 'feedback' from monitoring, as well as planning prior to introduction of the product.

The network planning introduced by bus operators in the 1970s and 1980s (but now largely confined, within Britain, to London, as described in Chapter 5) is a good example of this. Surveys establish existing customer behaviour and requirements. The plan aims to match these manifest demands with supply of services, at the same time identifying opportunities for innovations such as new limited-stop services, minibus conversion or cross-town through links.

The scale of such planning will depend upon the length of time needed for preparation – clearly greatest where new infrastructure is involved – and the scale of change. Where the change is mainly that of bus services using existing road networks, it could therefore be initiated at the level of an individual bus company, given a sufficiently large catchment area and expertise in network planning methods. Duration and scale are not necessarily correlated. For example, creating new bus priority schemes of the type described in Chapter 3 involves little expenditure and only modest additional infrastructure (except for new busways *per se*) yet the timescale may be a fairly long one, as other changes in traffic management, access arrangements for shops, etc. may be required. Conversely, introduction of a city-wide travelcard may require only a short planning timescale (although prior attention to sales outlets is essential, and often overlooked), yet may involve very large cash flows. Here, the main requirement may be to monitor sales after introduction and take appropriate action.

It is striking that the Travelcard in London, an innovation with much greater impact than many schemes carefully planned over a long period, involved a planning timescale of no more than about two years (1981–3), although successful monitoring of the scheme has come about not only through the operators' routine data, but also the user surveys conducted by London Transport.

Within private sector firms of the size traditionally found in the bus and coach industry, planning and investment are typically on fairly short timescales, yet here also effective planning may be needed to ensure success. Many of the long-distance coach services introduced by independents after the 1980 Act had little impact, despite modest fares and high-quality vehicles, owing to lack of suitable terminals, and sales outlets.

Given the approach outlined above, 'planning' can be seen as a process involving all sectors of transport, rather than one unique to the larger, public sector bodies. There are of course differences of degree – in timescale, and resources involved – but not necessarily of kind.

What framework does such a planning concept imply? Clearly, much of the system will be set up within the specific businesses concerned, but part also will fall within the public domain. This will include that dealing with large infrastructure projects only handled by the public sector, or in which the government is involved owing to the political implications even if some funding is from the private sector (the Channel Tunnel Rail Link is an obvious example). Most road and rail infrastructure schemes thus fall within the public sector.

Since 1986, local bus services have been operated largely through company structures, either in private ownership, or still in public ownership but with financial responsibilities similar to those in the private sector. Here, much planning is internal, but public sector planning remains important in respect of infrastructure, traffic management and the implications of other types of planning (such as the location of new housing development) on the public transport operators. This is recognized in the 'quality partnership' concept, in which operators seek to improve service quality and renew their fleets, while public authorities would in return provide improved infrastructure for bus services.

Transport and 'choice'

Transport demand is essentially a derived demand – for access to activities such as work, education, shopping and so forth. It may be argued that the real freedom of choice lies in the range of such activities that an individual can reach within constraints of time and income. For example, in comparing trips by those with and without cars available, the former generally display much higher rates, as illustrated through the National Travel Survey. Except in certain congested situations, the car will offer a faster door-to-door journey time and hence a wider range of activities over a larger radius within a given total time budget. Short-run perceived cost may display similar features. There is, of course, a secondary aspect of 'freedom' associated with car ownership, namely the choice of model, size and colour of the car itself. However, there is little if any correlation between this and the amount of travel (except for patterns of use of 'company cars'), in contrast with the order-of-magnitude differences between trip rates of car users and non-users. The high level of car use does, of course, impose externalities in the form of congestion, pollution and energy consumption, and hence the need to improve public transport as an acceptable alternative.

Applying this to public transport, one might see freedom as being maximized through an extensive network of reliable services, accompanied by comprehensive information systems and simple through ticketing. In some cases, direct competition between operators, or – more likely – initiatives taken by local management – might augment the quality and range of services on specific routes. The location of activities also plays an important role, in ensuring that they can be reached easily by public transport services.

Taking the current situation in Britain, this suggests that something like the approach we have in London produces better results than that in the other large cities. At the same time, a rather centralized bus network planning system exists, which could be augmented (but not replaced) by local initiatives, through the managements of local bus operators.

These issues may be illustrated by comparing Britain with other advanced, industrialized countries. The less rigid regulatory system in Britain has encouraged innovations such as higher quality long-distance and commuter coaches, new types of rural service, and high-frequency urban minibus operation. Yet in other respects, innovation lags behind that in more strictly regulated economies. The first automated urban railway, Docklands Light Rail, did not come into operation until 1987, four years after VAL in Lille (see Chapter 4). In The Netherlands and Belgium the vast majority of public transport ticketing is through prepaid forms, and conversion to nationwide electronic systems should be a relatively simple step.

Another aspect of the relationship between planning and competition is that some planning may be needed for competition to be effective. For example, the lack of adequate terminal facilities for long-distance coach services, especially in London, limited the impact of the Transport Act 1980, both by restricting total capacity, and giving independent operators few opportunities. Victoria Coach Station has now been substantially upgraded (although ironically, the reduced volume of coach movements after 1986 made it easier to find space for better passenger facilities), but remains poorly sited for the major coach flows.

With such considerations in mind, the external factors likely to influence transport demand, and policy changes which could be made both by government and transport operators, will be discussed.

Population trends

The starting point for any transport forecast must be the population served, and its composition. Changes in trip rate may then be considered separately, as influenced by factors such as price, car availability or service frequency (discussed earlier in Chapter 2).

Worldwide population is growing at about 1.5 per cent per annum, and generally at higher rates in developing countries (around 2.0 per cent per annum, compared with a stable or declining trend in many parts of Europe). Coupled with rural to urban migration in the latter, urban growth rates of 5 to 10 per cent may be commonplace. The main problem for the public transport operator in such cases becomes that of simply coping with demand. Conversely, in Europe, not only is total population virtually static, but that in urban areas, especially older cities, is falling.

Within Europe, an ageing population is developing, with implications for economic activity rates (subject to changes in retirement age levels). The proportion aged over 80 is anticipated to rise somewhat faster, with implications for accessibility and ability to use public transport services.

Spatially, a continued shift toward more prosperous regions is likely, with a continued outward shift within each region from traditional major cities to suburban fringe areas, and self-contained smaller towns (although London could be a marked exception to this). However, the rate of city population decline slowed down in the 1980s and 1990s, and such outward movement is no longer an aim of land-use planning policy.

The implications for public transport are that greater efforts will be needed to sustain patronage, with more attention paid to the levels of service in medium- to low-density suburban areas. Inner city radial routes will not necessarily require their existing level of peak capacity (although scope for shift from conventional bus to busway or light rail on high-density corridors remains). Better inter-suburban links will be required. In the long-distance market, city-centre to city-centre travel may become less important, and the need for good suburban interchanges will become greater. Cross-city links, especially in the London region, will become relatively more important as movements take place between regions around cities: these elements can be seen in the 'Thameslink' route's growing role since its reopening, and plans for 'Crossrail'. Growing medium-sized centres will require better cross-country links.

Insofar as future employment growth is in the service industries, this could be to the benefit of public transport, in that office employment in city centres may expand.

Energy

When the first edition of this book appeared in 1976, energy was undoubtedly one of the main 'fashionable' issues. Despite the further sharp rise in oil prices in 1979, its importance diminished, following the substantial fall in worldwide oil prices in real terms from the mid-1980s. Demand declined as a result of cuts in energy intensive heavy industry, and improved efficiency elsewhere – for example, in heating – have alleviated this problem for the time being. Further technical improvement in private car design is continuing, and scope for gains through measures such as reduced vehicle weight and regenerative braking systems in public transport modes have been outlined in Chapters 3 and 4.

None the less, complacency would be ill-advised, as finite limits exist to oil and other natural resources worldwide. There is also concern regarding the 'greenhouse effect' arising from increased atmospheric CO_2 emissions.

An increasing proportion of oil output is devoted to transport uses. For example, in the 'EU-30' transport represents about one-quarter of total energy consumption (from all primary sources), but is rising more rapidly than energy consumption as a whole. In terms of oil as such, 98 per cent of transport energy consumption is oil-based, and transport represents 67 per cent of final oil demand.[1] Overall, electricity would appear to offer a greater flexibility through use of alternative primary sources such as nuclear or coal, or renewable sources such as wave energy. Despite recent improvements and promised gains, the energy density of battery vehicles remains poor. The weight of the batteries, and the need for frequent replacement, increases their costs. Electrically powered vehicles using a continuous external supply, such as trolleybuses or rail vehicles, thus offer substantial gains. Other fuels have been proposed for private vehicles, such as hydrogen, but these themselves would require considerable energy inputs to convert them into a convenient form for on-vehicle use. At present, few efficient alternatives to the internal combustion engine appear in prospect, although experiments are in progress with fuel-cell buses.

Such constraints should not be viewed as giving rise to some overnight catastrophe, in which public transport would gain windfall traffic from the demise of the private car. However, they do favour a long-run approach designed to discourage a very low density land-use pattern which becomes almost entirely dependent upon the private car. A planning policy encouraging higher densities would enable public transport, and non-motorized modes for short trips to offer an alternative to car use, and in turn stimulate a greater level of public transport patronage.

Within Britain, such policies are evident in Planning Policy Guidance note 13 (popularly known as 'PPG13'), which first appeared in 1993, and in its latest form in 2001.[2] It now links up with other aspects of transport and land-use planning policy in encouraging the use of non-motorized modes and public transport, as a means for reducing energy consumption and pollution. The trend towards lower densities of settlement, and more dispersed activity centres, has clearly been to the detriment of public transport, and has further stimulated private car use. As argued in Chapter 5, higher densities would assist public transport in providing larger catchment populations within walking distance of a given route. Planning authorities are advised to bear such factors in mind in location of new development, and their response to proposals they receive.

Within PPG13, development within existing urban areas, of higher densities, is encouraged. Activity centres should be placed near public transport nodes. New, lower-density development is discouraged. Retention of existing waterway and rail alignments is suggested.

However, much of the advice is of a rather generalized form. That on shopping (also to be found in related guidance note PPG6), in particular, has come after a marked shift toward out-of-town centres during the 1980s and early 1990s. The ability of local authorities to influence land use is restricted both by the general shift toward deregulation in many aspects of the economy. The generalized nature of the British government proposals contrasts with the much firmer targets which have been set in Dutch planning and transport policy, for example.[3]

Taxation, public expenditure and equity

Despite reductions in financial support to public transport in recent years, a substantial proportion of operating costs, around 30 per cent, is met from public expenditure for both bus and rail systems (this figure includes payments for concessionary fares, specific services and school transport). So far as national railways are concerned, this is funded almost entirely through central government directly, apart from some payments via the PTAs (see Table 1.1). The bus industry is supported partly through central government (the partial fuel tax rebate on local services), but largely through local authorities, albeit under strong constraints imposed by central government.

This proportion of support is somewhat lower than found elsewhere in Europe or North America, where around 50 per cent would be typical. Nonetheless, it is important to ask how such expenditure affects the net incomes users and taxpayers thereby receive, in contrast to that where full-cost fares applied.

Rail users receive a much greater support per trip (and to a less marked extent, per passenger-km) than bus users, yet it can be shown that rail users in general have much higher income than bus users. In the London case, for example, an almost exact mirror image can be seen when Underground and bus users are stratified by decile income groups, bus users being concentrated at the bottom end of the scale, rail at the upper.[4]

Having said this, an increasingly high proportion of the net support to rail services is devoted to regional services, rather than London and South East, or Intercity, services, and these are less likely to be attractive to higher-income groups. Within the bus industry, cross-subsidy has been reduced since deregulation, although it could be argued that expenditure on tendered services tends to be directed, within urban areas, to those parts which display higher income and car ownership levels, and hence cannot support reasonable bus frequencies (in parts of Merseyside, for example). However, it does not necessarily follow that those dependent upon such tendered services are of high income themselves – users of a service within a low-density suburb are unlikely to be typical car owners, but those of lower incomes within such an area, who need access to employment, schools and shops outside it.

While public transport support has been cut back, and cost-based pricing thereby encouraged, progress has been slow in the implementation of road pricing in major cities as a means of similarly matching supply and demand for road space by private vehicles, although extensive studies both of the technology, and likely traveller response, are now in progress. Powers under the Transport Act 2000 should encourage local authority initiatives, and hopefully these may come to fruition in London and other centres such as Edinburgh or Bristol.

A major contrast between Britain and other industrialized countries lies in the taxation of user benefits on public transport. In many, employers may provide a season ticket without the recipient being taxed upon the benefit thereby gained, at any rate up to a certain level. Japan is the main example, but the practice is also common in Europe, sometimes through employers contributing directly to a lower ticket price, as in Paris. Although some attempts have been made to market travelcards via employers in this fashion, the tax imposed makes it unattractive both to employer and recipient, in contrast to the benefits given through the company car or free parking (albeit reduced in recent years, with the latter potentially subject to workplace user charging under the Transport Act 2000).

National taxation structure also affects the ability of local government to pursue its policy objectives. The limited scope for raising revenue through the council tax, reliance upon central government grants, and more centralized imposition of limits on total spending of local authorities by central government, have left very little local autonomy (see Chapter 1). Elsewhere, local or regional income taxes may play a major role – as in Sweden – or specific taxes can be raised for transport purposes, such as the 'versement transport' in most French cities, or taxes approved through local referenda in the US. British local authorities have no freedom to establish such means of raising funds, and an increasingly centralized policy has been adopted by central government in contrast with decentralization of urban finance and policy making in many other countries.

Such local decisions could be seen as a form of 'collective purchase' of transport services, yet creating much closer links between the voters and those affected than is the case in national policy decisions on the rail passenger network, for example. The question of equity would still remain, of course. Would those on higher incomes benefit more than lower-income residents of the inner city? An assessment by Turner[5] suggests that this would not be the case for London. Taking fare levels and rates (the form of local government taxation applying at the time) in 1984–5, the higher rates paid by higher income groups, and their lower off-peak use of public transport, offset the greater benefits a longer-distance peak-period user might gain from a general fares reduction. Were a progressive local income tax to replace the council tax as the main source of finance for such public expenditure, the relative gains to lower income groups would be further improved.

Any local income tax system would have to be based either on the home or work location of earners, preferably covering areas in which a fairly self-contained pattern was found of both, i.e. journey-to-work catchment areas. This would imply, for example, a somewhat larger area than the present Greater London, and certainly larger areas than the unitary authorities.

The 'sustainability' issue

The concerns about energy use and environmental impacts may be brought together under the broader concept of 'sustainability', i.e. an aim that present levels of activity do not unduly damage the prospects of future generations by depleting resources, and damaging the environment (a variety of definitions is in circulation). In transport terms this may imply, first, reducing environmental pollution emitted by all modes taken together. Second, it implies reducing the rate at which finite resources are consumed without replacement.

Considerable progress is already being made in reduction of pollutants at the localized level, such as sulphur, carbon monoxide and particulates (see, for example, the discussion of standards being applied to new buses in Chapter 3). Further progress, both in public transport and private car technology, is likely to enable such trends to continue. Hence, impacts on health and other aspect such as corrosion of buildings are likely to diminish. Within the public transport sphere, the critical factor may be the rate of fleet renewal, or retrofitting of existing stock.

A broader issue is the emissions of CO_2 as a 'greenhouse gas' rather than a 'pollutant' as such. Here, the overall volume of carbon-based fuels consumed becomes the issue rather than local changes. As in the case of localized emissions, technological changes may assist through improvement of fuel efficiency, and development of alternative resources. However, finite limits still apply to the stock of carbon-based fuel available. It is in this sphere that more radical changes may be needed in policy and individual behaviour. Reduction of the need to travel and a shift to more energy efficient modes both assist in this respect. Policies such as those in PPG13, and set out in treaties such as Kyoto, illustrate the changes required.

Increased fuel tax on private vehicles is perhaps the most obvious and simple mechanism by which to encourage more efficient use of energy, while leaving individuals free to determine their own travel priorities. It also assists in encouraging technical changes to improve efficiency (such as regenerative braking systems) and of smaller, more fuel efficient vehicles to attain the same travel objectives (hence a greater elasticity may be found with respect to fuel price than vehicle-km as such). However, constraints apply to this process. If one country seeks to move ahead of others, as was the case with the 'fuel duty escalator' in Britain in the late 1990s, this may create difficulties in terms of competitiveness, and more directly in the public reaction, evident in the fuel tax protests in the autumn of 2000. Even within Europe, wide disparities in fuel price exist, let alone the much lower levels found in the USA and some other countries. There are also concerns about impacts in rural areas, although as discussed in Chapter 8, this may have been exaggerated.

A degree of harmonization may thus be necessary in order to make such policies acceptable and consistent in their application. A noteworthy omission to date has been aviation, whose fuel is subject to very little tax, and to which environmentally based taxes have also seen little application. Yet it is the fastest-growing mode of transport, with a cumulative annual expansion of about 5 per cent. It would clearly be inconsistent to deter, for example, local car use through high fuel duties while ignoring the role of air travel growth.

A number of these issues were examined in a recent study by the Centre for European Policy Studies.[6] It suggested that curbing growth in energy use might be much easier in the passenger than the freight sector, given that the latter has already experienced major restructuring of manufacturing and distribution patterns which even radical increases in fuel costs would do little to reverse. Conversely, personal travel may be more flexible in the longer term, responding to price changes and other policy measures. Given the relatively high mobility already found (*vis-à-vis* worldwide averages) and high population density, enabling easier access to facilities (compared with the USA for example) Western Europe should be able to accommodate such changes in trends more easily than many other parts of the world.

The role of the European Union

A growing role in transport and related policies is being taken by the European Union (EU) following its initially more limited role as the 'Common Market' (European Economic Community, or EEC). Several aspects may be identified:

1   Adoption of common technical standards, enabling easier inter-operability between systems, and greater economies of scale in manufacture of vehicles and equipment. Examples include measures to improve inter-operability of international rail services (such as in signalling technology), and common standards of bus and coach design.
2   Adoption of a common institutional framework which should enable greater inter-operability and fairer competition within and between modes. The railway directive 91/440, requiring separate accounting for infrastructure and operations (and its further development) may be seen as an example. However, the degree to which this is followed within member states may vary greatly. For example, Britain took the concept much further than other states by creation of 'Railtrack' as a privatized infrastructure supplier.
3   Encouragement of greater safety in transport, accompanied by common speed limits, vehicle design standards, and measures such as common maximum alcohol limits for drivers.
4   Policies to encourage moves towards sustainability and environmental protection in transport. These may include measures to encourage use of public rather than private motorized transport, standards for fuel quality, and taxation policies towards fuel.
5   Provision of common technology, notably the proposed 'Galileo' satellite navigation system, complementing those available through USA and Russia.
6   Perhaps more controversially, a greater involvement has been evident in recent years in local transport policies, at the level of urban and regional systems, in addition to the issues of international movement or harmonization of technical standards. Examples include the current proposals for much

greater competition in the local public transport sector, including compulsory competitive tendering at five-year intervals. While this could be seen as part of the 'market' concept inherent in the original EEC, it may also contradict the concept of 'subsidiarity' in which policies should be determined at no higher a level in the institutional hierarchy than necessary.

At the time of writing, a Transport White Paper is being finalized but not yet published by the Commission. The planning framework for a ten-year period to 2010 parallels that within Britain, with similar expectations of trend projections, i.e. the greatest growth would be in air transport, followed by private cars and road freight. Policies to encourage sustainability, offsetting growth in congestion that would otherwise occur, and stimulating the rail and inland waterway sectors, are likely to be emphasized.[7]

'Mobility' or 'access'?

In conclusion, what is the main aim of providing public transport services? As suggested in Chapter 2, the output may be measured most readily by passenger trips, passenger-km or revenue. These are all measures of 'mobility', i.e. the amount of travel. Given a fixed pattern of land uses and activities, increased mobility will represent increased access: a wider range, and/or lower cost of activities. For example, a greater distance in commuting from home to work may represent a wider range of job opportunities, or of lower housing costs. Mobility as such is not a benefit, but represents a cost, which is offset by the benefits of activities made possible.

Although, broadly speaking, greater mobility represents improved access, and may indeed be essential simply to maintain access to the same range of facilities (for example, as village schools are closed), the standard of living enjoyed by an individual will not necessarily be in direct proportion to their mobility. Someone living in a small town with employment, shops and schools close at hand may well enjoy much greater access to activities than a person in a poorly served housing estate of a large city, despite the much greater mobility the latter may display.

Changing the location and timing of activities may also be a means of improving access rather than transport changes as such. The cases cited in Chapter 8 on rural transport illustrate this: medical facilities could be more conveniently located, and their timings changed to improve access by users of existing bus services. School transport, in particular, is very costly to provide, and involves awkward duration and timing of trips from the viewpoint both of parents and children. A full evaluation of transport costs (both financial, and of the travelling time involved) could lead to smaller, more local, school catchment areas being defined.

However, it is important to direct doubts about the benefits of ever-growing mobility to their true target, i.e. the tendency of activities to be located further from the customer, and for many marginal trips to be generated as incomes and car ownership rise. Like many ecological or environmental arguments, they may be used all too easily by those now enjoying the high level of material wealth produced by the present industrial system while living in what remains of small-scale communities, and applied only to others.

Even at the present levels of centralization of employment, shopping and other facilities, a substantial increase in rural public transport provision could be justified to improve the minimum levels of access for non-car-owners. In many urban areas, similar deficiencies are arising, especially as evening and weekend services have been curtailed. Pressures on concessionary fares budgets are resulting in curtailment of free off-peak travel passes for pensioners, and restrict the ability to retain low fares for peak child travel, which could hit low-income households.

This debate is also relevant to priorities being set by national organizations within the public transport sector. For example, in seeking to attain the growth forecast for rail travel set out in the ten-year plan, is there is tendency for the SRA to give greater emphasis to additional high-speed intercity links, generating new travel, rather than improved local services within major conurbations which could do more to speed day-to-day commuting travel and help reduce peak road congestion?

Notes

1 Green Paper, *Towards a European Strategy for the Security of Energy Supply*, Directorate-General for Energy and Transport, European Commission, Brussels, May 2001, p. 16. The term 'EU-30' refers to the existing fifteen member states plus those in Eastern and Central Europe aspiring toward membership, within which transport demand is likely to grow more quickly than in Western Europe.

2 Department of Transport, the Regions and the Environment PPG13 Planning Policy Guidance, *Transport*, March 2001.

3 Sturt, A. and Bull, D. (1993) 'Putting broad accessibility principles into planning practice', *Town and Country Planning*, October 1993, vol. 62, no.10, pp. 268–72.

4 Grayling, T. and Glaister, S. (2000) *A New Fares Contract for London*, Institute of Public Research, London, January 2000.

5 Turner, R.P. (1985) *Rates fair? An Evaluation of Revenue Support, Rates and Bus/ Underground Fares in Greater London*. Discussion Paper No. 14, Transport Studies Group, Polytechnic of Central London.

6 *Mobility in Europe: Forging a Sustainable EU Transport Policy*. Report for a CEPS Working Party, Centre for European Policy Studies, Brussels, April 2000.

7 UITP *Euro Express*, news bulletin, February 2001 issue, pp. 3, 4.

Index

Note: Figures and Tables are indicated by *italic page numbers*

LIVERPOOL JOHN MOORES UNIVERSITY
Aldham Roberts L.R.C.
TEL. 0151 231 3701/3634